Alan Bush, Modern Music, and the Cold War

This book, the first major study of Alan Bush, provides new perspectives on twentieth-century music and communism. British communist, composer of politicised works, and friend of Soviet musicians, Bush proved to be a lightning rod in the national musical culture. His radical vision for British music prompted serious reflections on aesthetics and the rights of artists to private political opinions, and influenced the development of state-sponsored music-making in East Germany. Rejecting previous characterisations of Bush as political and musical Other, Joanna Bullivant traces his aesthetic project from its origins in the 1920s to its collapse in the 1970s, incorporating discussion of modernism, political song, music theory, opera, and Bush's response to the Soviet music crisis of 1948. Drawing on a wealth of archival sources, including recently released documents from MI5, this book constructs new perspectives on the 'cultural Cold War' through the lens of the individual artist.

JOANNA BULLIVANT has held academic posts at the University of Oxford, University of Nottingham, and King's College London. She has published widely on British composers, modernism, and music and politics. This is her first book.

Music since 1900

GENERAL EDITOR Arnold Whittall

This series – formerly *Music in the Twentieth Century* – offers a wide perspective on music and musical life since the end of the nineteenth century. Books included range from historical and biographical studies concentrating particularly on the context and circumstances in which composers were writing, to analytical and critical studies concerned with the nature of musical language and questions of compositional process. The importance given to context will also be reflected in studies dealing with, for example, the patronage, publishing, and promotion of new music, and in accounts of the musical life of particular countries.

Titles in the Series
Jonathan Cross
The Stravinsky Legacy
Michael Nyman
Experimental Music: Cage and Beyond
Jennifer Doctor
The BBC and Ultra-Modern Music, 1922–1936
Robert Adlington
The Music of Harrison Birtwistle
Keith Potter
Four Musical Minimalists: La Monte Young, Terry Riley, Steve Reich, Philip Glass
Carlo Caballero
Fauré and French Musical Aesthetics
Peter Burt
The Music of Toru Takemitsu
David Clarke
The Music and Thought of Michael Tippett: Modern Times and Metaphysics
M.J. Grant
Serial Music, Serial Aesthetics: Compositional Theory in Post-War Europe
Philip Rupprecht
Britten's Musical Language
Mark Carroll
Music and Ideology in Cold War Europe
Adrian Thomas
Polish Music since Szymanowski
J.P.E. Harper-Scott
Edward Elgar, Modernist

Yayoi Uno Everett
The Music of Louis Andriessen
Ethan Haimo
Schoenberg's Transformation of Musical Language
Rachel Beckles Willson
Ligeti, Kurtág, and Hungarian Music during the Cold War
Michael Cherlin
Schoenberg's Musical Imagination
Joseph N. Straus
Twelve-Tone Music in America
David Metzer
Musical Modernism at the Turn of the Twenty-First Century
Edward Campbell
Boulez, Music and Philosophy
Jonathan Goldman
The Musical Language of Pierre Boulez: Writings and Compositions
Pieter C. van den Toorn and John McGinness
Stravinsky and the Russian Period: Sound and Legacy of a Musical Idiom
David Beard
Harrison Birtwistle's Operas and Music Theatre
Heather Wiebe
Britten's Unquiet Pasts: Sound and Memory in Postwar Reconstruction
Beate Kutschke and Barley Norton
Music and Protest in 1968
Graham Griffiths
Stravinsky's Piano: Genesis of a Musical Language
Martin Iddon
John Cage and David Tudor: Correspondence on Interpretation and Performance
Martin Iddon
New Music at Darmstadt: Nono, Stockhausen, Cage, and Boulez
Alastair Williams
Music in Germany since 1968
Ben Earle
Luigi Dallapiccola and Musical Modernism in Fascist Italy
Thomas Schuttenhelm
The Orchestral Music of Michael Tippett: Creative Development and the Compositional Process
Marilyn Nonken
The Spectral Piano: From Liszt, Scriabin, and Debussy to the Digital Age
Jack Boss
Schoenberg's Twelve-Tone Music: Symmetry and the Musical Idea
Deborah Mawer
French Music and Jazz in Conversation: From Debussy to Brubeck

Philip Rupprecht
British Musical Modernism: The Manchester Group and Their Contemporaries
Amy Lynn Wlodarski
Musical Witness and Holocaust Representation
Carola Nielinger-Vakil
Luigi Nono: A Composer in Context
Erling E. Guldbrandsen and Julian Johnson
Transformations of Musical Modernism
David Cline
The Graph Music of Morton Feldman
Russell Hartenberger
Performance and Practice in the Music of Steve Reich
Joanna Bullivant
Modern Music, Alan Bush, and the Cold War: The Cultural Left in Britain and the Communist Bloc

Alan Bush, Modern Music, and the Cold War

The Cultural Left in Britain and the Communist Bloc

Joanna Bullivant
University of Oxford

Shaftesbury Road, Cambridge CB2 8EA, United Kingdom

One Liberty Plaza, 20th Floor, New York, NY 10006, USA

477 Williamstown Road, Port Melbourne, VIC 3207, Australia

314–321, 3rd Floor, Plot 3, Splendor Forum, Jasola District Centre, New Delhi – 110025, India

103 Penang Road, #05–06/07, Visioncrest Commercial, Singapore 238467

Cambridge University Press is part of Cambridge University Press & Assessment, a department of the University of Cambridge.

We share the University's mission to contribute to society through the pursuit of education, learning and research at the highest international levels of excellence.

www.cambridge.org
Information on this title: www.cambridge.org/9781009158794

DOI: 10.1017/9781139519656

© Joanna Bullivant 2017

This publication is in copyright. Subject to statutory exception and to the provisions of relevant collective licensing agreements, no reproduction of any part may take place without the written permission of Cambridge University Press & Assessment.

First published 2017
First paperback edition 2022

A catalogue record for this publication is available from the British Library

Library of Congress Cataloging-in-Publication data
Names: Bullivant, Joanna Louise, 1983–
Title: Alan Bush, Modern Music and the Cold War : the cultural left in Britain and the communist bloc / Joanna Bullivant.
Description: Cambridge, United Kingdom ; New York, NY : Cambridge University Press, 2017. | Series: Music since 1900 | Includes bibliographical references and index.
Identifiers: LCCN 2017012142 | ISBN 9781107033368 (alk. paper)
Subjects: LCSH: Bush, Alan, 1900–1995 – Criticism and interpretation. | Music – Great Britain – 20th century – History and criticism. | Bush, Alan, 1900–1995 – Political activity. | Music – Political aspects – Great Britain – History – 20th century. | Communism and music – Great Britain – History – 20th century.
Classification: LCC ML410.B978 B85 2017 | DDC 780.92–dc23
LC record available at https://lccn.loc.gov/2017012142

ISBN   978-1-107-03336-8   Hardback
ISBN   978-1-009-15879-4   Paperback

Cambridge University Press & Assessment has no responsibility for the persistence or accuracy of URLs for external or third-party internet websites referred to in this publication and does not guarantee that any content on such websites is, or will remain, accurate or appropriate.

Contents

List of Figures		*page* viii
List of Music Examples		ix
Acknowledgements		xv
List of Abbreviations		xvii
	Introduction	1
1	Bush as Modernist: Material and Performance	17
2	Bush as Activist: The Idea of Workers' Music	62
3	Bush as Outsider: Music and Communism in Wartime	96
4	Building in the Rubble: *The Winter Journey* and *Lidiče*	116
5	Bush as Stalinist: The Year 1948	139
6	Bush and the Self: *Wat Tyler*'s Rituals of Becoming	177
7	Bush and East Germany: Opera, Sex, and the Communist Body	205
	Appendix 1 Developments in CPGB Policy, 1939–41	245
	Appendix 2 Bush, Selected Works, 1939–47	246
	Appendix 3 Wat Tyler, Characters and Synopsis	249
	Select Bibliography	252
	Index	264

Figures

4.1	Schema of Bush, *The Winter Journey*.	*page* 120
5.1	Compositions employing the thematic method.	162
5.2	Structure and tonality in Bush, *English Suite*, 'Fantasia'.	166
7.1	Productions of Bush's operas in the Communist Bloc.	211

Music Examples

1.1	Bush, Quartet for Strings and Piano, opening, op. 5 by Alan Bush, BL/AB MS Mus. 350 © Copyright 1925 Estate of Alan Bush. Reproduced by permission.	*page* 27
1.2	Bush, String Quartet in A minor, opening, op. 4 by Alan Bush © Copyright 1925 by Stainer & Bell. Reproduced by permission of Stainer & Bell Ltd, London, England, www.stainer.co.uk.	28
1.3	Bush, *Concert Piece* for Cello and Piano, opening, op. 17 by Alan Bush © Copyright 2004 by Peters Edition. Reproduced by permission.	29
1.4	Bush, *Relinquishment*, bb. 69–72, op. 11 by Alan Bush © Copyright 1929 by Oxford University Press. Extracts reproduced by permission. All rights reserved.	30
1.5a	*Relinquishment*, opening, op. 11 by Alan Bush © Copyright 1929 by Oxford University Press. Extracts reproduced by permission. All rights reserved.	31
1.5b	*Relinquishment*, bb. 32–8, op. 11 by Alan Bush © Copyright 1929 by Oxford University Press. Extracts reproduced by permission. All rights reserved.	31
1.5c	*Relinquishment*, bb. 79–80, op. 11 by Alan Bush © Copyright 1929 by Oxford University Press. Extracts reproduced by permission. All rights reserved.	31
1.6a	Bush, *Dialectic* for String Quartet, opening, op. 15 by Alan Bush © Copyright 1938 by Boosey & Hawkes Music Publishers Ltd. Reproduced by permission of Boosey & Hawkes Music Publishers Ltd.	32
1.6b	*Dialectic* for String Quartet, second subject, bb. 31–3, op. 15 by Alan Bush © Copyright 1938 by Boosey & Hawkes Music Publishers Ltd. Reproduced by permission of Boosey & Hawkes Music Publishers Ltd.	32
1.7	*Concert Piece* for Cello and Piano, piano, bb. 40–8, op. 17 by Alan Bush © Copyright 2004 by Peters Edition. Reproduced by permission.	41
1.8	*Concert Piece* for Cello and Piano, bb. 253–6, op. 17 by Alan Bush © Copyright 2004 by Peters Edition. Reproduced by permission.	43
1.9	*Concert Piece* for Cello and Piano, bb. 153–5, op. 17 by Alan Bush © Copyright 2004 by Peters Edition. Reproduced by permission.	44
1.10	Bush, Piano Concerto, i, opening, piano only, Concerto for Piano and Orchestra, with Baritone Solo and Male Voice Chorus in the last movement, text by Randall Swingler, op. 18 by Alan Bush © Copyright	

	1938 by Joseph Williams Ltd. Reproduced by permission of Stainer & Bell Ltd, London, England, www.stainer.co.uk.	48
1.11a	Bush, Concerto for Piano and Orchestra, with Baritone Solo and Male Voice Chorus in the last movement, i, trumpet (sounding) and trombone, 1 before Fig. 107, op. 18 by Alan Bush, text by Randall Swingler © Copyright 1938 by Joseph Williams Ltd. Reproduced by permission of Stainer & Bell Ltd, London, England, www.stainer.co.uk.	49
1.11b	Concerto for Piano and Orchestra, with Baritone Solo and Male Voice Chorus in the last movement, i, horns (sounding), 6 after Fig. 109, op. 18 by Alan Bush, text by Randall Swingler © Copyright 1938 by Joseph Williams Ltd. Reproduced by permission of Stainer & Bell Ltd, London, England, www.stainer.co.uk.	50
1.12	Concerto for Piano and Orchestra, with Baritone Solo and Male Voice Chorus in the last movement, i, piano only, 4 after Fig. 103, op. 18 by Alan Bush, text by Randall Swingler © Copyright 1938 by Joseph Williams Ltd. Reproduced by permission of Stainer & Bell Ltd, London, England, www.stainer.co.uk.	51
1.13	Concerto for Piano and Orchestra, with Baritone Solo and Male Voice Chorus in the last movement, i, piano only, 5 before Fig. 106, op. 18 by Alan Bush, text by Randall Swingler © Copyright 1938 by Joseph Williams Ltd. Reproduced by permission of Stainer & Bell Ltd, London, England, www.stainer.co.uk.	53
1.14	Concerto for Piano and Orchestra, with Baritone Solo and Male Voice Chorus in the last movement, iv, strings, opening, op. 18 by Alan Bush, text by Randall Swingler © Copyright 1938 by Joseph Williams Ltd. Reproduced by permission of Stainer & Bell Ltd, London, England, www.stainer.co.uk.	54
1.15	Concerto for Piano and Orchestra, with Baritone Solo and Male Voice Chorus in the last movement, iv, piano and violin I, 1 after Fig. 402, op. 18 by Alan Bush, text by Randall Swingler © Copyright 1938 by Joseph Williams Ltd. Reproduced by permission of Stainer & Bell Ltd, London, England, www.stainer.co.uk.	55
1.16	Concerto for Piano and Orchestra, with Baritone Solo and Male Voice Chorus in the last movement, iv, chorus, 2 after Fig. 414, op. 18 by Alan Bush, text by Randall Swingler © Copyright 1938 by Joseph Williams Ltd. Reproduced by permission of Stainer & Bell Ltd, London, England, www.stainer.co.uk.	57
2.1	Hanns Eisler, 'Solidaritätslied', bb. 5–10, aus dem Tonfilm *Kuhle Wampe*, op. 27 no. 1 by Hanns Eisler, words by Bertolt Brecht, Klavierauszug von Erwin Ratz © Copyright by Deutscher Verlag für Musik Leipzig and Edition Peters Group. Reproduced by permission.	70
2.2	Bush, 'To the Men of England', opening (reduction), op. 10 by Alan Bush, poem by Percy Bysshe Shelley © Copyright 1928 by Curwen. Reproduced by permission.	71

List of Music Examples

2.3	'To the Men of England', bb. 27–31, op. 10 by Alan Bush, poem by Percy Bysshe Shelley © Copyright 1928 by Curwen. Reproduced by permission.	73
2.4	Bush, 'Make Your Meaning Clear', opening, music by Alan Bush, words by Randall Swingler © Copyright 1939 by the Workers' Music Association. Reproduced by permission.	74
2.5a	Bush, *Three Contrapuntal Studies*, III (Fugue), fingering instructions, op. 13 no. 2 by Alan Bush, BL/AB MS Mus. 352 © Copyright 1931 Estate of Alan Bush. Reproduced by permission.	80
2.5b	*Three Contrapuntal Studies*, III (Fugue), opening, op. 13 no. 2 by Alan Bush, BL/AB MS Mus. 352 © Copyright 1931 Estate of Alan Bush. Reproduced by permission.	80
2.6	Bush, 'Machine Ballet', opening [reduction], from *Pageant of Co-operation*, music by Alan Bush, BL/AB MS Mus. 398 © Copyright 1938 Estate of Alan Bush. Reproduced by permission.	90
3.1	Bush, 'Unite and Be Free', bb. 3–8, words and music by Alan Bush © Copyright 1941 by the Workers' Music Association. Reproduced by permission.	107
4.1	Bush, *Lyric Interlude* for Violin Solo with Pianoforte Accompaniment, bb. 1–11, op. 26 by Alan Bush © Copyright 1975 Estate of Alan Bush. Reproduced by permission.	117
4.2	*The Winter Journey*, 'The City', bb. 75–84, Cantata for Soprano and Baritone Soli and Mixed Chorus, with accompaniment for String Quintet and Harp, op. 29 by Alan Bush, words by Randall Swingler © Copyright 1947 by Joseph Williams Ltd. Reproduced by permission of Stainer & Bell Ltd, London, England, www.stainer.co.uk.	122
4.3	*The Winter Journey*, 'The Sleepers in the City', bb. 1–22, Cantata for Soprano and Baritone Soli and Mixed Chorus, with accompaniment for String Quintet and Harp, op. 29 by Alan Bush, words by Randall Swingler © Copyright 1947 by Joseph Williams Ltd. Reproduced by permission of Stainer & Bell Ltd, London, England, www.stainer.co.uk.	125
4.4	*The Winter Journey*, 'The Sleepers in the City', bb. 38–40, Cantata for Soprano and Baritone Soli and Mixed Chorus, with accompaniment for String Quintet and Harp, op. 29 by Alan Bush, words by Randall Swingler © Copyright 1947 by Joseph Williams Ltd. Reproduced by permission of Stainer & Bell Ltd, London, England, www.stainer.co.uk.	126
4.5	*The Winter Journey*, 'Final Chorale', bb. 40–9, Cantata for Soprano and Baritone Soli and Mixed Chorus, with accompaniment for String Quintet and Harp, op. 29 by Alan Bush, words by Randall Swingler © Copyright 1947 by Joseph Williams Ltd. Reproduced by permission of Stainer & Bell Ltd, London, England, www.stainer.co.uk.	127

4.6	Bush, *Lidiče* for Mixed Voices, opening, by Alan Bush, words by Nancy Bush © Copyright 1947 by the Workers' Music Association. Reproduced by permission.	134
4.7	*Lidiče* for Mixed Voices, closing bars, by Alan Bush, words by Nancy Bush © Copyright 1947 by the Workers' Music Association. Reproduced by permission.	135
5.1	Schoenberg, *Klavierstück*, op. 33a, Bush's analysis of the opening chord.	156
5.2	*Dialectic* for String Quartet, first and second subjects as quartal collections, op. 15 by Alan Bush © Copyright 1938 by Boosey & Hawkes Music Publishers Ltd. Reproduced by permission of Boosey & Hawkes Music Publishers Ltd.	157
5.3	*Dialectic* for String Quartet, closing bars, op. 15 by Alan Bush © Copyright 1938 by Boosey & Hawkes Music Publishers Ltd. Reproduced by permission of Boosey & Hawkes Music Publishers Ltd.	157
5.4a	Bush, *English Suite* for String Orchestra, 'Fantasia', cantus firmus, op. 28 by Alan Bush © Copyright 1950 by Joseph Williams Ltd. Reproduced by permission of Stainer & Bell Ltd, London, England, www.stainer.co.uk.	165
5.4b	*English Suite* for String Orchestra, 'Fantasia', opening, op. 28 by Alan Bush © Copyright 1950 by Joseph Williams Ltd. Reproduced by permission of Stainer & Bell Ltd, London, England, www.stainer.co.uk.	165
5.5	*English Suite* for String Orchestra, 'Fantasia', 5 before Fig. 3, op. 28 by Alan Bush © Copyright 1950 by Joseph Williams Ltd. Reproduced by permission of Stainer & Bell Ltd, London, England, www.stainer.co.uk.	167
5.6	Bush's transcription of 'Lowlands, my Lowlands', by Alan Bush, ABH © Copyright Estate of Alan Bush. Reproduced by permission.	170
5.7	*English Suite* for String Orchestra, 'Soliloquy on a Sailor's Song', opening, op. 28 by Alan Bush © Copyright 1950 by Joseph Williams Ltd. Reproduced by permission of Stainer & Bell Ltd, London, England, www.stainer.co.uk.	171
5.8	*English Suite* for String Orchestra, 'Passacaglia', 'Cutty Wren' ground bass, op. 28 by Alan Bush © Copyright 1950 by Joseph Williams Ltd. Reproduced by permission of Stainer & Bell Ltd, London, England, www.stainer.co.uk.	173
5.9	*English Suite* for String Orchestra, 'Passacaglia', introduction, op. 28 by Alan Bush © Copyright 1950 by Joseph Williams Ltd. Reproduced by permission of Stainer & Bell Ltd, London, England, www.stainer.co.uk.	174
6.1	Bush, *Wat Tyler*, 'Minstrel song', VS, p. 181, an Opera in Two Acts with a Prologue by Alan Bush, libretto by Nancy Bush © Copyright 1959 by Novello & Co Ltd. Reproduced by permission.	190

List of Music Examples   xiii

6.2   *Wat Tyler*, VS, p. 36, an Opera in Two Acts with a Prologue by
      Alan Bush, libretto by Nancy Bush © Copyright 1959 by
      Novello & Co Ltd. Reproduced by permission.   192
6.3   *Wat Tyler*, VS, pp. 207–8, an Opera in Two Acts with a Prologue
      by Alan Bush, libretto by Nancy Bush © Copyright 1959 by
      Novello & Co Ltd. Reproduced by permission.   193
6.4   *Wat Tyler*, VS, closing bars, an Opera in Two Acts with a Prologue
      by Alan Bush, libretto by Nancy Bush © Copyright 1959 by
      Novello & Co Ltd. Reproduced by permission.   194
6.5   *Wat Tyler*, VS, p. 154, an Opera in Two Acts with a Prologue by
      Alan Bush, libretto by Nancy Bush © Copyright 1959 by
      Novello & Co Ltd. Reproduced by permission.   198
6.6   *Wat Tyler*, VS, pp. 242–3, an Opera in Two Acts with a Prologue by
      Alan Bush, libretto by Nancy Bush © Copyright 1959 by
      Novello & Co Ltd. Reproduced by permission.   200
6.7   *Wat Tyler*, VS, pp. 205–6, an Opera in Two Acts with a Prologue
      by Alan Bush, libretto by Nancy Bush © Copyright 1959 by
      Novello & Co Ltd. Reproduced by permission.   202
7.1   Bush, *The Sugar Reapers* or *Guyana Johnny*, wedding scene,
      VS 228–9, Opera in Two Acts (Six Scenes) by Alan Bush, libretto
      by Nancy Bush © Copyright 1965 Estate of Alan Bush. Reproduced by
      permission.   226
7.2a *The Sugar Reapers* or *Guyana Johnny*, Sumintra's scale and *raga*,
      Opera in Two Acts (Six Scenes) by Alan Bush, libretto by Nancy
      Bush © Copyright 1965 Estate of Alan Bush. Reproduced by permission. 229
7.2b *The Sugar Reapers* or *Guyana Johnny*, Panasar's scale and *raga*,
      Opera in Two Acts (Six Scenes) by Alan Bush, libretto by Nancy
      Bush © Copyright 1965 Estate of Alan Bush. Reproduced by permission. 229
7.2c *The Sugar Reapers* or *Guyana Johnny*, Ganesh Maraj's scale and *raga*,
      Opera in Two Acts (Six Scenes) by Alan Bush, libretto by Nancy
      Bush © Copyright 1965 Estate of Alan Bush. Reproduced by permission. 229
7.3   *The Sugar Reapers* or *Guyana Johnny*, Act I Scene 2, VS 78–9,
      Opera in Two Acts (Six Scenes) by Alan Bush, libretto by Nancy
      Bush © Copyright 1965 Estate of Alan Bush. Reproduced by permission. 230
7.4   *The Sugar Reapers* or *Guyana Johnny*, Act I Scene 1, VS, 42, Opera in
      Two Acts (Six Scenes) by Alan Bush, libretto by Nancy
      Bush © Copyright 1965 Estate of Alan Bush. Reproduced by permission. 231
7.5   Bush, *Joe Hill: The Man Who Never Died*, Act I Scene 3, 'Casey Jones',
      Opera in Two Acts by Alan Bush, libretto by Barrie Stavis, after his play
      The Man Who Never Died © Copyright 1967 Estate of Alan Bush.
      Reproduced by permission.   236
7.6   *Joe Hill: The Man Who Never Died*, Act I Scene 2, Opera in Two
      Acts by Alan Bush, libretto by Barrie Stavis, after his play *The Man*

	Who Never Died © Copyright 1967 Estate of Alan Bush. Reproduced by permission.	237
7.7	*Joe Hill: The Man Who Never Died*, Act II Scene 3, Opera in Two Acts by Alan Bush, libretto by Barrie Stavis, after his play *The Man Who Never Died* © Copyright 1967 Estate of Alan Bush. Reproduced by permission.	239
7.8	*Joe Hill: The Man Who Never Died*, Act II Scene 6, Joe's soliloquy, Opera in Two Acts by Alan Bush, libretto by Barrie Stavis, after his play *The Man Who Never Died* © Copyright 1967 Estate of Alan Bush. Reproduced by permission.	241

Acknowledgements

Many people have influenced and aided the process of writing this book. First and foremost, Dr Rachel O'Higgins, Alan Bush's daughter and curator of a large collection of his papers, has been constantly supportive, informative, helpful, and generous with her time. She allowed me to make several long trips to examine the material and kindly shared her memories of the journey she undertook with her father to British Guiana in 1959. Many other people have taken the time to share their memories of Alan Bush, some of whom have since passed away, and I am particularly grateful to John Jordan of the Workers Music Association, and the late Paul O'Higgins, Ronald Stevenson, Aubrey Bowman, and John Amis.

This project has involved a significant amount of archival research. Dr Nicolas Bell and other staff at the British Library were unfailingly helpful in navigating Bush's correspondence and manuscripts at a time when the catalogue consisted of a single sheet of A4. I am also indebted to the staff of, in London: the National Archives and the Victoria and Albert Museum; in Berlin: the Stiftung Archiv der Akademie der Künste, the Deutsche Rundfunkarchiv, and the Bundesarchiv; and in Leipzig: the Stadtarchiv.

My work on Alan Bush originated as a doctoral dissertation and has been pursued at academic posts in a number of other institutions. I am extremely grateful to the Arts and Humanities Research Council for funding my doctoral work, and to the Leverhulme Trust and the University of Nottingham for funding the Early Career Fellowship, which made the monograph possible. My doctoral supervisor, Jonathan Cross, and my editor, Arnold Whittall, have provided expert advice and encouragement on numerous occasions. Many other colleagues at Oxford, Nottingham, and elsewhere have read drafts and gamely participated in discussion of my research, including Robert Adlington, Simon Desbruslais, Larry Dreyfus, Annika Forkert, Pauline Fairclough, Daniel Grimley, Ben Harker, Sarah Hibberd, Esperanza Rodrigues-Garcia, and Martha Sprigge. Annika Forkert, Burkhard Schwalbach, and Golan Gur all kindly discussed the translation and interpretation of East German documents with me, and any errors in the latter are my own. Members of the Music Department at Cambridge University Press, especially Victoria Cooper, Kate Brett, Fleur Jones, and Lorenza Toffolon, have been unreservedly helpful in bringing the book to publication. The Faculty of Music at Oxford generously awarded me the 2016 Donald Tovey Memorial Prize, enabling me to complete final revisions of the manuscript. Finally, Jordan Summers Young gave up her free time to undertake a huge amount of proofreading and formatting.

At a very early stage of my research into Alan Bush, the late John Lowerson, who was then researching his own book on Bush, took the trouble to befriend me and share his profound expertise and knowledge. He was unfailingly supportive up until his sudden death in 2009, and our discussions from, respectively, the perspective of social and economic history and musicology, proved invaluable to the development of my ideas. While he died before writing up his own manuscript, and while this book does not include many areas which he was to cover, I hope he would approve.

The communist composer may be a complete human being; so too may the musicologist. This book has been written in the course of numerous house moves, job changes, and the birth of two children. My constant companion, critic, proofreader, cheerleader, babysitter, and taxi through this has been my husband, Professor Stephen Bullivant. This book is dedicated to him, and to our daughters Grace and Alice, with love.

Parts of earlier versions of Chapters 1 and 7 have appeared in other publications: 'Modernism, Politics and Individuality in 1930s Britain: The Case of Alan Bush', *Music & Letters* 90/3 (August 2009), 432–52; 'The Socialist Composer in the "capitalist concert-hall": Hanns Eisler and Alan Bush in 1930s England', in Oliver Dahin and Erik Levi (eds.), *Eisler and England*, Eisler-Studien 5 (Wiesbaden: Breitkopf & Härtel, 2014), 33–50; 'Black, White and Red: Communism and Anti-Colonialism in Alan Bush's *The Sugar Reapers*', in Robert Adlington (ed.), *Red Strains: Music and Communism Outside the Communist Bloc*, Proceedings of the British Academy 185 (Oxford: British Academy/Oxford University Press, 2013), 193–212; '"A world of Marxist orthodoxy?" Alan Bush's *Wat Tyler* in Great Britain and the German Democratic Republic', in Pauline Fairclough (ed.), *Twentieth-Century Music and Politics: Essays in memory of Neil Edmunds* (Aldershot: Ashgate, 2013), 7–21.

Abbreviations

CEMA	Committee for Encouragement of Music and the Arts
CPGB	Communist Party of Great Britain
DASB	Deutsche Arbeiter-Sängerbund (German Workers' Singers' League)
DDR	Deutsche Demokratische Republik
ENSA	Entertainments National Service Association
GDR	German Democratic Republic
ISCM	International Society for Contemporary Music
LLCU	London Labour Choral Union
RAM	Royal Academy of Music
SED	Sozialistische Einheitspartei Deutschlands (Socialist Unity Party of Germany)
Stakuko	Staatliche Kommission für Kunstangelegenheiten (State Commission for Artistic Affairs)
VDKM	Verband Deutscher Komponisten und Musikwissenschaftler (Union of German Composers and Musicologists)
WMA	Workers' Music Association

Abbreviations of Archival Sources

ABH	Alan Bush Archive, Histon, Cambridge
AdK-O	Archiv der Akademie der Künste der DDR
BArch	Bundesarchiv, Berlin
BBC/WAC	BBC Written Archive Centre, Caversham
BL/AB	The British Library, Alan Bush Collection
SAAdK	Stiftung Archiv der Akademie der Künste, Berlin
SAPMO-BArch	Stiftung Archiv der Parteien und Massenorganisationen der DDR im Bundesarchiv, Berlin
TNA/PRO	The National Archives, Public Record Office

Introduction

Why Alan Bush?

Modernist nationalist. British communist. Intellectual populist. When attempting to sum up Alan Bush (1900–95), one is confronted by the contradictory impulses that defined his life and career. Bush was a contemporary of Benjamin Britten and Michael Tippett.[1] Born into a wealthy middle-class industrialist family, he studied at the Royal Academy of Music (RAM, 1918–22) and took private composition lessons with John Ireland (1922–7), the teacher who would later have a brief and unhappy working relationship with Britten. He was made Professor of Harmony and Composition at the RAM in 1925 and remained so until his retirement in 1978, producing a compositional textbook, *Strict Counterpoint in the Palestrina Style*, and teaching successive generations of student composers.[2] He was married to his wife Nancy for sixty years, had three children, and continued composing and playing the piano until his death.

In counterpoint with this conventional narrative stands Bush's lifelong radicalism. He spent long periods in Berlin between 1926 and 1931, studying piano with Artur Schnabel, and musicology and philosophy at Friedrich-Wilhelms-Universität (what would become the Humboldt University of Berlin), where his teachers included Max Dessoir and Friedrich Blume.[3] While there, he not only immersed himself in the rich artistic environment of the Weimar Republic, but also became acquainted with the city's large and vibrant radical working-class musical culture. Having dabbled with theosophy and theories of mechanical materialism in the 1920s, he became acquainted with the German émigrés Bertolt Brecht and Hanns Eisler, and Tippett's cousin Phyllis Kemp, in the 1930s. In 1935, he joined the Communist Party of Great Britain (CPGB) and remained an ardent Stalinist for the rest of

---

[1] There is no scholarly biography of Bush. For a useful biographical memoir that incorporates a survey of the works by Lewis Foreman, see Nancy Bush, *Alan Bush: Music, Politics and Life* (London: Thames Publishing, 2000).

[2] Alan Bush, *Strict Counterpoint in the Palestrina Style: A Practical Textbook* (London: Joseph Williams, 1948).

[3] Nancy Bush, *Alan Bush*, 20–3.

his life.[4] For the remainder of that decade, alongside his concert works, he was extremely active in radical working-class musical culture as Musical Adviser to the London Labour Choral Union (LLCU), a conglomerate of working-class choirs, and as the founder of the Workers' Music Association (WMA) from 1936. It was also at this time that he visited the Soviet Union for the first time (1938) and started composing concert works with ostensibly political content, beginning with the Piano Concerto (1935–7) and continuing with the First Symphony (1939–40) and a succession of wartime orchestral and choral works.

Bush achieved notoriety in 1941 when the BBC briefly banned his music because he was a signatory of the communist-led, anti-war People's Convention. While he was courted briefly during the period of the Anglo-Soviet wartime alliance as a leading expert on Soviet music and international popular song, from 1948 he was the subject of renewed suspicion and antagonism from various quarters. Such antagonism stemmed not only from a wider crackdown on known communists working for public institutions in Britain, but also from Bush's outspoken defence of Zhdanovism, and the subsequent changes in his own compositional style in favour of a national, more populist style influenced by English folk music. The immediate fruits of Bush's avowed conversion were his Second Symphony, *The Nottingham* (1949), and his first opera, *Wat Tyler* (1948–50). The latter, despite winning a prize in the Arts Council opera competition run in association with the 1951 Festival of Britain, was not performed in Britain until 1974, and then only in a semi-professional production mounted by the WMA. By this point, Bush had had a successful but much-criticised career as an opera composer in the German Democratic Republic (GDR), but he had never achieved a fully professional production of one of his operas in his own country.

This oxymoronic convergence of the conventional trappings of a teaching career at a British conservatoire and the anything-but-conventional career of a prominent communist is undoubtedly intriguing. Making a case for Bush as a significant case study in the history of modern British music is more difficult. As a communist, Bush stood on the margins of British culture, less central to the articulation of national identity than Elgar or Vaughan Williams, and less vital to the construction of a modern British music than Britten or Tippett. There are well-worn counter-arguments dating back into Bush's middle age: that his music represents a fine body of

---

[4] See Alan Bush, 'In My Eighth Decade' in *In My Eighth Decade and Other Essays* (London: Kahn & Averill, 1980), 17–20.

national opera and symphony that deserves further attention, or, more disturbingly, that he has been unfairly marginalised because of his politics.

The problem with these arguments is that Bush is one of a legion of British composers outside the canonical nexus of Elgar, Vaughan Williams, and Britten who can claim attention; what makes Bush distinctive? Should he, in fact, be properly situated within the seemingly endless ranks of twentieth-century British eccentrics? Regarding the claims of marginalisation, these must indeed be addressed, but so too must the criticism made frequently in Bush's lifetime that his work was *promoted* in East Germany on purely political grounds. Moreover, in both cases, the end point of these arguments is to make the case for spending more time listening to Bush's music. While a worthy cause, this is not the primary task of the music historian. And, for several reasons, Bush seems consigned to the margins of twentieth-century music history. From 1948, he was a self-proclaimed populist and anti-modernist, and, as J.P.E. Harper-Scott has argued, we 'find it difficult to dislodge modernism as the central aesthetic concern of the twentieth century'.[5] An aesthetic of accessibility, social use, and compositions employing shared national musical materials stands in contradiction to modernism's impulses towards technical innovation, alienation, and abstraction. Moreover, in the Adornian narrative of modernism that has proved so influential in musicology of recent decades, such social utility rejects the emancipatory potential of modernism as critique. From a more basic perspective, works so invested in a discredited ideology run the risk of landing, ironically, upon Trotsky's 'rubbish heap of history'. Even prior to his renunciation, Bush was in the equally problematic category of the British composer. As Philip Rupprecht has discussed, the notion of a 'time lag' between musical innovations on the Continent and their appearance in Britain has remained stubbornly persistent.[6] Problematic, too, are the historical claims that modernism is somehow antithetical to the British temperament, variously transgressive, ideological, and contrary to the British sense of caution. Harper-Scott's case study, Walton, is 'doubly dissociated from the vanguard of modernism by being both British and "conservative" [...] in his use of musical materials and processes'.[7] Bush scores the hat trick by adding Stalinism to this list of attributes.

---

[5] J.P.E. Harper-Scott, *The Quilting Points of Musical Modernism: Revolution, Reaction, and William Walton* (Cambridge: Cambridge University Press, 2012), xiii.

[6] Philip Rupprecht, *British Musical Modernism: The Manchester Group and Their Contemporaries* (Cambridge: Cambridge University Press, 2015), 33ff.

[7] Harper-Scott, *The Quilting Points of Musical Modernism*, xiii.

It is therefore unsurprising that much of his critical reception in his lifetime, and until relatively recently, consisted of either outright condemnation of the later music or of efforts to eliminate one of this trio of obstacles from consideration.[8] Writing on Bush in this period frequently reflects one or more of the following assertions: (i) Bush was a promising and cosmopolitan modernist who sacrificed his personal idiom for the sake of politics and wrote more/less successful works thereafter; (ii) meritorious works of his were unjustly shunned in Britain for purely political reasons; (iii) by continuing to pursue political music beyond the 1930s, he relinquished the possibility of the sort of broad musical humanism ascribed to Britten and Tippett. Thus Tippett himself wrote with not a little condescension that 'Alan lives in a world of Marxist orthodoxy and certainty, while I live in a world of humanist ambivalence and uncertainty'.[9] Peter J. Pirie could dismiss Bush as 'isolated in English music, for the reason that his music, centring round his Communism, is dedicated to furthering the class struggle', while Percy Young contrasted the 'landmark' of Bush's string quartet *Dialectic* with the 'triteness' of some of the later music.[10] More nuanced arguments by Malcolm Macdonald, Anthony Payne, and Colin Mason have made attempts to establish an apolitical basis for criticism.[11] Representing another line of defence of Bush's late music, Ronald Stevenson praised Bush's move 'from an amorphous cosmopolitan *imbroglio* of idioms to a well-defined national style'.[12] In each instance, Bush's relationship to modernism, to national identity, and to communism are in play, yet no attempt has adequately explained the interaction of these conflicting priorities within his work.

---

[8] More recent efforts in musicology to assess Bush include Nathaniel Lew, 'A New and Glorious Age: Constructions of National Opera in Britain, 1945–1951', PhD thesis, University of California, Berkeley (2001); Julie Anne Waters, '"Against the Stream": Intersections of Music and Politics in the Conception, Composition and Reception of Alan Bush's First Three Symphonies', PhD thesis, Monash University (2012); and Joanna Bullivant, 'Modernism, Politics and Individuality in 1930s Britain: The Case of Alan Bush', *Music & Letters* 90/3 (August 2009), 432–52. In each case, only part of the composer's career and selected works are examined.

[9] Michael Tippett, 'A Magnetic Friendship: An Attraction of Opposites' in Ronald Stevenson (ed.), *Time Remembered. Alan Bush: An 80th Birthday Symposium* (Kidderminster: Bravura Publications, 1981), 9.

[10] Peter J. Pirie, *The English Musical Renaissance* (London: Gollancz, 1979), 187–8; Percy M. Young, *A History of British Music* (London: Benn, 1967), 597.

[11] Malcolm MacDonald, 'The Music, to One Pair of Ears' in Stevenson (ed.), *Time Remembered*, 26; Anthony Payne, 'Alan Bush', *Musical Times* 105/1454 (April 1964), 264; Colin Mason, 'Alan Bush in High Middle Age', *The Listener*, 26 May 1960, 954.

[12] Ronald Stevenson, 'Alan Bush: Committed Composer', *Music Review* 25/4 (November 1964), 324.

British Modernism

How, then, might Bush be approached anew as a historical subject? One solution which has borne fruit in relation to other British composers is to interpret his music through the lens of a more encompassing understanding of modernism. Work on reception history and institutions has uncovered the extent to which 'ultra-modern' music was heard, performed, and debated in twentieth-century Britain.[13] Jenny Doctor has gone so far as to view its presence itself as modernist, drawing attention to the 'parataxis' of the juxtaposition of traditional concert procedure and new technologies, classics and 'novelties' at the wartime Proms.[14] Ongoing research reveals ever more evidence of the impact of Continental modernists upon British composers.[15] Alongside such scholarship, what Harper-Scott terms an 'expansionist' critical approach has drawn on a broader array of technical resources in order to elucidate instances of British modernism.[16] Alain Frogley's reading of Vaughan Williams's 'London' Symphony, drawing on H.G. Wells and the modernist preoccupation with the alienating metropolis; Daniel M. Grimley's account of the 'Pastoral' Symphony and its parallels with Paul Nash's fractured landscapes of wartime France; and Harper-Scott's own analysis of Elgar, which employs James Hepokoski's analysis of modernist sonata forms in Sibelius and others, are cases in point.[17] Musicologists have also benefitted from new theories of British modernism in literary studies, in which, similarly, the period following the high, cosmopolitan modernism of Pound, Eliot, Yeats, Woolf et al. has been seen as one of insularity and decline. In the most influential such

---

[13] See, for example, Malcolm Gillies, *Bartók in Britain: A Guided Tour* (Oxford: Clarendon Press, 1989); Jennifer Doctor, *The BBC and Ultra-Modern Music, 1922–1936: Shaping a Nation's Tastes* (Cambridge: Cambridge University Press, 1999); Jenny Doctor and David Wright (eds.), *The Proms: A New History* (London: Thames & Hudson, 2007).

[14] Jenny Doctor, 'The Parataxis of "British Musical Modernism"', *Musical Quarterly* 91/1–2 (Spring/Summer 2008), 110–12.

[15] See, for example, the discussion of the impact of Hindemith on British composers in Jürgen Schaarwächter, *Two Centuries of British Symphonism: From the Beginnings to 1945: A Preliminary Survey* (Hildesheim: Georg Olms Verlag, 2015), vol. II, 731–49.

[16] Harper-Scott, *The Quilting Points of Musical Modernism*, xiii.

[17] Alain Frogley, 'H.G. Wells and Vaughan Williams's *A London Symphony*: Politics and Culture in Fin-de-Siècle England' in Chris Banks, Arthur Searle and Malcolm Turner (eds.), *Sundry Sorts of Music Books: Essays on the British Library Collections Presented to O.W. Neighbour on His 70th Birthday* (London: British Library, 1993), 299–308; Daniel M. Grimley, 'Landscape and Distance: Vaughan Williams, Modernism and the Symphonic Pastoral' in Matthew Riley (ed.), *British Music and Modernism, 1895–1960* (Aldershot: Ashgate, 2010), 147–74; J.P.E. Harper-Scott, *Edward Elgar: Modernist* (Cambridge: Cambridge University Press, 2006).

study for musicologists, Jed Esty has read late works of Eliot, Woolf, and E.M. Forster as attempts, in response to Britain's transformation from imperial power to 'Little England', to retain the transformative powers of modernism within a national context.[18] Thus, in such works, a metropolitan, cosmopolitan, and alienated modernism operates in tension with the articulation of an idealised rural, organic, national community. While not always directly indebted to Esty, the exploration of these tensions has produced varied new perspectives from Heather Wiebe, Christopher Chowrimootoo, and Rupprecht, for example.[19]

The strengths of this body of work are the situating of aspects of musical style and technique within a complex historical and cultural context, an expanded analytical palette, and illuminating comparisons with a wealth of figures, such as Sibelius, who have themselves been incorporated into a diverse modernism beyond a putative Schoenberg/Stravinsky core. Yet in the case of Bush the category of British modernism must be handled with care. Rupprecht has traced the trope in British music criticism that perceived something 'indecent' or alien about the use of modernist techniques, and the marginal position of those composers – ranging from Frank Bridge to Dorothy Gow to Elisabeth Lutyens – who were most indebted to developments such as the twelve-note method.[20] Yet alongside this stands the vein of criticism demonstrated by the following vignette. Walter Leigh, another contemporary of Bush, studied composition with Hindemith in the 1920s and was influenced by the radical aesthetic experimentation of Weimar Berlin. In Leigh's obituary, Hubert Foss remarked that in comparison with his teacher 'Leigh's [music] was hardly what is called *gebrauchsmusik*: it was less terrifying, less self-conscious'.[21] While Leigh himself did not live to see such a time, others who showed a 'less terrifying' absorption of modernism – such as Alan Rawsthorne, Bush himself, and even Lutyens to an extent – formed part of what Calum Macdonald would come to denote a 'lost generation' of composers.[22]

---

[18] Jed Esty, *A Shrinking Island: Modernism and National Culture in England* (Princeton and Oxford: Princeton University Press, 2004).

[19] Heather Wiebe, *Britten's Unquiet Pasts: Sound and Memory in Postwar Reconstruction* (Cambridge: Cambridge University Press, 2012); Christopher Chowrimootoo, 'The Timely Traditions of *Albert Herring*', *Opera Quarterly* 27/4 (2011), 379–419 and 'Bourgeois Opera: *Death in Venice* and the Aesthetics of Sublimation', *Cambridge Opera Journal* 22/2 (2011), 177–218; Rupprecht, *British Musical Modernism*, 48ff.

[20] Rupprecht, *British Musical Modernism*, 45–7.

[21] Hubert J. Foss, 'Walter Leigh', *Musical Times* 83/1194 (August 1942), 255.

[22] Calum Macdonald, 'Lost Generation', *The Listener*, 23 April 1987, cited in Neil Edmunds, 'William Glock and the British Broadcasting Corporation's Music Policy, 1959–73', *Contemporary British History* 20/2 (June 2006), 247.

This group, generally on the Left, fell between two stools of being too modernist when they were becoming established and too conservative for the more internationalist musical climate of the 1960s.

The notion of the 'lost generation' is worth pausing over because it highlights the slippage – almost impossible to avoid – into describing British composers as more or less modernist. The use of such language is intriguing. It is dangerous because it can imply a sort of Richter scale of modernism, and thus reinforce the very centralising model with Schoenberg at its centre that the concept of British modernism aims to challenge. It also reveals a longstanding trend of ambivalence in the discourse over British modernism. Foss implies, whether through bombast, insecurity, or generosity, a superiority on the part of Leigh, a level of confidence and authenticity missing in true *Gebrauchsmusik*. Yet as Rupprecht and Ben Earle have both identified, an opposing tradition of 'group self-contempt' towards British modernism is equally venerable.[23] Earle's assertions that this notion needs revision notwithstanding, his closing statement that Humphrey Searle was 'the British composer, perhaps more than any other, who genuinely deserves to be called a modernist' suggests that the 'discourse of national doubt' is by no means finished.[24]

Directly related to the long history of self-examination in discussions of British modernism is the question of what cultural work is being done when we claim a composer or work for modernism. As Harper-Scott writes, 'labelling music as modernist or not is not a neutral aesthetic judgment but always a political act'.[25] He identifies, in addition to the 'expansionist' response to modernism, a 'positive' response (of which the expansionist is a variant) and a 'democratic' response.[26] The positive response is a post-Adornian position, which posits modernism as the most vital and emancipatory response to human existence in the twentieth century. The democratic response, with which Harper-Scott especially associates the work of Richard Taruskin, presents modernism as bourgeois, elitist, and repudiated by the emergence of popular forms of music disseminated via modern technologies and media. It is striking that efforts to resituate British composers in the context of modernism almost always involve ethical rehabilitation as much as an expanded technical vocabulary: Elgar's ambivalence towards Empire, the radical socialist roots of Vaughan Williams's Englishness, Holst's Eastern spiritualism. The 'positive' view is

---

[23] Ben Earle, '"The real thing – at last?" Historicizing Humphrey Searle' in Riley (ed.), *British Music and Modernism*, 300.
[24] Ibid., 325; Rupprecht, *British Musical Modernism*, 48.
[25] Harper-Scott, *The Quilting Points of Musical Modernism*, xii.   [26] Ibid., xiii.

perhaps historically nowhere more evident in British music studies than in the body of work on Britten, notably in the work of Philip Brett, that connected his adoption of aspects of Continental modernism to his artistic and moral project of addressing the plight of the alienated individual, and subjecting those societies which oppress the outsider to critique.[27]

This is not to question the veracity of any of the composer-focused work just mentioned. What must be observed is how uneasily Bush sits within this expansionist, positive model of British modernism. He is precisely in the category of composers who made limited inroads into modernist techniques and who are thus vulnerable to the narrative of national self-doubt, and his virulent Stalinism and conservatism are antithetical to recuperation based on a model of modernism associated with Adornian values of individual emancipation.

Communists

Returning to the question of how to approach Bush as historical subject and bearing these issues in mind, another profitable line of investigation is to examine Bush through the lens of the large respective bodies of work on music and communism and on British communism. In the field of Cold War musicology, scholarship by Marina Frolova-Walker, Peter J. Schmelz, Anne C. Shreffler, and others has drawn attention to such central issues as the incoherence of socialist realism as an aesthetic and the wide-ranging interpretations it provoked; the non-identity between socialist individuals and states; the complexity of processes of political oversight of musicians (in opposition to myths surrounding the relationship between Stalin and Shostakovich, say); the competing Cold War rhetoric and programmes of arts patronage that surrounded claims to such contested categories as 'freedom' and 'modernity'; the nuanced position occupied by politically radical modernists such as Luigi Nono, Cornelius Cardew, and Louis Andriessen; and the permeability of the aesthetic and ideological 'Nylon Curtain'.[28] Such work has

---

[27] See, for example, the essays on Britten reproduced in Philip Brett, *Music and Sexuality in Britten: Selected Essays*, ed. George E. Haggerty (Berkeley and Los Angeles: University of California Press, 2006).

[28] The literature here is too broad to give more than suggestions. On Nono, Cardew, and Andriessen, see Carola Nielinger-Vakil, *Luigi Nono: A Composer in Context* (Cambridge: Cambridge University Press, 2015); John Tilbury, *Cornelius Cardew (1936–1981): A Life Unfinished* (Matching Tye, Essex: Copula, 2008); Robert Adlington, *Louis Andriessen: De Staat* (Aldershot: Ashgate, 2004). On music and communism, see Anne C. Shreffler, 'Berlin Walls: Dahlhaus, Knepler, and Ideologies of Music History', *The Journal of Musicology* 20/4

established a framework within which the individual agency of communist composers (in both the East and West) can be examined and the ideological binarism that forms a barrier to serious investigation of a composer like Bush can be dismantled.

The study of British communism has produced little on musicians, a situation eminently fair given the tiny size of the Party and even smaller cohort of musicians within it, yet this also offers fresh perspectives.[29] An important and continuing strain of British communist memoir – most recently added to by David Aaronovitch's *Party Animals* – has emphasised the elements of otherness, insularity, delusion, even tragicomedy, which characterised British communism.[30] The titles of these memoirs – *Party Animals, The Lost World of British Communism, I Believed* – variously evoke the exotic curiosity of the phenomenon when viewed strictly from the outside, the sense of disillusionment experienced by so many who left the Party, and the uniformity and collective nature of their experiences. As Raphael Samuel has asserted:

> To be a Communist was to have a complete social identity, one which transcended the limits of class, gender and nationality. Like practising Catholics or Orthodox Jews, we lived in a little private world of our own, or, like some of the large or extended families of the period, 'a tight ... self-referential group'. A great deal of our activity – Communists of the period were nothing if not 'politically active' – for all the urgency of its occasions, might be seen retrospectively as a way of practising togetherness.[31]

(Autumn 2003), 498–525 and '"Music Left and Right": A Tale of Two Histories of Progressive Music' in Robert Adlington (ed.), *Red Strains: Music and Communism Outside the Communist Bloc*, Proceedings of the British Academy (Oxford: Oxford University Press, 2013), 67–88; Marina Frolova-Walker, '"National in Form, Socialist in Content": Musical Nation-Building in the Soviet Republics', *Journal of the American Musicological Society* 51/2 (1998), 331–71 and *Stalin's Music Prize: Soviet Culture and Politics* (New Haven and London: Yale University Press, 2016); and a special Cold War issue, edited by Peter J. Schmelz, of the *Journal of Musicology* 26/1 (Winter 2009). For the phrase the 'Nylon Curtain', see Györgi Péteri (ed.), *Nylon Curtain: Transnational and Trans-Systemic Tendencies in the Cultural Life of State-Socialist Russia and East-Central Europe* (Trondheim, Norway: Program on East European Cultures and Societies, 2006).

[29] Some partially successful attempts to open discussion on music in the CPGB may be found in several chapters of Andy Croft (ed.), *A Weapon in the Struggle: The Cultural History of the Communist Party in Britain* (London: Pluto, 1998).

[30] Examples include David Aaronovitch, *Party Animals: My Family and Other Communists* (London: Jonathan Cape, 2016); Alexei Sayle, *Stalin Ate My Homework* (London: Sceptre, 2010); Raphael Samuel, *The Lost World of British Communism* (London and New York: Verso, 2006); Douglas Hyde, *I Believed: The Autobiography of a Former British Communist* (London: Heinemann, 1950).

[31] Samuel, *The Lost World of British Communism*, 13.

In the field of history rather than memoir, however, a more nuanced picture of communist identity and experience is emerging. Rather than exotic Others, British communists were a diverse group who occupied various positions with respect to national identity, and who embraced different group identities in addition to their communism through intellectual and cultural activity, work, trade unionism, family life, and friendship. Thus Bush was married to a non-communist, worked with the BBC, maintained his longstanding teaching position in the heart of the British musical establishment, and was, eventually, able to see past Tippett's Trotskyism and the composer Bernard Stevens' exit from the Party to maintain his friendships.

On the one hand, such work on communism and culture offers a route into the complexity of Bush's experiences and aesthetic positions, and the possibility of a more nuanced view of his relationship with British culture than simply conceiving of him as the outsider variously marginalised by his modernism, his conservatism, or his politics. On the other hand, care must be taken that evidence of his embeddedness in British culture does not efface the very real suspicion and ostracism of communists in Cold War Britain, nor Bush's genuine political radicalism, which remains problematic. In new accounts of British communist culture, Bush invariably emerges as excessively willing to embrace the Party line even by its own rigorous standards. Not only did he throw himself into all manner of Party work, but was unfailingly willing to defend the Party and, to an even greater extent, the Soviet Union at the lowest moments of its history. Just as Bush sits uneasily within British modernism, he remains problematic as the subject of a rehabilitated picture of Western communism.

Modernism and Communism: A Theoretical Solution

As a final starting point for approaching Bush, there stands Harper-Scott's adumbration of a theoretical relationship between communism and British modernism. Harper-Scott interprets modernism, after Alain Badiou, as an '*Event* that institutes a new form of knowledge', that evinces a variety of responses, both 'faithful' and 'reactive' (thus producing faithful or reactive subjects, a designation that may variously refer to a piece of music or a group of composers, for example).[32] For Harper-Scott, the fundamental revolution of musical modernism is the emancipation of dissonance, because it established an order outside the ancient binary of consonance and dissonance in Western music. Consequently, the faithful

[32] Harper-Scott, *The Quilting Points of Musical Modernism*, xiii and 159ff.

subject position may be exemplified by works, such as *Moses und Aron* or *Lulu*, in which 'music is no longer understood in terms of the binary of consonance and dissonance – a mimesis of ideological binaries in whose confines the human subject "must" constitute itself – but in terms of a radical communism of notes, guaranteed by more or less extreme intellectual rigidity'.[33] In the case of the reactive subject, there may be palpable signs of the effects of the emancipation of dissonance, yet the music is still governed by 'the presumption of tonicity'.[34] Bound up with this analysis of modernism is the broader Badiouvian idea of communism as the Event driving human history, an idea based on a radical egalitarianism that was partially articulated by, and yet transcends, the failed communist experiments of the twentieth century and is still vital.[35] Introducing a British dimension, Harper-Scott's case study is the composer William Walton. Drawing on Esty, Harper-Scott interprets Walton's turn from faithfulness to reaction – a transformation instantiated in the First Symphony (1931–5) – as the adumbration of the (ideal communist) new community that was writ large in Britain's disintegrating imperialist vision.

There are attractions to Harper-Scott's model. The concept of faithful and reactive responses suggests a route to addressing the more/less modernist problem that is central to understanding Bush. The prospect of a conception of communism that is non-identical with the dictatorships of the twentieth century is also potentially fruitful for a composer who developed his own brand of English musical communism. Yet Harper-Scott's approach will not be mine. Above all, it is the nuances of Bush's experience as historical subject that fascinate and provoke reflection on such matters as British communist identity or the reception of modernism, and it is in the detail of the past, rather than theory for the future, that Harper-Scott's study proves problematic. For example, in his overview of Walton's works, Harper-Scott states that 'the theatrical (if not the musical) gestures of [the first version of] *Façade* indicate his early faithfulness'.[36] Yet outside the framework of emancipation of dissonance as the hallmark of musical modernism, it is not clear how this translates to theatricality and whether similar conclusions may be drawn about other works which may be considered gesturally but not musically faithful (Weill's stage works, for instance). *Façade* also presents a case in which, arguably, the division of Badiouvian responses hinders rather than helps historical and aesthetic

---

[33] Ibid., 179.   [34] Ibid., 179.
[35] See also Alain Badiou, 'The Idea of Communism' in Costas Douzinas and Slavoj Žižek (eds.), *The Idea of Communism* (London and New York: Verso, 2010), 1–14.
[36] Harper-Scott, *The Quilting Points of Musical Modernism*, 222.

insight. In Harper-Scott's schema, jazz, along with minimalism and pop is relegated to the 'obscure' response, as music which 'simply rejects the principle of emancipated dissonance outright', asserting that '[t]he correspondence between this tendency and its increased saleability is surely not fortuitous'.[37] Yet the reception of jazz was strongly bound up with that of contemporary music in inter-war Britain, because of the association of both with the experience of late modernity through international cultural products primarily introduced to Britain via modern technology, and because of their marriage in works of Stravinsky, for example.[38] Both modernism and jazz were also crucial influences upon the young Walton and his circle, as evidenced by both *Façade* and the preceding String Quartet (1919–22). These observations do not necessarily dent Harper-Scott's ultimate aim, which is to establish a theoretical framework for a modernist musicology that can critique a globalised, neoliberal age. Yet they do expose its shortcomings as a model for historical investigation. In an intriguing parallel, the feminist writer Toril Moi has challenged the legitimacy of Lacan's theory of femininity, remarking that 'We need more historically specific, more situated, and far more clearly defined accounts of women's lived experience and women's subjectivity than femininity theories can produce'.[39] An account of communism and British modernism that draws primarily on a composer totally divorced from communist states and parties may legitimately avoid the lived experience of communism. A study of Alan Bush – a composer who, even when cultivating a specifically English communism, remained deeply inspired by and committed to the realities of the communist state in the Eastern Bloc – cannot. We need historically detailed accounts of figures who engaged with communism and modernism to understand how these categories operated in Britain. And few accounts can provide such a wealth of historical detail as that of Alan Bush.

An Alternative Approach: Bush and Modern Selfhood

My approach, then, is the reverse of Harper-Scott's, in that where he constructs a theory of the relationship between modernism and communism and works inwards, I start with this historically specific 'lived experience' and work outwards. The first priority in appreciating the aesthetic and political tensions that underpin Bush's career is to reconstruct what he

---

[37] Ibid., 186.   [38] Bullivant, 'Modernism, Politics, and Individuality in 1930s Britain', 436.
[39] Toril Moi, 'From Femininity to Finitude: Freud, Lacan, and Feminism, Again', *Signs: Journal of Women in Culture and Society* 29/3 (Spring 2004), 845.

thought and did, how he composed, and how he was received by others at crucial points in his career. Fortuitously, both Bush himself and some of the key institutions with which he worked were voracious hoarders of records and correspondence, which, since the collapse of the Soviet Union, and Bush's death in 1995, has become available. Bush's enormous collection of letters and manuscripts has been deposited in the British Library and was catalogued over the course of my doctoral research. Bush's daughter, Dr Rachel O'Higgins, has maintained an invaluable archive of other material, including details of CPGB Musicians' meetings in the 1940s (to my knowledge not extant elsewhere), concert programmes, reviews, and unpublished articles. Bush's MI5 file was recently released, providing a wealth of concrete information that was previously a matter of speculation. The archives of the BBC and CPGB, and East German official documents now held by the Bundesarchiv, Berlin, have provided additional insights. Consequently, it has been possible to reconstruct in great detail the formation of Bush's ideas, his relationship with bodies like the CPGB and BBC, and the discourse that emerged surrounding his provocative works. From these sources, it is possible to build the anatomy of a British communist artist in all its complexity. Bush's relationships with others in the CPGB, his experiences with cultural bureaucracies and powerful individuals in East Germany, and his exasperating efforts to reform workers' music in interwar Britain all attest to the non-identity of communist individual, Party, state and ideology. Such examples, among others, show the extent to which Bush as an individual negotiated these intersecting spheres of communism, as did numerous others he encountered both in Britain and the communist bloc.

It is from this rich body of evidence that a new and coherent account of his relationship to modernism, communism, and British identity emerges, one which not only elucidates the apparent contradictions of Bush's career, but also offers insights into British communism and communist music more widely. The critical responses to Bush cited previously frequently characterise his music by employing binary oppositions around a central point of aesthetic reversal, imprecisely dated to around 1948: modern/not modern, political/apolitical, narrowly political/broadly humanist. In fact, he pursued a remarkably coherent aesthetic strategy from the 1930s onwards, one which encompassed composition, music theory, and cultural planning. As a Marxist, Bush perceived himself to be a historically and socially situated subject, committed to bringing about a new era of world socialism. His interests in modernist music and the year-to-year fluctuations of communist policy, while important, were ultimately subordinate to this commitment.

The idea of Bush as self-aware subject is a crucial one. Communism has been associated with the effacement of the individual, as witnessed by everything from the demand for total identity between the individual and the state, to the stipulation for composers to use national musical materials as a form of collective expression, to ludicrous accounts of East German toddlers being taught proper social behaviour through synchronised use of the potty. In both the Adornian concept of modernism and Cold War discourse, there has been an equally strong association between modernism and the articulation of the individual self. While inadequate, as has already been discussed, these associations have coloured Bush's reception, rendering his turn to a more national, popular style both a renunciation of musical selfhood and a decidedly anti-modernist gesture; at worst, a straightforward invitation to the Soviet leadership to do his thinking for him. Yet there is much evidence of a more nuanced model of communist selfhood. For example, Jochen Hellbeck, examining diaries from the Stalinist period, has revealed the efforts of ordinary Soviet citizens to chart their personal, self-conscious struggle towards identity with the goals of socialism.[40] Furthermore, Charles Taylor has identified three major facets of modern identity:

> first, modern inwardness, the sense of ourselves as beings with inner depths, and the connected notion that we are "selves"; second, the affirmation of ordinary life which develops from the early modern period; third, the expressivist notion of nature as an inner moral source.[41]

While Taylor is focusing on the modern period writ large, and traces aspects of this identity back to Augustine, it is applicable because the historical accusation against Bush, and communist values in general, is not that they are *less* modern but somehow antithetical to the very state of being modern. On the contrary, all these qualities are exhibited in Bush's longstanding efforts to find a musical language that could encompass and fuse what he valued in mass culture and modernism: his sense of his own interior journey mirroring and guiding outward actions; his own espoused belief in his self-criticism and correction in favour of nationalism in the 1940s; and his recourse to notions of musical nature in forging his theory of music. Moreover, the self is not formed *ex nihilo*, but through continual encounters with others and society as a whole. Bush's artistic self was forged not only through his own self-consciousness of his responsibilities

---

[40] Jochen Hellbeck, *Revolution on My Mind: Writing a Diary under Stalin* (London and Cambridge, MA: Harvard University Press, 2006).

[41] Charles Taylor, *Sources of the Self: The Making of Modern Identity* (Cambridge: Cambridge University Press, 1989), x.

as a communist artist, but also through repeated encounters with the revolutionary events through which he lived: the rise of fascism, the outbreak of the Second World War and the schizophrenic positions of the CPGB; the events of 1948; and the emergence of an East German socialist state.

Having introduced the assertion that Bush was a self-aware subject attempting to engage with the historical and social circumstances of modernity, it is now possible to reformulate his relationship with modernism. I contend that Bush engaged with musical modernism as a phenomenon that carried specific political and cultural connotations at different times, and that offered both opportunities for cultural work and for the construction of a new music appropriate to a new historical era of socialism. Thus, between 1933 and 1939, modernist works could be performed as part of specifically anti-Nazi agitations, but the twelve-note method also offered deeper inspiration as an alternative to a tonal system that Bush, at this time, associated with bourgeois capitalism. Furthermore, I argue that modern music was a contested and politicised category, through which Bush evaluated with British and East German culture, and which he used to make claims about the legitimacy of his aesthetics. It is unnecessary to claim that Bush or individual works are or are not modernist. Far more revealing is to chart the tensions that emerged in his efforts to forge a path to a modern, socialist music, and the responses that task provoked in different contexts. Not only does this cast new light on his relationship to modernism, but it reveals why Bush is such a rewarding case study for those interested in modern British music and communism more widely. While Bush's artistic path was idiosyncratic and provoked much antagonism in Britain, the questions he engaged with – the construction of a modern national culture, the legacy of war and renaissance of British music, the meaning and significance of musical modernism, freedom of political and artistic expression – stood at the centre of twentieth-century British musical culture. Thus Bush was – and is – a lightning rod for considering how those themes unfolded in policy, composition, and through the experience of individuals beyond the canonical core of Elgar, Vaughan Williams, and Britten. Bush is a focal point, an instantiation of the intersections of modernism, communism, and British identity, who demonstrates how these conflicting categories might be brought into a meaningful relationship.

Given the wealth of material and the nascent state of research, it has been impossible for this book to attempt a comprehensive survey of Bush's works and career in addition to the aims already stated. Many interesting and significant works – notably the 'Byron' Symphony and the works for voice and piano – have been omitted, as have important areas of Bush's activity such as his teaching. Instead, the book is structured around the most trenchant controversies in Bush's career: his engagement with modernism; his workers' music; his experiences in wartime, including the notorious BBC ban; his actions in 1948; his aesthetics of national opera; and his experiences in East Germany. From the consideration of these issues – each of which is assigned a chapter – a narrative emerges of Bush's modern-national aesthetic project, through its most complete expression in *Wat Tyler*, to its decline in the new cultural climate of the 1960s. Through each chapter, too, not only Bush's own ideas and practice, but also his response to events and the actions of others, shall be brought into focus. Thus, while an exhaustive account is yet to written, what will emerge is a portrait of the prominent communist whose music proved so provocative in British culture and whose career illustrates such a complex interaction of categories central to twentieth-century music.

1 Bush as Modernist: Material and Performance

The period dating from Bush's studies with John Ireland (1922–7) to the outbreak of the Second World War was crucial to his political and aesthetic formation. It was then that he joined the Communist Party, experienced the cultural life and extreme politics of Weimar Berlin, began his lifelong association with workers' organisations, and made many of the acquaintances – not least the émigrés Brecht, Eisler, Ernst Hermann Meyer, and Georg Knepler – who would decisively influence his ideas. Yet this phase of Bush's career also witnessed extremes of opinion and activity that are difficult to reconcile, and this difficulty has been reflected in critical accounts. Ian Kemp's unflattering comparison of the composer with Tippett implies that the later 1930s was the starting point for the incursion of politics into Bush's music, to resoundingly negative effect:

> Politics had [...] introduced [Tippett] to a breadth of human feeling he felt able to reach through his music. [...] If the primitive rhythms and acceptance of Soviet cultural dogma in Eisler's workers' songs seemed to him to have an enervating effect on the music of Alan Bush (who joined the Communist Party in 1936), then at least this sharpened [Tippett's] own instincts for a simplicity of real individuality.[1]

Tippett's political engagement, then, gave him 'human feeling' and 'real individuality', whereas Bush learned from Eisler a 'primitive' musical simplicity, the acceptance of political dogma, and, it is implied, relinquishment of individuality. Suzanne Robinson, too, has argued that whereas Bush 'modelled himself on Eisler', Tippett was unable to 'advocate the submission of the individual conscience to mass action or [...] to any political dogma'.[2]

This view of Bush in this period stands in contrast to the body of opinion which considers Bush's pre-war works – notably *Relinquishment*, op. 11 (1928) for piano solo; *Dialectic*, op. 15 (1929) for string quartet; and the *Concert Piece* for Cello and Piano, op. 17 (1936) – to demonstrate a degree

---

[1] Ian Kemp, *Tippett: The Composer and His Music* (Oxford and New York: Oxford University Press, 1987), 38–9. In fact, Bush joined the CPGB in 1935.

[2] Suzanne Robinson, 'From Agitprop to Parable: A Prolegomenon to *A Child of Our Time*' in Suzanne Robinson (ed.), *Michael Tippett: Music and Literature* (Aldershot: Ashgate, 2002), 85, 107.

of complexity comparable to those of Schoenberg. Wilfrid Mellers identified a disparity between Bush's 'deliberately simple and direct' workers' music and the 'highly sophisticated, complicated, intellectual' art music.³ Peter Evans associated *Dialectic* with a 'capacity for taut argument' and 'the rigour of much European music'; Percy Young went so far as to refer specifically to the quartet's 'affinities with dodecaphony'.⁴

On the one hand, then, Bush is described as relinquishing his individual compositional voice in favour of crude and simplistic political music in the 1930s. On the other, he is associated with the technical sophistication of the most radical of the pre-war modernists. Evans' comments, in particular, recall Lutyens' famous assertion that to use a technique [the twelve-note method] associated with Schoenberg was 'un-English [...] we were writing in what was considered a "mittel-European" style'.⁵

These two bodies of opinion are not necessarily mutually exclusive. After all, Kemp and Robinson are, on the whole, discussing amateur workers' songs rather than Bush's more conventional concert repertoire. Yet given that those two areas of Bush's musical activity were happening at the same time, how can the workers' songs be seen as a simplification of a single, unified style? Moreover, why should politics in Bush's case in the 1930s be a barrier to self-expression, whereas for Tippett, in Kemp's view, it was the impetus for 'real individuality'? This question is even more urgent when comparing views of Britten's musical and political affinities in the 1930s with those of Bush. Like Tippett's, Britten's political interests have been associated with his lifelong musical celebration of the individual. Moreover, these political interests have been connected with Britten's exploration of European modernism. The story of Britten's plans to study with Berg being quashed on 'moral' grounds is indicative of the association drawn between Britten's musical and political 'otherness'.⁶ Philip Brett writes of *Our Hunting Fathers* (1936) that 'the acerbic, disjointed orchestral gestures, the almost hysterical vocal cadenza on the word "Rats," and the uncomfortable musical motive that follows, with

---

³ Wilfrid Mellers, 'A Note on Alan Bush and the English Tradition' in Edward Clark (ed.), *Tribute to Alan Bush on His Fiftieth Birthday* (London: Workers' Music Association, 1950), 21–2.
⁴ Peter Evans, 'Instrumental Music I' in Stephen Banfield (ed.), *The Blackwell History of Music in Britain: The Twentieth Century*, vol. 6 (Oxford: Blackwell, 1995), 216; Young, *A History of British Music*, 597.
⁵ Cited in Rupprecht, *British Musical Modernism*, 40.
⁶ For a discussion of the affair, see Donald Mitchell and Philip Reed (eds.), *Letters from a Life: The Selected Letters and Diaries of Benjamin Britten 1913-1976*, vol. I (London: Faber, 1991), 394–5.

percussion exploding everywhere like gunfire, locates the piece quickly enough in anti-fascist discourse'.[7] Brett also connects the 'harsh-sounding, "political" side of Britten's work' to his difficulties in coming to terms with his homosexuality.[8] Brett's reading emphasises that, musically and politically, Britten is an isolated, individual voice, one that reached its fullest expression in *Peter Grimes* (1945), just as Tippett was able to combine a political statement and lament for the individual in *A Child of Our Time* (1944).

It would be wrong to equate Bush's experience with Britten's, yet at the very least, readings of Bush's contemporaries – not to mention the affinity between the personal and the political in works by, say, Berg and Hindemith – demand a much more nuanced consideration of Bush's negotiation of political and musical influences in this period, and how these pertained to the expression of selfhood. As shall be demonstrated, in interwar Britain, the social and political associations of modern music were still being negotiated, not least on the radical Left. Bush, far from unthinkingly swerving towards political propaganda, was a prolific and thoughtful commentator who placed modern music and politics at the heart of his aesthetic concerns. Even more significantly, in both popular debates and Bush's own musings on music and politics in the decade, the self-conscious articulation of the individual self was a matter of prime importance. Thus, the 1930s not only reveal the complexity of Bush's nascent ideas about the relationship between modern music on the one hand and radical politics on the other, but also that the vexed question of his personal role in this process was asked from the outset of his engagement with communism.

Meanings of Modernism

Contemporary reactions to modern music were more varied and complex than can be adequately reflected here, not least in the array of terms surrounding the work of Schoenberg, Stravinsky, and other modernists. 'Extremism' and 'ultra-modernism' were common but imprecise in meaning, as some sources suggest the latter is a relative rather than an absolute term. Richard Capell, for example, wrote in 1934 of comparing the 'ultra-Modernism of 100 years ago and today'.[9] 'Contemporary' was a loaded term thanks to the International Society for Contemporary Music (ISCM) and the BBC Contemporary Music concerts. Yet both 'contemporary' and

---

[7] Philip Brett, 'Auden's Britten' in *Music and Sexuality in Britten*, 191.   [8] Ibid., 191–2.
[9] R.C. [Richard Capell], 'Modernism Made Easy: How to Feel at Home in the Jungle', *Daily Telegraph*, 17 February 1934, 17.

'modern' could simply mean contemporaneous. A constant difficulty for writers was the inadequacy of these terms in view of the fact that Elgar and Ravel, say, were 'contemporary' composers, yet were perceived very differently from those composers associated with the ISCM. The only universal agreement was that modern music was *difficult* to define. And yet the recurrence of certain descriptive terms suggests that critics recognised a phenomenon that was nebulous, yet coherent enough to generate repeated attempts at definition. For convenience, I will simply use the term 'modern music'.

A number of British responses to the influx of modern music from Continental Europe in the 1930s are familiar. Modern music is perceived to break radically with the past: it 'does not add to musical progress but tries to start it all over again'.[10] It is considered ugly and dissonant – 'an unending succession of hideous noises' – and bewildering to audiences.[11] It is described as dry, cerebral, and unemotional: the 'preciousness and intellectuality of the cerebral, sterilised moderns' that 'obstructs true feeling and emotion'.[12] These statements are easily ascribed to a conservative outlook, yet closer scrutiny suggests deeper concerns. Several writers compare the new compositional techniques such as the twelve-note method to Esperanto. Gerald Abraham wrote that 'spontaneous musical ideas can hardly be expressed in an artificial language, that this "Esperanto" can only express ideas as purely brain-spun as itself'.[13] Abraham's statement recalls Wittgenstein's assertions regarding Esperanto: 'Esperanto. The feeling of disgust we get if we utter an invented word with invented derivative syllables. The word is cold, lacking in associations, and yet it plays at being "language"'.[14] Just as Wittgenstein is repelled by 'a language without any feeling, without richness',[15] Abraham questions the possibility that an artificial musical language can be truly expressive: both existing languages and tonality are thus perceived to be a *natural* form of expression. The Esperanto comparison also reveals the strain of criticism that saw modern music as individualist to an extreme, as a private, esoteric

---

[10] McN. [William McNaught], 'London Concerts', *Musical Times*, 74/1081 (March 1933), 270.
[11] Edward J. Dent, *TERPANDER or Music and the Future* (London; New York: K. Paul, Trench, Trubner; Dutton, 1926); repr. as *The Future of Music* (Oxford: Pergamon Press, 1965), 1.
[12] Ernest Chapman, 'Ernest Bloch', *Musical Times*, 75/1092 (February 1934), 121–3.
[13] Gerald Abraham, *This Modern Stuff: A Fairly 'Plaine and Easie' Introduction to Contemporary Music* (London: D. Archer, 1933), 41.
[14] Ludwig Wittgenstein, *Culture and Value: A Selection from the Posthumous Remains*, ed. Georg Henrik von Wright and Heikki Nyman, trans. Peter Winch (Oxford: Blackwell, 1998), 60e.
[15] Cited in Stanley Stewart, 'Was Wittgenstein a Closet Literary Critic?', *New Literary History*, 34/1 (2003), 57.

language. This theme was taken up by Arthur Bliss, for example, who spoke of the 'ivory tower' composer for whom 'a distorted individualism results'.[16] Other writers reinforce Abraham's statement, suggesting that tonality is not only a natural, but also an evolving language. William McNaught praised Bliss's Clarinet Quintet (1932) because, despite modern elements, 'there is no suggestion in it of a deliberate cutting away from the past, of a denial of the old language, and a consequent necessity of making up a new one'.[17] And he condemned modernists who 'discard everything that has happened before and start progressing with nothing to progress from'.[18]

An account of new compositional systems by Leonid Sabaneev indicates that the belief that modern music was artificial provoked deeper anxieties than a fear that it stifled natural expression:

> The European has his own music [...] to which cultured thought will always return. When we have ceased to be Europeans, and have reverted to barbarism and forgotten the culture of the past, it may be possible to erect some new thing – ultrachromaticism, let us suppose – on the space left vacant. [...] Ultrachromaticism no longer seems to me an organic possibility of culture, a stage in its inevitable development, as temperament undoubtedly was; it is an artificial excrescence of civilization.[19]

For Sabaneev, the 'organic' growth of tonal music is connected to the growth of civilisation. The parallel between modern music and perceived threats to European civilisation was pursued by Capell in the *Daily Telegraph*. Discussing the arbitrary nature of the twelve-note system, Capell wrote:

> Here as elsewhere Nature is no egalitarian. Schönberg's 'dodecaphony' – a doctrine of musical communism or, better perhaps, musical anarchy – is up against a fact of nature as irresistible as seasons or tides. [...] It is no doubt a generous impulse of Schönberg's to stand up for the disinherited: to 'liquidate' perfect octaves and fifths in the interests of their bastard brothers. But, alas for our musical Marxes and Bakunins, Nature ordained in the days of the Creation that perfect octaves and fifths and major thirds were to have privileged positions for ever and a day.[20]

---

[16] Arthur Bliss, 'Aspects of Contemporary Music' [1934] in Gregory Roscow (ed.), *Bliss on Music: Selected Writings of Arthur Bliss 1920–1975* (Oxford: Oxford University Press, 1991), 91.

[17] William McNaught, 'Gramophone Notes', *Musical Times*, 77/1118 (April 1936), 325–6.

[18] Ibid., 326.

[19] Leonid Sabaneev, 'The Possibility of Quarter-Tone and Other New Scales', *Musical Times*, 70/1036 (June 1929), 504.

[20] Richard Capell, 'The Problem of Problems: Modern Musicians and the Quest for Inspiration', *Daily Telegraph*, 19 December 1936, 19.

Capell's analogy with communism is metaphorical, yet clearly parallels Sabaneev's. Moreover, Cecil Gray perceived 'a more than superficial analogy between atonalism in music and communism in the political world'.[21] Gray argued that Sibelius was favoured in Britain and America because those countries adhered to 'the ideal of sane and orderly progress and development in continuation of the past'.[22] Communism and fascism were 'represented symbolically by the atonalism of Schönberg on the one hand and the neo-classicism of Stravinsky on the other'.[23] Gray thus makes Capell's implication concrete: he perceived a direct correspondence between upheavals in modern music and those in modern politics.

Yet modern music, particularly in relation to Stravinsky, could be perceived very differently. In contrast to those composers who create an isolated, individualistic 'Esperanto', Bliss described others who 'shout their wares in the middle of the market-place',[24] while Sabaneev characterised Stravinsky as the 'musical [Henry] Ford'.[25] These associations with materialistic values were linked to the perception that the music of Stravinsky and Hindemith was lacking in a spiritual element. One writer criticised Stravinsky's music as being purely physical.[26] Another contrasted art that uplifted the soul with that which reflected the 'trivial' and 'material' 'spirit of the age'.[27] Similarly, Hindemith's music especially was associated not merely with modern machinery, but with an array of aspects of modern life: speed, efficiency, disdain for nature, and – significantly in relation to the spiritual – cynicism and absence of belief. His music, Abraham argued, 'expresses with diabolical accuracy the modern spirit of hurry, of mechanical efficiency, of cynical belief-in-nothing'.[28] Hindemith's assault on art, in contemporary views, lay in reducing music to the tawdry level of modern life.

The perceived physicality of Stravinsky's music suggests another parallel with the spirit of the age, as this was a criticism made of jazz. D.L. LeMahieu has observed that jazz was perceived to be a rebellion of the primitive against European civilisation: the parallel with Sabaneev's critique of

---

[21] Cecil Gray, *Predicaments, or Music and the Future: An Essay in Constructive Criticism* (London: Oxford University Press; Humphrey Milford, 1936), 182.
[22] Cecil Gray, 'The Enduring Art of Sibelius', *The Listener*, 30 July 1937, 11.   [23] Ibid., 11.
[24] Bliss, 'Aspects of Contemporary Music', 93.
[25] Leonid Sabaneev, 'Dawn or Dusk? Stravinsky's New Ballets "Apollo" and "The Fairy's Kiss"', *Musical Times*, 70/1035 (May 1929), 403.
[26] See 'London Concerts', *Musical Times*, 77/1125 (November 1936), 1035.
[27] Arthur T. Froggatt, 'The Spirit of the Age', *Musical Times*, 70/1038 (August 1929), 708–9.
[28] Gerald Abraham, 'Hindemith is as Bracing as Skegness', *Radio Times*, 17 March 1933, 660.

'ultrachromaticism' is clear.[29] Moreover, both jazz and Stravinsky's music were associated with materialism and commercialism. Correspondingly, jazz was associated with the primary means of its dissemination and mass-market appeal: the new gramophone and wireless technologies. Similarly, as Huxley remarked of Stravinsky: 'Beethoven was transcendental in the direction of heroism, of the soul, of infinity. Stravinsky's "Ragtime" is transcendental in the direction of soullessness and of mechanics. In this respect the work is remarkably expressive of the contemporary *weltanschauung*'.[30] Finally, jazz was international: exotically American and disseminated worldwide, it transcended class and national boundaries. Schoenberg's modernism was associated with fears of international communism. Stravinsky and Hindemith's brand of modernism provoked anxiety about the capitalist variety of internationalism: standardisation and the eradication of national and individual differences. A frequent criticism of ISCM festivals was that all the music sounded alike, lacking distinct individual and national characteristics.[31] Furthermore, Gray observed that 'the liberal, democratic era of which the individualistic tendency in art was the counterpart, is definitely over, for the time being, at least'.[32] He predicted that music in the future would be 'objective and impersonal', rather than subjective, personal, and emotional.[33] Gray's description 'objective and impersonal' demonstrates how far the different fears of capitalist and communist standardisation may have been conflated in responses to modernism.

Despite the brevity of this survey, several observations may be made. Both radical, and especially communist, politics and the idea of the individual were recurrent and important tropes within the discourse surrounding musical modernism in 1930s Britain. Although some composers were seen to exhibit an extreme, inaccessible individualism, Capell and Gray rejected twelve-note music as the counterpart of communism not only for its artifice, but also for its eradication of individual difference. This fear of the end of the cherished principle of individuality through political upheaval was equalled by comparable anxieties about the threat to culture posed by the new mass, mechanised, popular culture of the post-war period. Bliss encapsulated these twin fears, stating that 'it is on the firm preservation of [...] individuality that the very

[29] D.L. LeMahieu, *A Culture for Democracy: Mass Communication and the Cultivated Mind in Britain between the Wars* (Oxford: Clarendon Press, 1988), 116–7.
[30] Cited in Basil Hogarth, 'Aldous Huxley as Music Critic', *Musical Times*, 76/1114 (December 1935), 1080.
[31] See, for example, Irving Schwerké, 'The I.S.C.M. Festival at Paris', *Musical Times*, 78/1133 (July 1937), 651.
[32] Gray, *Predicaments*, 164.   [33] Ibid., 222.

existence of the artist depends. [...] Art at the mercy of a soulless mechanical materialism ceases to exist just as surely as when basely used as material for political or social causes'.[34]

Yet modern music's perceived rejection of traditional values and the potential correlation between modernism and a mass audience were not always expressed negatively. Edward J. Dent remarked that 'music which is intentionally destructive may help to clear the ground and sweep away some of the romantic rubbish that still encumbers the minds of us who listen'.[35] Robin Hey argued not only that modernism should reflect the spirit of a mechanical age, but that a mass, untrained audience might be an appropriate audience for modern music:

> The musical layman [...] is likely to be fairly prompt in response to this expression of the Zeitgeist. It is not, necessarily, that he is more in tune with the 'spirit of the age' than is the critic; it is simply that, since art means less to him than life, he is more freely iconoclastic about it and, further, he is able to sense where it reflects the colours of the life about him.[36]

Discussion of music in the left-wing press had a self-evident concern with reaching the masses, yet more surprisingly, the value and mass relevance of modern music was also considered. Ben Short in the far-left *Daily Worker* discussed the need for music 'which seeks to stir and provoke the workers' senses to consciousness of vital developments'.[37] Drawing on the arguments of Eisler, exiled in Britain for part of the decade, Short made the accusation that conventional music might be considered 'bourgeois' and 'reactionary'. Referring to Eisler's reading of Schoenberg's music as 'a reflection of the problems of capitalism', he argued for a space for modern music in the workers' movement.

Spike Hughes of the *Daily Herald* was also optimistic about modern music:

> Shostakovich's opera, 'Lady Macbeth', would be far too modern for the most sophisticated Covent Garden audience. In Leningrad, every performance is sold out. Why? Because the artist in Russia [...] has for his public a nation which is naturally artistic and, since the revolution, entirely unprejudiced by traditions and that dreadful attitude of 'I-don't-know-any- thing-about-art-but-I-know-what-I-like'.[38]

Hughes suggests, like Hey, that the mass audiences of post-revolutionary Russia are unprejudiced by tradition and thus receptive to modernism.

---

[34] Bliss, 'Aspects of Contemporary Music', 89.   [35] Dent, TERPANDER, 35.
[36] Robin Hey, 'Music that Expresses Contemporary Life', *Radio Times*, 10 July 1931, 59.
[37] Ben Short, 'Problem: Tunes that Lull or Words that Inspire', *Daily Worker*, 8 June 1936, 7.
[38] Spike Hughes, 'Land without "Box-Office" Art', *Daily Herald*, 8 June 1934, 10.

Consequently, modernism may not be incompatible with the aims of socialism; a revolutionised state may embrace revolutionary music.

Echoing Short, Stuart Fletcher wrote of Vaughan Williams's Fourth Symphony:

> The terseness and starkness of this F minor Symphony, first performed two years ago, its two warring themes [...] are very much of the world we live in to-day. [...] I don't like this symphony any more than I like books about the Distressed Areas, Hitler's Germany, or the Spanish War, but I feel that it demands my attention, and, having got it, holds it.[39]

Fletcher, unlike Hughes, does not perceive modern music to be of inherent artistic value, yet it is perceived to have a propagandistic value as a reflection of the crisis-ridden (capitalist) world. This view is echoed in a *Left Review* article on socialist realism in Shostakovich's *Lady Macbeth*. The opera is favourably compared with Berg's *Wozzeck*, because in contrast to Berg's, Shostakovich's music is seen as 'objective psychopathy':

> It does not charm or fascinate in an escapist sense. The dramatic intensity, the satire and depth of psychological meaning originate in the theme of a disordered society, and make of the music a polished weapon hard and bright. It does not in fact depict the crime and callousness of capitalist society. It reflects it, and it reflects it, as in a world struggling towards Socialism it should reflect it, right back at the audience.[40]

The author, James Findlay Hendry, again raises the possibility that a modern idiom may be valuable to socialism as a reflection of capitalism. Yet his statement is more sophisticated than Fletcher's: the difference suggested between *Wozzeck* and *Lady Macbeth* has not to do with style, but the effect upon the audience. Where Berg charms the listener into 'escapism', suggesting a passive response, Shostakovich, by presenting the phenomenon objectively, forces the listener to maintain emotional distance and think about the subject presented. As Hendry remarked, 'realism should presumably pin the spectator down and permit of no escape from the social problem awaiting solution in actual fact'.[41]

The commentators cited in the foregoing discussion are not equal in their depth of knowledge and critical acumen. The writers in left-wing periodicals in particular make some very crude analyses of the relationship between modern music and modern politics. Nevertheless, the range of

---

[39] Stuart Fletcher, 'On the Gramophone', *Daily Herald*, 13 January 1938, 19.
[40] James Findlay Hendry, 'Lady Macbeth of Mzensk', *Left Review*, 2/6 (March 1936), 273.
[41] Ibid., 272.

assertions reveal not only that there was a rich discourse surrounding the social and political meanings of modern music in inter-war Britain, but that in left-wing circles, ignorance of developments in the Soviet Union and the fact of associations between modern music and radical politics led to arguments that Berg or the Shostakovich of *Lady Macbeth* could indeed prove to be the music of socialism, suitable for a mass audience. It is noteworthy too that Short and Hendry both associate modernism with provoking thought and action rather than a passive emotional response. In a 1935 critique of the bourgeois literary tradition Stephen Spender famously asked whether it was possible for the 'artist to discover a system of values that are not purely subjective and individualistic, but objective and social'.[42] In left-wing musical circles, too, this was a crucial question.

Bush and Modernism

In considering how this debate may contribute to a richer understanding of Alan Bush in the 1930s, it is significant that notions of emotional expression and individuality loom large in later accounts, drawing parallels with the trope of 1930s British criticism particularly directed at Schoenberg. Ronald Stevenson discerns a divide in Bush's music not only between 'modernism' and 'nationalism' but also between unconscious individualism and a self-conscious desire to express the collective feelings of the workers. Stevenson argues that Bush, raised on Debussy and the notion of music as 'as an individual expression',[43] had to contend not only with the 'petty bourgeois' notion of music 'as an escape either in entertainment or in abstraction', but also with his own essentially refined, introverted character: one not ideal for rousing the masses.[44] Correspondingly, a 1946 article in the left-wing journal *Our Time* remarked that early works such as the song-cycle *Songs of the Doomed*, op. 14 (1932–3) 'have a cold, grey quality that may reflect an emotional state or an absorption with experiments'.[45] Like Stevenson, the author implies introversion and individual concerns in the early works at the expense of wider social ones.

There are compelling reasons to question this notion of an opposition between an instinctive or unconscious modernism and the self-conscious cultivation of populist idiom. A most important observation to be made is that Bush's earliest works show little influence of the most avant-garde

---

[42] Cited in Samuel Hynes, *The Auden Generation: Literature and Politics in England in the 1930s* (London: Bodley Head, 1976), 164.
[43] Stevenson, 'Alan Bush: Committed Composer', 325.   [44] Ibid., 328.
[45] Robert Gill, 'Composers of Today 6: Alan Bush', *Our Time*, 6/2 (1946), 31.

music of the time. The Piano Sonata in B minor, op. 2 (1921), which Bush withdrew along with all works that predate his studies with Ireland, is technically accomplished, but it is essentially within the sphere of the Romantic piano sonata in its harmonic idiom and its pianism.[46] The Quartet for Strings and Piano, op. 5 (1924–5) displays Bush's early interest in Ravel and Debussy, yet this is again within a conventional framework, as indicated by the clear tonal implications and Brahmsian phrasing of the opening (Ex. 1.1). The opus immediately preceding the Piano Quartet, the String Quartet in A minor (1923), is equally striking from the perspective of associations between Bush and European modernist models. The lyrical, Dorian opening phrase betrays English rather than Continental influences (Ex. 1.2).

Ex. 1.1 Bush, Quartet for Strings and Piano, opening.

[46] See Lisa Hardy, *The British Piano Sonata, 1870–1945* (Woodbridge: Boydell, 2001), 93–4.

Ex. 1.2 Bush, String Quartet in A minor, opening.

In contrast, from 1928 Bush produced a series of works which were, to paraphrase Daniel Albright, more immediately *difficult* than those just cited.[47] In the *Concert Piece*, for example, the prominence of the diminished fifth in the Bartókian opening undermines the sense of the tonic (Ex. 1.3). Furthermore, phrasing, sonata structure, and the thematic unity of the piece – which it shares with the Quartet for Strings and Piano – are frequently disrupted on the surface by shifts of texture, speed, and dynamic. The work repeatedly reaches moments of crisis, which are then replaced by a new and contrasting section. In the last few minutes of the piece, the music is alternately highly fragmented or consists of the insistent reiteration of small intervallic sets. The effect, rather than reinforcing the

[47] Daniel Albright (ed.), *Modernism and Music: An Anthology of Sources* (Chicago and London: University of Chicago Press, 2004), 5.

Ex. 1.3 Bush, Concert Piece, opening.

Ex. 1.4 Bush, *Relinquishment*, bb. 69–72.

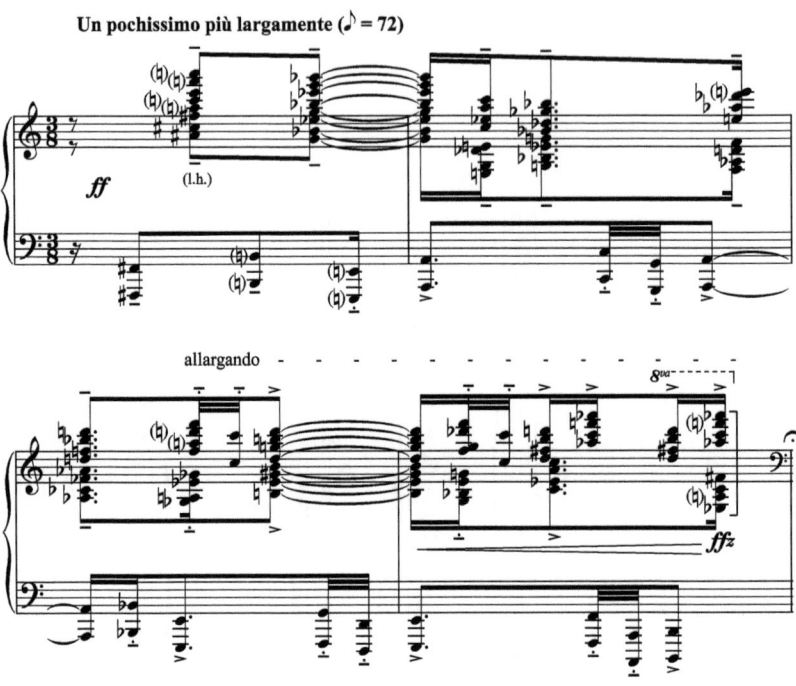

tonal conclusion, makes the last, tonally unambiguous bars sound rather perfunctory.

Relinquishment, op. 11 (1928) for piano and *Dialectic*, op. 15 (1929) for string quartet show, similarly, both the surface fragmentation and dissonance of modern music and compositional procedures that may be linked to specific modernist models (Ex. 1.4). In contrast to the conventional homophony of the Quartet for Strings and Piano, *Relinquishment* employs formal and motivic techniques associated with Bartók and Schoenberg. The work is a process of continuous contrapuntal development of a four-note figure, x, adopting the palindromic 'arch' form associated with Bartók (A B [a + b] C B^1 [b + a] A^1). Ex. 1.5 shows the derivation of sections B and C from the opening material. Section B retains the motif x in a new contrapuntal combination of voices, while Section C derives from a constitutive interval of x: the perfect fourth. While *Dialectic* returns to sonata form, it shares with *Relinquishment* the obsessive development of a four-note figure which dictates both the thematic and harmonic dimensions of the music, as may be seen in a comparison of the first and second subjects (Ex. 1.6).

Ex. 1.5a *Relinquishment*, opening.

Ex. 1.5b *Relinquishment*, bb. 32–8 (Section B begins at bar 35).

Ex. 1.5c *Relinquishment*, bb. 79–80 (start of Section C).

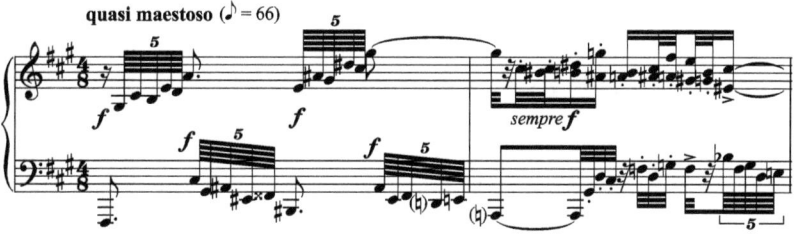

The argument that there was a shift in Bush's works of the 1920s and 1930s towards a greater engagement with modernist techniques is supported by contemporary reviews. A review of the String Quartet, op. 4 refers to the 'pleasing use' of the 'idiom of folk-song' and similarities to Vaughan

Ex. 1.6a Bush, *Dialectic*, opening.

Ex. 1.6b *Dialectic*, second subject, bb. 31–3.

Williams's 'contemplative feeling'.[48] In contrast, Bush's *Symphonic Impression*, op. 8 (1926–7) provoked the criticism that 'some parts had the pungency in which young composers of to-day find delight, others harked back to less sophisticated days'.[49] Reviewers in both England and Germany at the turn of the decade associated Bush with modernism. The *Monthly Musical*

---

[48] *Morning Post* concert review, undated, Alan Bush Archive, Histon (ABH).
[49] *Liverpool Post* concert review, 12 September 1930, ABH.

Record felt that Bush 'is much too anxious at the moment to be thought a terrifyingly progressive composer', while the critic of the *Deutsche Allgemeine Zeitung*, following a concert of Bush's works in Berlin in 1928, wrote that Bush was 'entirely a child of our time, writing atonality unashamedly'.[50] Also notable in these reviews is the fact that, in contrast to more recent writers, these critics view Bush's 'pungent' idiom as forced or insincere. This idea is pursued in a review of the *Concert Piece* by M.D. Calvocoressi:

> My impressions of the previous hearing [of the Concert Piece] would be represented accurately by a question mark. Now, I still wonder what the composer's purpose was. [...] The tone is the reverse of detached, and many intentions are perceptible apart from that of contrasting the two instruments as sharply as possible, jerkily at times, with rare brief moments of close co-operation between the two which only increase the atmosphere of contrast, and to rely on accents and dynamic effects but not at all on colour. The key note is, at times, grim meditation; more often, anger and rebellion.[51]

Calvocoressi finds the work baffling not because it is inexpressive, but because the expressive purpose is unclear amid the violent contrasts. Correspondingly, the *Musical Times* review observes:

> Bush is a strong thinker in music, whose promulgations of aesthetic and political doctrine are every now and then submerged by ripples of inspiration. No one, hearing his Piece, can doubt it expresses an extended train of ideas; for the most part fierce and satiric, yet with moments of real beauty, and therefore of emotion.[52]

This reviewer associates the most overtly modernist elements of the work – its dissonant and fragmented surface – with Bush's political beliefs. Furthermore, he opposes the modernist, political, and 'satiric' with the traditional, lyrical, and 'emotional' moments in the piece, the latter being perceived as the only instance of true expression.

This survey of Bush's early works and their reception indicates clearly the flaws in Stevenson's argument; Bush did not display an instinctive modernism, but rather he started to engage with aspects of modern music from Continental Europe in the late 1920s. To further dismantle the notion of an individualistic modernism supplanted by a populist style, this very period was significant for Bush both musically and politically. The year 1928 – in which he composed *Relinquishment* – was when Bush moved to Berlin and began experiencing what Nono called 'the historical, cultural and political importance of Berlin in the years before 1933', something

---

[50] Eric Blom, 'In the Concert Room', *Monthly Musical Record*, 60 (1930), 303; N. Bush, *Alan Bush*, 20.
[51] M.D. Calvocoressi, 'From My Note-Book', *Musical Opinion*, 60/715 (April 1937), 590.
[52] 'London Concerts', *Musical Times*, 78/1128 (February 1937), 166-7.

Nono himself absorbed secondhand a generation later via Hermann Scherchen.[53] Having already begun working with the LLCU in 1926, alongside his fellow English communist composer Rutland Boughton, Bush sought out both radical music and radical politics in Berlin. He attended both the Berlin premiere of Stravinsky's *Oedipus Rex* in 1928 and a performance of Brecht and Eisler's masterpiece of political theatre *Die Massnahme*.[54] As his fellow student in philosophy, Egbert Hildebrandt, would later attest, such outings 'were always the occasion of serious discussions on fundamental artistic and aesthetic questions and on problems of world outlook, over which we struggled to come to a clear understanding'.[55] Nor was there an abrupt division of music and politics in Bush's works. *Songs of the Doomed*, the song-cycle denigrated by Robert Gill as reflecting 'an absorption with experiments', set the poetry of the former miner F.C. Boden, which included vivid and outspoken descriptions of miners' experiences.[56] As this makes clear, radical politics did not supplant modernism for Bush; rather, he discovered them at the same time within a cultural discourse with which modern music and politics were constantly associated. As a final comment on views which cast Bush's modernism as instinctive, to make such an assertion is to present Bush as a naïve and unreflective figure within this discourse. As may now be demonstrated, nothing could be further from the truth.

Bush as Writer

Bush was a prolific commentator on modern music and its social and political context, writing and speaking in such varied settings as *Left Review* and the Musical Association, as well as being an active promoter of modern music. He founded the RAM New Music Society, an organisation aiming to perform any works which 'were thought to have some characteristic which differentiated them from Nineteenth Century music',[57] and which put on works by Stravinsky, Bartók, and

---

[53] Nielinger-Vakil, *Luigi Nono*, 13.
[54] While Nancy Bush indicates that Bush heard the first performance of *Oedipus Rex*, it is probable that he actually saw the first Berlin performance, given on 25 February 1928 at the Kroll Opera, two nights after the opera's premiere as a fully staged work in Vienna (following a concert performance in Paris on 30 May 1927). It is not clear when Bush saw *Die Massnahme*, but it is likely he saw a very early performance, given that its premiere took place in Berlin in December 1930.
[55] Egbert Hildebrandt, 'A Student Friendship in Berlin', in Stevenson (ed.), *Time Remembered*, 71.
[56] Robert Gill, 'Composers of Today 6: Alan Bush', 31.
[57] Alan Bush to F.T. Durrant, 4 March 1934, British Library, Alan Bush Collection (BL/AB), MS Mus. 653, Royal Academy of Music New Composers' Society.

Schoenberg. His music was performed at festivals of the ISCM, and he wrote favourable reviews of two festivals for major publications.[58] Bush wrote in 1930 of his admiration for Stravinsky's *Les Noces* and Bartók's 'truly remarkable' Second Violin Sonata.[59] In 1934, he was analysing Schoenberg's works, including the twelve-note *Klavierstück*, op. 33a. He also defended modernism in lectures and articles in the 1930s. The *Western Australian* reported of some 1932 lectures on modern music given in Perth that Bush 'was unblushingly a propagandist' of modern music, speaking 'in high praise' of Schoenberg and Stravinsky.[60] In a 1936 paper, Bush defended Schoenberg against the charges of musical barbarism, arguing that twelve-note composition was 'a method of composing by following out principles which evolve from rather than contradict those of the late romantic period'.[61]

Yet Bush also made criticisms of modern music, Schoenberg in particular. In the same 1936 paper, he wrote of 'the crisis in the modern musical world which makes itself apparent in the bewilderment and dislike of audiences in the face of an apparently esoteric cult'.[62] He argued that on any *technical* basis, Schoenberg was the most modern music at present, yet then remarked, 'how loath we all would feel at being forced to yield the palm to music which seems both arid and hysterical'.[63] In a 1937 essay, Bush explained 'the present anarchy in musical theory and practice [and] the bewilderment and hostility of audiences when faced with the works of the leading composers of the present day' as 'the counterparts in the musical world of the conflicts and contradictions which beset the capitalist system as it staggers from one crisis to the next'.[64]

It is possible to view these conflicting statements as a crisis of confidence that began after Bush joined the Communist Party in 1935, as he allied himself to the cultural policies and example of the Soviet Union. Neil Edmunds has

---

[58] Bush reviewed the 1935 (Prague) and 1939 (Warsaw) festivals. See Alan Bush, 'The I.S.C.M. Festival at Prague', *Musical Times* 76/1112 (October 1935), 940–2; Alan Bush and Arnold Cooke, 'The Prague International Festival', *Daily Telegraph*, 7 September 1935, 7; Alan Bush, 'The I.S.C.M. in Poland: Composers from Fourteen Lands at the Warsaw Festival', *Daily Telegraph*, 6 May 1939, 11.

[59] Alan Bush to Edward Clark, 7 January 1930, BBC Written Archive Centre, Caversham (BBC/WAC), RCONT1: Composer, Alan Bush, File 1A (1928–1941).

[60] 'Modern Music: Some Problems Discussed', *The Western Australian*, 4 October 1932, ABH.

[61] Alan Bush, 'What Is Modern Music?', *Proceedings of the Musical Association*, 63rd Session (1936–7), 22.

[62] Ibid., 25.   [63] Ibid., 26.

[64] Alan Bush, 'Music' in C. Day-Lewis (ed.), *The Mind in Chains: Socialism and the Cultural Revolution* (London: Frederick Muller, 1937), 125–6.

claimed that, in the light of policy changes in the Soviet Union, it was 'no coincidence that Bush began to simplify his idiom [...] during the mid-1930s'.[65] Certainly, Bush's interest in Soviet music dates from the second half of the 1930s. Yet his knowledge of events in the Soviet Union and the doctrine of Socialist Realism was, at this stage, limited. He only visited the country for the first time in 1938, and he did not correspond with Russians regularly before this date. The phrase 'Socialist Realism' does not appear in his writings until the early 1940s. Moreover, Bush asserted in 1937 that, in the Soviet Union and under Socialism, 'composers would not be restricted in any way with regard to the matter or style of their compositions'.[66]

A far more important influence at this stage in Bush's development were the ideas of Brecht and Eisler. In Berlin, as he recounted later, Bush had not only heard *Die Massnahme* but also encountered Eisler's 'remarkable militant songs' being sung by workers' choirs.[67] When Brecht and Eisler spent time in England as émigrés from Nazism, Bush became acquainted with them and later cited them as a strong influence in his political conversion to communism.[68] He made efforts throughout the decade to mount performances of Eisler's music, most notably the first English performances of *Die Massnahme* in 1936.

Eisler himself articulated a relatively sophisticated, Marxist, dialectical conception of music history, interpreting broad changes in practice in terms of large-scale social and historical shifts from feudalism to bourgeois capitalism and on to the imminent new period of world socialism. In his essay 'The Builders of a New Musical Culture' (1931), Eisler identified the key feature of bourgeois music in its principle of contrast, a style which is 'appropriate, as no other, for appealing to the individual experience and to the individual imagination. [...] an attempt is made to excite [the listener], to entertain him and to create associations for him'.[69] He criticised the decline of this principle from its initial revolutionary statement of individual freedom in Beethoven's symphonies, into 'pure stimulant'.[70] Where audiences had thus 'become dependent upon a music that easily

---

[65] Edmunds, 'William Glock and the British Broadcasting Corporation's Music Policy', 258.
[66] Bush, 'Music', 143.
[67] Alan Bush, 'Hanns Eisler as I Knew Him' [English draft for special publication in memory of Eisler], Stiftung Archiv der Akademie der Künste, Berlin (SAAdK), Archiv der Akademie der Künste der DDR (AdK-O), File 1585: Sonderheft 'Hanns Eisler' 1963–4.
[68] R. Murray Schafer, *British Composers in Interview* (London: Faber & Faber, 1963), 55–6.
[69] Hanns Eisler, 'The Builders of a New Musical Culture' [1931] in Manfred Grabs (ed.), *Hanns Eisler: A Rebel in Music. Selected Writings of Hanns Eisler* (1978; repr. London: Kahn & Averill, 1999), 46.
[70] Ibid., 38.

gratifies in a time of difficult and precarious economic conditions', Eisler sought a music which would foster an active response on the part of the listener.[71] The audience participation in communist hymns envisaged in *Die Massnahme* represents one realisation, yet is by no means the most sophisticated method. To give one example of the latter, Brecht felt that Eisler's song from *Die Mutter*, 'In Praise of Dialectics', 'which might easily give the effect of a purely emotional song of triumph, is kept in the sphere of the rational by the music'.[72] Rather than supporting the drama by creating mood or emotion, Eisler set up his music in opposition to the text, thus aiming to place the listener at an objective distance from the drama. Similarly, 'change in dynamics, tempo and the system of accompaniment is a way of using musical "alienation" to emphasise a particular idea'.[73] By creating a jarring contrast or interruption in the music, such techniques of alienation prevented emotional identification from the listener.

During his Berlin years, Eisler had consciously rejected his teacher Schoenberg's modernism: while Schoenberg has revolutionised musical material (as the *Materialrevolutionär*), true revolution demanded the transformation of musical function.[74] By the time Bush first met Eisler in London in 1935, he had modified this position somewhat due to the Nazis' response to modern music. In the face of attacks on leading modern composers, Eisler urged collaboration between workers' movements and modernist composers.[75] Rejecting Georg Lukács' conservative realist stance, he defended the continual material progress of music.[76]

Eisler's influence upon Bush's emerging political-musical aesthetic is evident. In a 1935 article, 'Arbeiterbewegung und moderne Musiker', Bush echoed Eisler's directly by analysing the difficulty of the gulf between

---

[71] Ibid., 37–8.
[72] Cited in Günter Mayer, Sleeve Notes to *Hanns Eisler: Historic Recordings*, Boris Blacher, cond., Gesang Studioorchester (Berlin Classics BER 92302, 1996), 24.
[73] Ibid., 22.
[74] For discussion of this concept see Günter Mayer, 'Leben und Kunst unter dem Primat der Politik: Über zwei Konflikttypen bei Hanns Eisler' in *Komponisten, auf Werk und Leben befragt: ein Kolloquium*, ed. H. Goldschmidt, G. Knepler, K. Niemann (Leipzig: Deutscher Verlag für Musik, 1985), 289.
[75] Hanns Eisler and Ernst Bloch, 'Avantgarde-Kunst und Volksfront' [1937] in Günter Mayer (ed.), *Hanns Eisler: Musik und Politik. Schriften 1924–1948* (2nd edn, Leipzig: Deutscher Verlag für Musik, 1985), 397–405.
[76] Hanns Eisler and Ernst Bloch, 'Die Kunst zu Erben' [1938] in Mayer (ed.), *Hanns Eisler: Musik und Politik*, 406–14.

modern musicians and workers and calling for greater cooperation.[77] In a 1936 article, he argued that workers' music 'should be built up by means of rational constructive elements rather than by fanciful harmonic or colour devices'. This would 'suggest as correct a scientific and objective outlook, rather than a romantic and subjective one'.[78] Crucially, here, Bush reveals his concern with what kind of musical material could foster new effects. Elsewhere, it becomes clear that certain aspects of contemporary music presented one solution. Bush referred in lecture notes to the 'non-drugging effects of contemporary music'.[79] We have seen that *Left Review* considered the 'objective' qualities of Shostakovich's *Lady Macbeth*, its effect on the audience, to be its primary achievement. Significantly, Bush praised *Wozzeck* in similar terms following an attack by Boughton, who claimed that Schoenberg and his followers 'intended to cut emotion out of music':[80]

> I do not think that this statement is meant in the obvious way in which Mr. Boughton interprets it, namely as a consciously willed divorce of emotion from music; it means rather the intention to avoid those emotion-producing, sensuous effects of which earlier music, especially that of the later nineteenth century, made such a feature. What is attempted in *Wozzeck* [...] is a musical representation of the psychic impressions made by the events in the outer world upon Wozzeck's mind, distorted as they would be by his nervous, overstrained condition.[81]

Bush discerned in *Wozzeck* the same quality of objective distance from the subject which Hendry perceived in *Lady Macbeth*.

The significance of this observation becomes clear if we re-examine Bush's ambivalence towards Schoenberg. Bush condemned Schoenberg's music as 'arid and hysterical'; he went on to criticise *Erwartung* as 'an expression of the personal-psychological reactions of the composer, as though they were all important in despite of the widespread misery and physical need of the exploited populations of the world'. Accordingly, the work represented 'the last stage of a decadent romanticism, whose function it is to provide an avenue of escape from reality'.[82] Yet in 1942 Bush wrote:

---

[77] Alan Bush, 'Arbeiterbewegung und moderne Musiker' [1935] in *1ʳᵉ Olympiade Ouvrière Européenne: de musique et de chant. 8–10 Juin 1935, Strasbourg* [festival programme], 19–27, ABH.

[78] Alan Bush, 'Music and the Working-Class Struggle', *Left Review* 2/2 (November 1935), 650.

[79] Alan Bush, 'Understanding Modern Music', handwritten MS, undat. [1930s], ABH.

[80] Rutland Boughton, 'Music. Wozzeck: Opera without Emotion', *New Britain* 2/44 (21 March 1934), 543.

[81] Alan Bush, 'Wozzeck', *New Britain* 2/46 (4 April 1934), 619.

[82] Bush, 'What is Modern Music?', 29.

> Arnold Schoenberg's 12-tone system was a revolutionary attempt to break the deadlock of pre-1923 modern music, of the hyper-emotional and hysterical Wagnerian, Scriabinian, Franckian schools [...] His vital contribution was the introduction of the principle of methodic construction into modern music. His system was [...] altogether based on strictly logical deduction, on extreme economy of thematic material and on the elimination of that bombastic and opportunist confusion which was spread about by so many of his contemporaries. [...] His method had to stand up against almost the entire musical opinion of his time, and yet was *quite in keeping with the endeavour of the most progressive elements in society to clarify, enlighten and 'de-dope' human brains, to teach them again to think logically.*[83]

Bush suggests here that regardless of style, the heightened subjectivity of *Erwartung* disqualified it from being a modern work. Conversely, the twelve-note method was the first truly modern music because it was rooted in a logical system. It is not simply that a modern technique may foster objective audience responses; rather, objectivity is the very definition of modern music. Furthermore, Bush's last statement about the twelve-note method reveals that music that embraced modern techniques need not be unsuitable for the egalitarian culture of a future state of socialism, despite technical unfamiliarity. In both workers' music and modern music, objectivity was a desirable quality, because it could encourage the listener to think. The principle of a logical and objective constructive basis for composition in the twelve-note method was its most valuable feature. Not only did this permit a future for art music that was not grounded in musical 'anarchy', but it challenged an aesthetic that privileged the emotional and individual. Accordingly, modern music by Bush's definition was inevitably political, as an objective music would not merely challenge capitalist aesthetic ideals, but it could also present an alternative experience to what Bush called 'the "anodyne" way of listening [...] officially encouraged by the cultural overlords of most countries'.[84]

Bush's Modernism

If, then, in Bush's view, elements of modern music could foster an objective, active form of listening that could help to bring about social and

---

[83] Alan Bush, 'Marxism and Music', typewritten MS, undat. [1942], 7–8, ABH (my emphasis).
[84] Bush, 'What Is Modern Music?', 23.

political transformation, to what extent were these ideas realised in his works of the 1930s? In the remainder of the chapter, two case studies – Bush's *Concert Piece* and his Piano Concerto, op. 18 (1934–7) – will be used in order to examine these questions in detail.

Concert Piece for 'Cello and Piano, op. 17 (1936)

The *Concert Piece* belongs, with *Dialectic* and *Relinquishment*, to the group of early works which, unlike many of Bush's later compositions, have no overt political content in the form of texts and programmes. It shares with those works a dissonant, in places fragmented, surface. Unlike those works, however, the *Concert Piece* constituted a return to chamber and piano music, following a lengthy break,[85] at the very time when Bush was writing prolifically about his aesthetic and political ideas. It therefore provides an ideal case for considering the relationship between his ideas about modern music and his aesthetic position.

Like *Dialectic* and *Relinquishment*, the *Concert Piece* is constructed with rigorous economy from an initial thematic cell (see Ex. 1.3) which has both thematic and harmonic implications. It is a modified, 'three-in-one' sonata form consisting of a slow introduction, exposition/first movement with codetta, 'slow movement', development, recapitulation, and extended coda. The initial set of a semitone and diminished fifth is immediately presented in inversion in the piano. Thereafter, the piano line continues to derive material from the cello theme, thereby introducing a new theme which is gradually modified to reach its definitive form at bar 25. The first subject is also derived from the opening theme, placing more emphasis on the minor third. This then produces a further repeating demisemiquaver theme first heard at bar 104. The work is thus really a process of developing variation. Moreover, as Ex. 1.3 and Ex. 1.7 indicate, the thematic material determines not only the horizontal but also the vertical aspect. The music is frequently contrapuntal, yet even purely accompanying material is derived from the original theme. After Bush's definition, the *Concert Piece* is constructed with the objectivity he associated with the twelve-note method, due to the economy and 'logical deduction' of material.

Yet in other respects, the work seems to refute Bush's desire to avoid 'the cult of individuality, of personal expressionism'.[86] As Calvocoressi

---

[85] Between 1930 and 1935, the only chamber music Bush composed was the *Three Contrapuntal Studies* for Violin and Viola (1931).
[86] Bush, 'Music and the Working-Class Struggle', 650.

Ex. 1.7 *Concert Piece*, piano, bb. 40–8.

Violoncello

Ex. 1.7 (cont.)
Piano

observed, the music 'is the reverse of detached', often highly impassioned or lyrical in tone. Bush claimed in an undated programme note that, at the time of writing, 'Hitler fascism was already beginning to threaten the peoples of Europe. This menacing atmosphere may explain the grave and rather turbulent expression of the work'.[87] This assertion prompts the question of whether the *Concert Piece* reveals a gap between Bush's espoused rationalist aesthetic and its realisation in his music. However, Bush denied any programmatic reading at the time, asserting that it was intended to be a 'piece of elegant entertainment music',[88] and in contrast to later works, he gave no programmatic indication in his abstract, functional choice of title. Most significantly,

---

[87] Cited in Rachel O'Higgins (ed.), *The Correspondence of Alan Bush and John Ireland, 1927–1961* (Aldershot: Ashgate, 2006), 68.

[88] Alan Bush to E.D. Needham, 29 March 1937, BL/AB MS Mus. 453, Miscellaneous Correspondence 1937–8.

Ex. 1.8 *Concert Piece*, bb. 253–6.

Bush never stated an intention to eradicate emotion from music. His outlook may rather be understood, like Brecht's, as a shift of emphasis from the purely 'emotionally suggestive' towards the 'rationally persuasive'.[89]

Rather than asking how the work distances the listener, we might ask how the listener is drawn in on an emotional level. As previously stated, there is much surface contrast, for example in the passage of rhythmic disruption, motivic fragmentation, and registral contrasts at bar 253 (Ex. 1.8). One possibility is that Bush sought to preclude the 'drugging' effect of his music partly through a violent, disrupted surface which resisted immediate apprehension of its logical motivic development. Yet a subtler facet may also be discerned. During the first statement of the first subject (bars 40–7), the tonic is heard variously. The initial dyad in bar 40 has a bare quality reinforced by the percussiveness of the piano. At three other points, bar 41^3, bar 43 and bar 46^3, the third of the chord

---

[89] Cited in Ernst Fischer, *The Necessity of Art: A Marxist Approach*, trans. Anna Bostock (Harmondsworth: Penguin, 1963), 14.

Ex. 1.9 *Concert Piece*, bb. 153–5.

is only present in one instance. Moreover, in addition to the fact that each statement is an appoggiatura, the leading note (C♯) is never used in approaching the tonic (or, indeed, anywhere in this section). The two appearances of the tonic chord with the distinctive E♭-D appoggiatura at the start of the section fail to assert the tonic because of the conflicting harmonic implications (towards C) in the right hand. In the passage as a whole, the tonic is never established through a conventional dominant preparation and resolution; it is rather emphasised by the reiteration of three prominent chords. Bush's harmonic idiom in this passage thus avoids the harmonic richness and directional impetus of the most characteristic tonal intervals in favour of a sparser harmony intensified by the high, percussive piano writing. In bar 141, too, the initial cello theme of the 'slow movement' is marked *cantabile*, and the many chromatic inflections suggest a highly expressive melody. Yet the jagged and harmonically austere piano motif invests the cello theme with a quality of restraint and distance. Consequently, the moment of expressive lyricism supported by a newly homophonic piano accompaniment that arrives in bar 154 has an extraordinary quality of distance in another sense (Ex. 1.9). This isolated instance of the emotional lyricism denied hitherto has a quality of strangeness, a sense of being in quotation marks, comparable to the 'ancient scent' of the final song in *Pierrot Lunaire*.

To what extent, then, does the *Concert Piece* realise Bush's aesthetic of modern music? Bush felt scepticism towards the emotionalism, sentimentality and subjective listening he perceived in late-nineteenth-century musical experience. In elements of Schoenberg and Eisler's modernism, he identified technical means of realising an aesthetic which inspired thought and action rather than a passive emotional response. Aspects of the *Concert Piece* – its relentless development of the initial thematic cell, its austere harmonic idiom, its disrupted surface – may be interpreted as an attempt on Bush's part to deploy these technical means in one of his own abstract concert works.

Yet this is not to suggest that the *Concert Piece* is a radically modernist work. The contrast between a violent, palpably modernist passage like that at bar 253 and the immensely nostalgic, lyrical quality of the central episode at bar 154 – a contrast that seem more urgent than comparable examples in *Dialectic* – leaves a suggestion of doubt about Bush's agenda. The effects of the work are subtle; it is by no means a radical rejection of emotion. At passages such as bar 154, does the subsequent abandonment of the emotional or lyrical climax suggest an ironic debunking? Or does it imply a tension between a politically influenced ideal of modern music and nostalgia for a passionate expressionism that Bush no longer condoned? These questions crystallise the significance of the *Concert Piece* for understanding Bush's music in the 1930s. It is richly suggestive of Bush's politically motivated aesthetic, yet it also points to the tensions between his radical rhetoric and its realisation in practice.

Concerto for Pianoforte and Orchestra, op. 18 (1937)

In contrast to the *Concert Piece*, Bush's next work has been viewed, by Edmunds for example, as a decisive step away from modernist influences and towards a simplified idiom.[90] Bush wrote to the BBC that 'the idiom is the reverse of difficult or obscure'.[91] It is a new departure in its introduction of an overtly political text in the final movement following three purely instrumental movements. The text boldly interrupts the initial

---

[90] Edmunds, 'William Glock and the British Broadcasting Corporation's Music Policy', 258 n99.
[91] Alan Bush to Kenneth Wright, 11 July 1937, BBC/WAC RCONT1: Composer, Alan Bush, File 1A.

instrumental section of the finale, embarks on a critique of the function of music under capitalism, and ultimately urges the audience not to passively enjoy the concert but to take action against war and social injustice in the present day.[92] In these respects it may be seen to support the conventional narrative of Bush's musical development as a rejection or relinquishment of modernism for political ends. This act of relinquishment is also suggested by Bush's choice of a genre associated with virtuosity, popular appeal, and the staging of an opposition between individual and collective forces. Contemporaneous British piano concertos by Britten and Alan Rawsthorne also incorporated musical-political content, in Rawsthorne's case directly citing the 'Bandiera Rossa' of the Spanish Republicans.[93] Whereas those concertos were small-scale, neoclassical affairs, Bush's is epic in scale, symphonic in construction, rich in topical allusions, and suggests as its models (in view of the choral finale) Beethoven's Ninth Symphony and Choral Fantasia and Busoni's Piano Concerto. Yet it is above all, the affinities with his later music that has informed appraisals of the work, just as Britten's several explicitly political works of the late 1930s (for example, *Our Hunting Fathers, Russian Funeral, Ballad of Heroes*) have been interpreted as leading to the universalism of his mature works. Bush's concerto invites programmatic interpretations as a narrative of a turbulent struggle of the individual and collective, thus distancing it from the abstract world of the *Concert Piece* and suggesting greater parallels with the portrayals of heroic individuals in, for example, Bush's later opera *Wat Tyler* and his *Byron Symphony*. Certainly, the work was perceived to be an act of propaganda at the time of the oft-recounted premiere.[94] Tippett later recalled 'the surprise and perhaps even dismay which Alan experienced when Adrian [Boult], to counter what he thought the somewhat left-wing slant of the vocal finale, forced the applause to end by unexpectedly performing the National Anthem'.[95]

---

[92] The full text of the final movement is reproduced in Stevenson (ed.), *Time Remembered*, 66–7.

[93] For discussion of these issues in Britten's Piano Concerto, see Eric Roseberry, 'Britten's Piano Concerto: The Original Version', *Tempo* 172 (March 1990), 10–18, and his essay 'The Concertos and Early Orchestral Scores: Aspects of Style and Aesthetic' in Mervyn Cooke (ed.), *The Cambridge Companion to Benjamin Britten* (Cambridge: Cambridge University Press, 1999), 236–7.

[94] This took place at Broadcasting House on 4 March 1938 (it was broadcast simultaneously) with Alan Bush (piano), Dennis Noble (baritone), Adrian Boult (cond.), BBC Male Voice Chorus, BBC Symphony Orchestra.

[95] Michael Tippett, 'A Magnetic Friendship: An Attraction of Opposites' in Stevenson (ed.), *Time Remembered*, 9. It is not clear whether this was in fact an impromptu decision by Boult or a decision made earlier by the BBC. Certainly the corporation expressed prior

Yet other evidence suggests that the Piano Concerto may bear a more complex relationship to Bush's previous music. While it was first performed in 1938, when Bush was deeply entrenched in political-musical activism, the work was begun as early as April 1934 and the first three movements had been written, but not orchestrated, by May 1935.[96] Most of the work thus predates the *Concert Piece*, so may hardly be seen as a politically motivated rejection of its idiom. The finale – the locus of the work's overt political content – was by contrast completed only in August 1937 when Alan and Nancy were staying near Svendborg, Denmark in the company of Brecht and Eisler.[97] This raises questions about the relationship between the first three movements and the finale. Indeed, Bush wrote much later of the last movement:

> I had no thought of Busoni in mind. My object, to turn a piece of concert music into a vehicle of political [sic] was forced upon me by the political circumstances of the time. [...] I felt that the world situation was too urgent to permit a musician to expend a great deal of time, unless the resulting work had some immediate impact.[98]

The finale, then, may be an abrupt *volte-face* in the midst of a work that began as an abstract conception, at the height of Bush's interest in modernism.

In support of this possibility, Ates Orga has drawn attention to aspects of the style and structure of the concerto which reveal its similarities to *Relinquishment, Dialectic*, and the *Concert Piece*. Like *Relinquishment*, the first movement is a Bartókian 'arch' form.[99] Orga has also traced the derivation of the thematic material of the entire work from the two contrasting themes declaimed by the piano at the very opening of the concerto, which he labels A and B (Ex. 1.10).[100] Like the *Concert Piece*, the first movement is a process of developing variation. The chorale-like theme that begins 6 after Fig. 109, for example (Ex. 1.11b), is derived from the preceding music (Ex. 1.11a), which in turn derives from Theme B (Ex. 1.11). The fact that the majority of the thematic material of the work originates in the 'European

---

concern over the text and it was not a regular feature of concerts to perform the Anthem at the end. See also Lewis Foreman (ed.), *From Parry to Britten: British Music in Letters 1900–1945* (London: Batsford, 1987), 203–4 and 209–10.

[96] O'Higgins (ed.), *The Correspondence of Alan Bush and John Ireland*, 48; Alan Bush to Edward Clark, 4 May 1935, BBC/WAC RCONT1: Composer, Alan Bush, File 1A.

[97] Nancy Bush, *Alan Bush*, 39.

[98] Alan Bush, undated typescript, BL/AB MS Mus. 448, Correspondence with Ronald Stevenson, vol. 4. I am indebted to the late John Lowerson for bringing this to my attention.

[99] Ates Orga, 'The Concertos' in Stevenson (ed.), *Time Remembered*, 47–8, 50.

[100] Ibid., 47–8.

Ex. 1.10 Bush, Piano Concerto, i, opening, piano only.

chromatic' Theme B, rather than the 'English Aeolian modal' Theme A, also points to the affinities between the Piano Concerto and the works already discussed.[101] Theme A itself, with its associations of folk song, may be taken as evidence of the conscious shift towards Soviet aesthetics perceived by Edmunds. Yet this judgment should be made with caution. Bush's proclivity for the interval of the perfect fourth within his themes could be a means of

---

[101] Ibid., 45–6.

Ex. 1.11a Bush, Piano Concerto, i, trumpet (sounding) and trombone, 1 before Fig. 107.

enriching his tonal vocabulary by generating dissonance, yet could also produce the characteristic modal flattened seventh of English music, as in the lyrical subject from *Dialectic* shown in Ex. 1.6b. Moreover, although Bush criticised folk song because of its 'romantic associations of an idyllic pre-capitalist era', he was not opposed to modal scales in general. He wrote pertinently of workers' music that it:

> must have some features that stamp it musically as of the present day. Either the scale should differ from the major or minor scales of the last three centuries, or the use of the intervals of those scales must be such as to contradict the practice of this previous music.[102]

He went on to assert the need for workers' music to be built up of 'rational constructive elements', on the same grounds as his arguments in favour of Schoenberg's music: to avoid the emotional, the sensuous and the passive response. The modal theme in the Piano Concerto, with its rigorous thematic development, may be interpreted in this light.

A more problematic issue, when considering the Piano Concerto against the backdrop of Bush's aesthetic of objectivity, is his choice of the genre of the concerto, given its associations of virtuoso display and the focus on individual expression via the solo instrument. One possibility is that Bush saw the concerto form as a potential vehicle for *critique* rather than display. One of Brecht and Eisler's means of presenting alternatives to bourgeois culture was the subversion of both existing forms and specific musical models. In his 1935 essay 'The Crisis in Music', Eisler identified one

---

[102] Bush, 'Music and the Working-Class Struggle', 649–50.

Ex. 1.11b Piano Concerto, i, horns (sounding), 6 after Fig. 109.

function of the 'larger musical forms' in a socialist musical culture as 'the destruction of conventional musical concepts'.[103] *Die Massnahme* is a classic example, constituting both a reinvention of Bach's Passions and an inversion of the Passions' social hierarchy. As Albrecht Betz observes: whereas in the Passion the hierarchy of values places 'Christ at the top, the mass of people at the bottom and the narrating Evangelist as the

---

[103] Hanns Eisler, 'The Crisis in Music' [1935] in Grabs (ed.), *Hanns Eisler: A Rebel in Music*, 117.

Ex. 1.12   Piano Concerto, i, piano only, 4 after Fig. 103.

intermediary', *Die Massnahme* places 'the masses (the examining chorus) as the highest, the Young Comrade the lowest [...] and the agitators in the middle as a small collective and as commentators'.[104] Bush was also reinterpreting older works in social and political terms in this period. In an essay on Chopin, he examined 'how his art reflects the consciousness of his period', concluding that 'in him we see a conflict of feeling and action which accounts for much that is sentimental and nostalgic in his other works and which is absent in those more directly inspired by his national consciousness'.[105] Bush wrote similarly of Beethoven 'openly associating himself with the ideals of the French Revolution' and of 'music sincerely trying to unite the warring classes of society' in Beethoven's work.[106]

In view of these statements, it is revealing to examine how Bush uses the concerto form itself, musical topics, and specific allusions to earlier composers. With regard to the former, at the outset of the concerto, rather than forming the basis of an orchestral ritornello or double exposition, the initial themes are presented by the sparsely accompanied solo piano. Subsequently, the piano and orchestra rarely engage in a dialogic relationship. Rather, for much of the movement and especially the opening sections they present material in contrasting blocks. The apportionment of material after the opening section is also significant. The orchestra never presents Theme B in either its original form or as shown in Ex. 1.12, while the piano after the opening bars never presents Theme A. Thus the piano is primarily limited to realisations of the Theme B material that are quiet and introspective in mood. When Theme B material is declaimed in the orchestra, it is initially in the form of a decisive fugue, and subsequently scored militaristically with full brass and side drum (the latter is shown in Ex.1.11a). The climax of this brass declamation of Theme B material is the full orchestral chorale (Ex. 1.11b),

---

[104] Albrecht Betz, *Hanns Eisler: Political Musician*, trans. Bill Hopkins (Cambridge: Cambridge University Press, 1982), 96.
[105] Alan Bush, 'Chopin', *Poetry and the People* 20 (1940), 19.   [106] Bush, 'Music', 131.

above which the piano adds ornamental figures. In interpreting this passage, Bush's description of Beethoven's *Missa Solemnis* is of particular interest:

> [Beethoven] precedes the words *dona nobis pacem* ('give us peace') with an orchestral interlude depicting the far off military music, drums and trumpet calls which come gradually nearer, until one of the soloists breaks forth into an agonised cry of '*Agnus Dei, qui tollis peccata mundi, dona nobis pacem*' [...] There could be no musical treatment which more unmistakably conveys Beethoven's intention that it was against the evils of war as well as the pain of the soul's unrest that his cry was directed.[107]

Given the prominence of the critique of capitalist war within the British Left in the 1930s, Bush's interest in a musical allusion that was critical of war is fitting.[108] His specific choice of the chorale as an instance of religious music is also revealing. Bush considered Bach's Protestant religious music to be 'a reflection in the religious sphere of the dissatisfaction with its material conditions of the class to which he belonged, the German middle class'.[109] Equally pertinently, Eisler remarked that:

> Music in the church is not directed towards the individual or his individual fate, but has the task of making all participants adopt a certain religious bearing. Thus, by allowing the listener to take part in the music himself later on, by joining in the chorale, he takes part in a kind of exercise and so is forced all the more effectively into a particular bearing.[110]

Eisler himself placed the chorale in a modern political context in the theatre work *Die Massnahme*: with the aim of uniting workers through active participation in singing.[111] In the context of the piano concerto, following the military music, the chorale can thus signify both collective suffering and collective expression in opposition to the (individual) piano.

In support of this reading, not only does the piano exclusively present the introspective Theme B material, but also repeatedly leads the music

---

[107] Alan Bush, 'The Greatness of Beethoven' [1953], in *In my Eighth Decade*, 57. Bush describes this passage in the same terms in 'Music', 131.

[108] This issue was, for example, the subject of Tippett's play *War Ramp* (1935).

[109] Bush, 'Music', 129. In a Marxist view, at this point in history the bourgeoisie constitutes the progressive, potentially revolutionary class.

[110] Eisler, 'The Builders of a New Musical Culture', 41.

[111] See John Willett, '*Die Massnahme*. The vanishing *Lehrstück*' in David Blake (ed.), *Hanns Eisler: A Miscellany* (Luxembourg: Harwood Academic, 1995), 82.

Ex. 1.13   Piano Concerto, i, piano only, 5 before Fig. 106.

to points of stasis. The section that begins with Ex. 1.12, for example, presents three repetitions of the material at successively higher registers, each ending as shown in Ex. 1.13. While in each repetition the bass fifth motion (though, typically, without raised leading notes) indicates the tonal progression, the repetition of the material creates a surface effect of failure to move forward that is alleviated by the succeeding orchestral fugue. The orchestral chorale ends with a restatement of material related to Ex. 1.13. In the second half of the movement, the restatement of Theme A at its original pitch at Fig. 121 is subjected to increasingly frequent interjections from the piano, leading to a collapse of the contrapuntal presentation of the material in the brass and a pedal A above which the piano again reiterates the Ex. 1.13 material. In the final bars, fragments of the chorale are ornamented by the piano before a brief virtuoso flourish and cadence in which neither the thematic conflict nor the opposition of individual piano and collective orchestra are resolved.

In addition to this evidence of Bush's use of topical references, his allusions to the specific model of Beethoven's Ninth are significant. Bush's concerto shares with Beethoven's symphony its overall schema (fast-scherzo-slow-fast) and key (D minor – major). Yet it is in the finale that Bush's Beethovenian model is most apparent. Like Beethoven's, Bush's finale initially revisits the conflicts of the opening movements, a moment in Beethoven's work that Stephen C. Rumph has compared to

Ex. 1.14 Piano Concerto, iv, strings, opening.

a concerto cadenza.[112] Not only does Bush's initial theme of the finale recall Theme A, but the opposition of virtuosity in the piano and urgent interjections in the orchestra is resumed (Ex. 1.14). At 1 after Fig. 402, for example, the piano embarks on elaboration of the theme reminiscent of the Scherzo, which it introduces at 2 after Fig. 401, and against which an interjection of the opening material is jarring (Ex. 1.15). Similarly, the final orchestral climax preceding the entry of the chorus is an abrupt interruption of a tranquil passage in A♭. This recalls the lyrical second theme of the third movement, which begins in G♭ immediately following the densely chromatic D minor opening theme derived from the first movement's Theme B. Subsequently, at the entry of the chorus, Bush creates a direct parallel with Beethoven's 'O Freunde, nicht diese Töne' in addressing the audience with 'Friends, we would speak a little of this performance'. There is also yet another musical parallel with the Ninth in that, while the final movement as a whole remains around the tonal centre of D, the music returns to D♭, thus resonating with the slow movement's second theme, on the words 'the giant man, enormous in freedom', which occur in the midst of a description of a world which has eradicated capitalism. Bush presents a sudden key change to indicate the sublime in a way comparable to Beethoven's B major modulation for the soloists near the end of the Ninth Symphony, immediately preceding the final 'wildest outburst of joy', in Donald Tovey's words.[113]

In the context of Bush's use of the concerto model to stage a conflict of individual and collective in this work, what did these parallels with the Ninth

---

[112] Stephen C. Rumph, *Beethoven after Napoleon: Political Romanticism in the Late Works* (Berkeley and London: University of California Press, 2004), 205.

[113] Donald Tovey, *Essays in Musical Analysis, Volume II: Symphonies (II), Variations and Orchestral Polyphony* (London: Oxford University Press, Humphrey Milford, 1935), 45.

Ex. 1.15 Piano Concerto, iv, piano and Vln. I, 1 after Fig. 402.

Symphony signify? Again, the model of Eisler is significant. Eisler perceived the Ninth Symphony to be of great importance in the contemporary situation:

> When this powerful Hymn to Joy bubbles up, climbs, and ends in jubilation, every class-conscious worker, filled with strength and confidence, can and must say to himself that these tones which now provide fighting workers with energy will only truly belong to us when we defeat the ruling class. Then

the masses of oppressed millions will cheer with Beethoven's song of triumph.[114]

Eisler's Beethoven, in the final movement, presented a utopia which was to be achieved on earth with the triumph of the working class. Bush, similarly, felt that in the symphony Beethoven 'speaks to the people directly; he has lost faith in the power of intention of heroic individuals or ruling-class governments to benefit mankind'.[115] Crucially, in the Piano Concerto, Bush does not mirror Beethoven directly. Bush's brief evocation of the sublime to depict the imagined socialist future gives way to the abrupt return to D minor and the reintroduction of side drum and brass. Bush's ending is an endorsement to action in the present crisis rather than a moment of apotheosis. Nevertheless, the evidence of Bush's ideas about the Ninth and the nature of the finale suggest that he viewed the Ninth as a model of how to express the need for collective action over the power of 'heroic individuals'. In this sense, the model of the Ninth represented an inversion of the model of the later nineteenth-century concerto, which accentuated the difference between soloist and orchestra and privileged virtuoso display. In Bush's concerto, rather than the finale representing the summation of individual display, the conflict of piano and orchestra is dissolved as both accompany the chorus. As the second section of the text comes to an end, we again hear one of the piano's virtuoso passages exemplified in Ex. 1.13. Whereas this was a forestalling of musical development and resolution in the preceding movements, here it has become an illustration of the aspirations of the cause. As the piano's virtuosity is now in service of the music as dictated by the choir, resolution of the musical conflicts is now possible and achieved in the final bars of the chorus on the words 'Man's future is to be fought for in our day'. The three-note arpeggiated motif first introduced at the end of the open-ended Theme A, but unresolved throughout the work, leads not to a dissonant hiatus and collapse of the musical momentum, but to resolution and a final flourish from both orchestra and piano.

This reading places the Piano Concerto firmly within what I have called Bush's pre-war aesthetic of objectivity. As with the *Concert Piece*, however, there is a question over how successful Bush was at realising his ideas in practice. The long gestation of the work remains problematic. We noted that the first movement has affinities with Bush's style in earlier works, particularly in its logical thematic construction and the use of

---

[114] David B. Dennis, *Beethoven in German Politics, 1870–1989* (New Haven and London: Yale University Press, 1996), 97.
[115] Bush, 'The Greatness of Beethoven', 56.

Ex. 1.16   Piano Concerto, iv, chorus, 2 after Fig. 414.

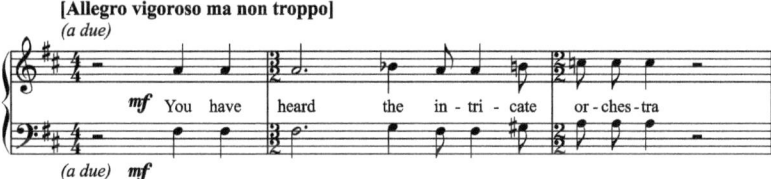

'non-tonal' and therefore, for Bush, modern elements such as a modal scale. These favoured procedures start to cause difficulties with the entry of the chorus. Although the use of material relating to the very opening of the concerto invests the work with unity, it is distinctly unlyrical, as Ex. 1.16, derived from Theme B, illustrates. In combination with the extremely long text, this weakens the impact of the choral finale as an exhortation to action.

It is worth pursuing the idea that these weaknesses in the final movement betray the incomplete state of Bush's political-musical aesthetic. We have already seen that Bush was feeling a sense of urgency about the need for political action against fascism in 1937. One manifestation of this was particular anxiety about the effect of abstract musical works in the concert hall. The Nazi Party's use of Beethoven at political rallies was of obvious concern in this regard,[116] but Bush by no means limited the targets of his disapproval to expressly fascist actions. In a letter to Britten of 1936, he argued:

> In the capitalist concert-hall the formalities of the procedure and costume of the players are the insignia of the ruling-classes; the present bourgeois aesthetic of 'art for art's sake' will be stressed (even where it contradicts the plainly expressed intentions of the composer these will be excused patronisingly away where they cannot be suppressed from notice) and the attention of the public will be directed especially to the 'neutral' artistic and subjective characteristics of the work.[117]

Bush considered the performance context of the concert hall to reinforce a capitalist point of view. He believed that the preservation of capitalism was leading to the destruction of culture under fascism. Bush asked Britten to consider of his own music: 'will the performance of this work in such and such circumstances aid in clarifying the minds of the audience in relation to the class-struggle?'[118]

---

[116] Bush, 'Music and the Working-Class Struggle', 646.
[117] Alan Bush to Benjamin Britten, 11 August 1936, BL/AB MS Mus. 452, Miscellaneous Correspondence, 1925–36.
[118] Ibid.

The finale of the Piano Concerto may be interpreted as an attempt at a solution to this problem, an experimental departure from the previous movements. The fact that the text was specially written by Swingler is of particular interest. A frequent collaborator with Bush, Swingler himself wrote extensively and theorised on ways of revolutionising art and re-establishing social function. He had also recently worked with Bush on *Peace and Prosperity* (1937), a revue 'combining satirical songs and economic statistics, naturalistic and allegorical drama, posters, dance and historical tableaux' in a critique of the National Government.[119] Although the music does not survive, the combination of elements illustrates the two artists' interest in the dramatic and performative element and in experimentation with different media.

The initial statement spoken by the chorus in the finale – 'Friends, we would speak a little of this performance' – introduces a dramatic element into the work. The direct address to the audience interrupts their absorption in the music in the same way that, in theatre, addresses to the audience break the illusion of the drama (the 'fourth wall'). The next part of the text consists of a description of the performance ('you have heard the intricate orchestra') and the effect of music on man. The text describes the 'power' of music to release human potential. The audience is thus compelled to think about the effect of music upon themselves, rather than simply experiencing the emotional effect of the music at this point. Most significant in this regard, however, are the words of the final section:

> What shall we do, then, other than sit and weep,
> Other than sink and let the music seep
> Through mind and marrow like a summer sleep?
>
> What shall we do, for whom no drug can still
> War's felt crescendo, and human ill
> And our own sense of helplessness most of all?
>
> Art is no drug, nor yet oblivion's river.
> Music is the mind-changer, the life-giver,
> The future's design, the release of new endeavour.

The earlier part of the text has underscored music's potential to move people to action. However, the question 'What shall we do [...] other than sink and let the music seep through mind and marrow' seems to make a direct reference to the conditions under which the piano concerto had thus far been experienced. The words suggest that it is not the musical text

---

[119] Andy Croft, *Comrade Heart: A Life of Randall Swingler* (Manchester and New York: Manchester University Press, 2003), 59.

so much as the audience's passive response which results in art becoming a 'drug'. The audience are thus exhorted to respond newly and actively to the music.

In view of the text, Bush's claim that the final movement was an immediate response to a pressing political problem takes on a new significance. Where Beethoven invited the listener to embrace more joyous sounds, Bush rather rejects the listener's conventional passive listening response to the first three movements in favour of a more critical engagement. The effect of the text, then, is alienating, as Bush calls into question the listener's experience of the music thus far. It is worth recalling at this point that Bush composed the final movement in the company of Brecht and Eisler. There are striking parallels between Brecht's comparisons of dramatic and epic theatre and Bush's statements at this time that are pertinent to the finale. Brecht, with reference to opera, compared dramatic and epic theatre thus:[120]

Dramatic theatre	Epic theatre
implicates the spectator in a stage situation	turns the spectator into an observer but
wears down his capacity for action	arouses his capacity for action
provides him with sensations	forces him to take decisions
experience	picture of the world
the spectator is involved in something	he is made to face something
suggestion	argument
instinctive feelings are preserved	brought to the point of recognition
the spectator is in the thick of it, shares the experience	the spectator stands outside, studies

Immediately clear are the resonances of Brecht's ideas in Bush's statements, particularly in Bush's association of 'sensations' with Romantic music, his condemnation of the appeal to instinct in capitalism and fascism, and the need for music to inspire action. Even beyond this suggestion of Brecht's influence on Bush's thought, the parallels with the text of the Piano Concerto are clear. The text is constructed so as to suggest possibilities for action. More significantly, the text's description of the mechanics of the performance 'turns the spectator into an observer'. Taking into account Bush's anxiety about the effect of concert performance on the political impact of works, and the influence of

---

[120] This table is an abbreviated form. For the full comparison see Brecht's essay 'The Modern Theatre is the Epic Theatre' [1930] in John Willett (ed. and trans.), *Brecht on Theatre: The Development of an Aesthetic* (London: Methuen, 1964), 37.

Brecht and Eisler throughout the decade, the finale of the Piano Concerto may thus be understood not as a lapse into propaganda but as a criticism of the bourgeois concert experience in line with Bush's ongoing aesthetic project.

This reading does not eradicate the problems with the work already identified. It remains the case that the final movement is an uneasy match with the first three movements, even if understood as a deliberate critique. Moreover, the concerto was undoubtedly unsuccessful in conveying these intentions at the first performance. The most common responses were that the words of the finale were indistinct and that the presence of politics in a concert work was objectionable. The text was also far too long for clarity. If the critics in the audience could only discern the words with the aid of a printed programme, for radio listeners the performance must have been unintelligible. Yet for all its faults, the Piano Concerto is emblematic of Bush's work in this decade because it embodies Bush's uncertainty regarding the way in which modern music could have a social and political effect. In contrast to his more entrenched aesthetic positions in later decades (although these too are open to much more nuanced interpretation), this was a period in which Bush by no means saw a modern musical idiom and a socialist outlook as incompatible. On the contrary, he regarded the former as indispensable to the latter. In the absence of a consensus regarding the relationship between music and politics among the British left-wing intelligentsia, and being exposed to a range of musical and aesthetic models, Bush experimented. The Piano Concerto is best understood as a memorable product of this experimentation, rather than an inevitable first step towards his later socialist realism.

Where does this leave Bush as modernist? Certainly, the image of Bush as an apolitical, individualistic, 'difficult' modernist who gave it up for politics must be rejected. Firstly, as we have seen, Bush's engagement with modern music and left-wing politics went hand in hand. Secondly, the mix of traditional and modern elements in Bush's music, the gap between often-radical theory and its realisation in practice, renders any unequivocal description of Bush as modernist problematic. Rather, Bush should be understood as engaging with various modernist aesthetics and techniques in the pursuit of a modern music appropriate to his aesthetic and political goals. Both Schoenberg and Eisler, in Bush's eyes, offered productive possibilities for subverting bourgeois musical culture: a goal that was socialist in seeking to expose the ideological foundation of that culture, and modernist in seeking a radical new function for the concert hall. How far the works of this period really achieved such a goal is open to question. And yet this is hardly surprising. Bush was certainly, like Tippett, late to reach compositional maturity. This was a period in which Bush, far from being insulated from contemporary developments in Britain, was embracing a whole host of modern music at the same time as he weighed into real debate over the possibilities of socialist music. In view of Bush's later anti-modernist pronouncements, it is easy to wrongly perceive his 'modernist' period through the lens of his post-war self-criticism. Above all, however, Bush's music in the 1930s was an incomplete project.

2 Bush as Activist: The Idea of Workers' Music

> I do not care about mixing propaganda and art and I do not quite see that the people who hold such particular political views should arrogate to themselves and none others the title of 'Workers'.
>
> Ralph Vaughan Williams[1]

Recalling a concert of Bush's music in the early 1940s, Mellers described an 'utterly disparate' programme. Bush had responded to Mellers' invitation to introduce a complete programme of his own works. On the one hand, there were piano pieces which were 'highly sophisticated, complicated, intellectual and [...] Central European rather than English in technique'; on the other, songs for amateur choir which were 'deliberately simple and direct in style'.[2] Mellers may be forgiven for struggling to reconcile the latter category with the former. The repertoire he described falls under the umbrella of what Bush himself described as 'workers' music', a term probably adapted from his encounters with organisations like the German Workers' Singers' League (*Deutsche Arbeiter-Sängerbund*; DASB) in Germany.[3] As Vaughan Williams perceived, the terminology carried definite political connotations, evoking a tradition of socialist mass song of which the apogee was 'The Internationale' (also the anthem of the Soviet Union throughout the inter-war period). For this reason, there is an argument for treating workers' music separately within evaluations of Bush's oeuvre and musical style. While the composer was writing political songs – 'Song to Freedom' (1930), 'Question and Answer' (1931), 'Song of the Hunger Marchers' (1934), 'Make Your Meaning Clear' (1939) – alongside his concert music throughout the late 1920s and 1930s, they occupied different performance spaces (mass rallies, political meetings, demonstrations), targeted different audiences, and were topical, occasional, and technically simple enough for amateur performance. However, the fact that Bush included such songs within diverse concert programmes suggests that he himself

---

[1] Ralph Vaughan Williams to Alan Bush, 13 July 1939, in Hugo Cobbe (ed.), *Letters of Ralph Vaughan Williams, 1895-1958* (Oxford and New York: Oxford University Press, 2008), 276.

[2] Mellers, 'A Note on Alan Bush and the English Tradition', 21-2.

[3] Bush employs the term in his articles 'Arbeiterbewegung und moderne Musiker', 21 and 'Music and the Working-Class Struggle', 650.

perceived common aesthetic ground between his 'sophisticated' and 'simple and direct' compositions. This has forced critics and musicologists like Mellers into attempting some form of joint musical appraisal likewise. In addition, the songs are easily associated, through their socialist content and simple style, with Bush's aesthetic shift around 1948. Consequently, the workers' music demands consideration as a potential precursor of Bush's turn to populism and nationalism and, as such, has proven vulnerable to dismissal as crude, musically trivial propaganda.[4]

Sympathetic writers, generally friends or colleagues of Bush, endeavoured to address these challenges by situating the workers' songs within his varied body of choral music.[5] While such accounts do something to assert the aesthetic value of this music, it is doubtful whether they seriously dent the association between the workers' songs and the post-1948 works. Where criticism is entirely technical, the simplicity of the repertoire will always be stark in comparison with works like *Dialectic*. Where, as in the case of Stevenson, a writer defends this simplicity on the basis of the socialist argument for greater popular appeal, the connection to later Soviet aesthetic policies is reinforced.[6] An alternative and more promising approach has been to resituate Bush's workers' songs within a sphere of activity radically different from the concert-based musical world inhabited by his other works. This is the theory at the heart of Ian Watson's study of song in workers' culture.[7] Influenced by an interview with Bush undertaken in the 1970s,[8] Watson posits the idea of a 'second culture' that was connected to radical politics and characterised by drastically different musical features, aims, performers, and repertoire from mainstream musical culture. The strength of this reading is that Bush's workers' music is indeed not reducible to the composition of a few songs, but rather it may act as a catch-all term for a vast amount of conducting, performing, organisation, theoretical writing, and practical experimentation undertaken from the late 1920s onwards. Bush's work leading the LLCU and WMA encompassed all these tasks and more, with the latter eventually moving into specialist

---

[4] As implied, for example, in Ian Kemp's comparison of Tippett, Eisler, and Bush discussed at the start of Chapter 1.

[5] Ernst H. Meyer, 'The Choral Works' in Clark (ed.), *Tribute to Alan Bush on his Fiftieth Birthday*, 32–4; Bernard Stevens, 'The Choral Music' in Stevenson (ed.), *Time Remembered*, 32–5; Stevenson, 'Alan Bush: Committed Composer', 323–42.

[6] Stevenson, 'Alan Bush: Committed Composer', 327–8.

[7] Ian Watson, *Song and Democratic Culture in Britain: An Approach to Popular Culture in Social Movements* (London: Croom Helm, 1983).

[8] Ian Watson, 'Alan Bush and Left Music in the Thirties: An Introduction and an Interview', *Gulliver* 4 (1978), 80–90.

performances of international working-class song, publishing, running a record label (Topic Records), and even cultural policy. He edited the *Left Song Book* (1938) with Swingler. He wrote voluminously on theories of workers' music and practical implications, and contributed to cultural discussions within the Communist Party. Finally, Bush was deeply involved in three major left-wing visual and musical spectacles of the 1930s: The Pageant of Labour (1934), 'Towards To-morrow': A Pageant of Co-operation (1938), and most notably the Festival of Music for the People in 1939.

However, important qualifications must be made to the 'second culture' concept. Watson's notion of an entirely distinct sphere of workers' music has already been subjected to serious critique by Duncan Hall, who observes the many points of intersection between high and low culture and the tension between motions for workers to enjoy 'the best music available' and to have 'art of their own'.[9] Among Bush's activities, the use of classical and modern music in the Festival of Music for the People and the LLCU's resurrection of Handel's *Belshazzar* are evidence of a similar ambivalence. It is significant, too, that Bush himself, for all the depictions of him during this decade as a bearded radical, straddled the worlds of conventional concert-giving and the nascent culture of inter-war radical socialism. We have seen in Chapter 1 that the Piano Concerto represented an attempt to disrupt the former; to what extent, then, was the workers' music not the Other of the concert music but another manifestation of a wholesale effort to transform musical culture?

An approach is needed which does not either eliminate or overemphasise the differences between Bush's pre-war concert music and workers' music, but which brings these two categories into a properly dialectical relationship. Like Bush's 'modernism', workers' music is an aesthetic-political label and consequently demands analysis which encompasses both musical content and political context. Furthermore, if both Bush's modernism and his workers' music were part of a cohesive vision of a future musical culture, it is right to examine them as spheres of activity – encompassing performance, theory, and composition – rather than corpuses of works. This redefinition not only expands the object of study, but also allows the exploration of tensions between what was imagined – both musically and politically – and the reality of the rapidly changing geopolitical situations, scant resources, conflicting opinions, and existing traditions of British socialist music-making with which Bush worked. While the *idea* of a 'second culture' exerted a powerful influence upon Bush's imagination when it came to workers'

---

[9] Duncan Hall, *'A Pleasant Change from Politics': Music and the British Labour Movement between the Wars* (Cheltenham: New Clarion, 2001), 17–21.

music of this period, the manifestation of that culture in practice proved halting, complex, and frequently contradictory.

Material and Function

Bush's earliest experiences of working-class music were English.[10] Dave Russell has asserted that although popular music-making in the Victorian period was vibrant and widespread, 'much [...] [of it] was probably in a [politically and socially] conservative direction'.[11] Bush echoed this argument in 1936, writing that brass bands, although exclusively working-class, had as yet made no contribution to the 'class-struggle', and that working-class choral organisations had only recently started to embrace a political role.[12] There was certainly no workers' choral movement in Britain to rival that of Germany, where, from the 1860s onwards, choral singing was closely associated with the rise of social democratic political parties.[13] Even the term 'workers' music' did not have the same currency in Britain. Nevertheless, by 1926 the Labour movement could boast some established musical practices and theoretical work on the role of music in Labour politics.[14] As Chris Waters has argued, late-Victorian socialists writing on music were influenced by two intellectual traditions: middle-class philanthropic social reform and utopian socialist thought.[15] Both camps were motivated to foster activity by the belief that music had the power to transform the individual's moral character. Whether the aim of this transformation was upward social mobility or radical social reform was, however, a matter of debate which had corresponding implications for musical activities. The desirability of promoting 'the best music available' in order to achieve moral transformation, or of fostering a distinctly working-class music, were subjects of much uncertainty.[16] Musical activities were also complicated by motivations of

---

[10] Prior to becoming Musical Adviser to the LLCU in 1929, a post that involved responsibility for selecting repertoire and organising some of the choirs' activities, Bush worked with the organisation in a junior capacity from 1926.

[11] Dave Russell, *Popular Music in England, 1840-1914, A Social History*, 2nd edn (Manchester and New York: Manchester University Press, 1997), 291.

[12] Bush, 'Music and the Working-Class Struggle', 648-9.

[13] See James Garratt, *Music, Culture and Social Reform in the Age of Wagner* (Cambridge: Cambridge University Press, 2010), 197ff.

[14] The Labour movement, broadly defined, encompasses 'the Labour Party, the trade unions and the co-operative movement [...] as well as the Communist Party and various small fringe socialist groups and parties'. Hall, 'A Pleasant Change from Politics', 2.

[15] Chris Waters, *British Socialists and the Politics of Popular Culture, 1884-1914* (Manchester: Manchester University Press, 1990), 100-1.

[16] Ibid., 101-2; Hall, 'A Pleasant Change from Politics', 17-21.

using music for purposes of fundraising, entertainment, or spreading the word ('pennies, pleasure and propaganda').[17] Thus by the 1920s there existed a variety of organisations promoting music for both practical and ideological reasons. For example, the only national choral body in the movement, the Clarion Vocal Unions, was both socialist in principle and held competitions and performed at celebrations, socials, and fundraisers.[18] Such varied activities were replicated across the country at a local level.

That Bush was initially influenced by this tradition is apparent from an examination of his earliest work in the field. An article written in 1929 describing the aims and achievements of the LLCU is indicative of Bush's conception of the role of workers' music at this juncture. Bush asserted that while these opportunities for show were important, the LLCU's most valuable work was behind the scenes:

> Our struggles to master the music, which is almost always of the very highest class and sometimes rather difficult, involve us in the practice of our discipline and in a constant endeavour to improve our gifts, from both of which we derive great benefits.[19]

This statement and the title of the article itself – 'Adventures in Self-Expression' – indicate the extent to which Bush then saw workers' music as primarily about personal edification. While this bears some affinity to Bush's later (Marxist) vision of a workers' music that promotes a transformed consciousness, it is at this stage more reminiscent of the Victorian socialist belief that music can transform the individual, who in turn may transform society. This is supported by Bush's indications of appropriate repertoire. Rather than endorsing a unique, non-bourgeois repertoire for workers, the important factor is singing 'music of the very highest class'. A sample of LLCU repertoire from 1929 supports Bush's notion of workers' music, consisting of a mixture of traditional songs like 'Ca' Hawkie' and the 'Song of the Volga Boatmen', sixteenth-century songs and madrigals such as John Mundy's 'Hey ho! chill go to plough no more', more recent choral favourites like Elgar's 'The Challenge of Thor' from *King Olaf*, and socialist songs such as Boughton's 'Song of Liberty' and the blandly satirical 'Lord Balbus'.

However, even at this early stage, there is evidence of Bush's dissatisfaction with the LLCU. As early as the beginning of 1930, Bush exchanged letters with Francesca Allinson, conductor of one of the LLCU's constituent

---

[17] Hall, *'A Pleasant Change from Politics'*, 46. [18] Ibid., 14.
[19] Alan Bush, 'Adventures in Self-Expression' [1929] [draft of an article on the LLCU intended for *The London News*], BL/AB MS Mus. 645, Correspondence relating to the London Labour Choral Union.

local choirs, lamenting the lack of good socialist music for use in the Labour movement and criticising some of the existing repertoire: 'I was delighted to get your letter, and to know that the L.L.C.U. possesses at least one conductor besides myself who does not consider Lord Balbus the ideal Socialist Song!'[20] It is not difficult to speculate about the nature of Bush's objections. 'Lord Balbus' is a musically slight part-song printed in Tonic Sol-fa, presumably partly warranting disapproval on grounds of his demand for music of good quality.[21] More importantly, the lighthearted text is political only in the broadest and mildest sense, contrasting the loneliness of a lord who refuses to share his wealth with the poor but happy people outside his gates. In his 1936 article, 'Music and the Working-Class Struggle', Bush railed against the tendency of working-class choirs to 'ape the middle-class musical societies' in repertoire he summed up as consisting of 'the sentimental part-songs of the nineteenth and twentieth centuries, together with folk-song arrangements and sixteenth-century madrigals'.[22] The aforementioned 1929 LLCU repertoire is an obvious target of this criticism: on these criteria there was little to distinguish the LLCU as distinctly working class. Clearly the organisation had made some commitment to the idea of singing specifically socialist songs like 'Lord Balbus'. At a 1924 rally, too (as opposed to the concert-based programme of 1929) they performed such stalwarts as 'the Marseillaise' and 'England Arise!' Yet both the repertoire as a whole and Bush's comments in 'Adventures in Self-Expression' suggest that the existing socialist idea of workers achieving moral transformation by singing 'music of the highest class' was still strongly in evidence. Moreover, it is not yet clear what a distinctly socialist repertoire might have meant, either to Bush or to LLCU. 'Lord Balbus' was musically conservative and textually socialist only in the broadest possible terms.

These uncertainties are discernible in Bush's initial efforts at changing the LLCU repertoire by drawing on the resources and example of the German workers' movement. He wrote in 1930 that he was 'revolving various plans in his mind which he believes will prove to be of some assistance to the development of the working-class movement in England, especially on the artistic and philosophical side',[23] and which he planned to develop whilst living in Berlin. He had already made contact with the DASB, which expressed interest in fostering links with England

---

[20] Alan Bush to Francesca Allinson, 3 March 1930, BL/AB MS Mus. 645.
[21] Algernon E. Anderson, *Lord Balbus: From Poems of Satire and Sentiment* (London: Joseph Williams, 1927).
[22] Bush, 'Music and the Working-Class Struggle', 648–9.
[23] Alan Bush to Annie J. Atkins, 30 June 1930, BL/AB MS Mus. 645.

and provided Bush with sample songbooks and material.[24] He was later successful in affiliating the LLCU to the *Internationale der Arbeitersänger* (International of Worker-Singers), an organisation whose objects were to 'promulgate international understanding between the workers of different nationalities, the creation of an international music-library of a socialistic character, and to assist countries where the workers' singing-movement is relatively weak in their development in the surmounting of their difficulties'.[25] He also wanted to create a company to publish workers' music in England with the aid of the German organisation. While this was unsuccessful, he was able to have English versions of several German songs published by the LLCU. One of the songs chosen, 'Bundeslied' (published by the LLCU in translation as 'The Call to Freedom') was certainly more appropriate to Bush's aims than 'Lord Balbus'. The text featured the combination of identifying a need and calling for action that would become a hallmark of Bush's own workers' songs. After describing the worker's life as one of unrelieved work and suffering, the final verse calls upon workers to awake and break the 'bondage of need'. It was also a long-standing choral favourite of the German social democratic movement. However, this embrace of the German movement was still not yet tantamount to a radical, modern socialist repertoire on the lines envisaged by Eisler. The DASB was a moderate, social democratic organisation which itself faced the same dilemmas as English socialist musical organisations over the relative claims of the classical tradition and *Kampfmusik* for inclusion in the repertoire.[26] Eisler, promoting the latter line, ultimately broke with the organisation.[27] Hans von Bülow's 'Bundeslied' itself, furthermore, is an 1863 four-part choral setting of Georg Herwegh's 'Bundeslied des Allgemeinen deutschen Arbeitervereins', a setting of the poem which had long attracted criticism in Germany due to its purportedly bourgeois, non-proletarian style.[28] It is not clear whether Bush was aware of such criticisms, but the incident does raise the question of how much consideration he had yet given to building a repertoire that was both politically and *musically* new and distinctive.

To what extent, then, did the workers' songs Bush wrote and performed in the later 1930s reflect the transformation of his aesthetic? There is ample

---

[24] Alan Bush to Editor, *Daily Herald*, 13 February 1930, BL/AB MS Mus. 645.
[25] Alan Bush to Annie J. Atkins, 30 June 1930, BL/AB MS Mus. 645.
[26] See W.L. Guttsman, *Workers' Culture in Weimar Germany: Between Tradition and Commitment* (New York, Oxford and Munich: Berg, 1990), 159ff.
[27] The group rejected a performance of *Die Massnahme*, prompting a group including Eisler to break away and form a separate organisation. See Betz, *Hanns Eisler*, 105–6.
[28] See Garratt, *Music, Culture and Social Reform*, 207–9.

evidence of a much stronger presence of modern songs in general among the repertoire Bush was disseminating. In 1930, Bush helped to edit *Twelve Labour Choruses*,[29] a volume produced by the Independent Labour Party, which provided choral settings of poems from *Labour's Song Book*, itself a collection of the texts of songs and hymns to be used in the Labour movement.[30] Notwithstanding some new or recent settings and the inclusion of 'The Internationale', the volume was both traditional and specifically English in its choice of socialist verse by, among others, William Blake, William Morris and the Leeds-born socialist Tom Maguire. Musically, the compilation was a mixture of traditional songs and melodies and largely hymn-like, strophic four-part settings mostly made by Boughton, Bush's predecessor as LLCU Musical Advisor. *The Left Song Book* of 1938 represented a striking departure. In contrast to the more abstract benefits of singing described in 'Adventures in Self-Expression', Bush and Swingler emphasised the necessity for songs that were 'as clearly related to our movement as possible'.[31] In addition to a highly international selection of traditional workers' songs, the editors included an array of topical workers' songs from different countries, including Eisler's 'Einheitsfrontlied'. They also provided topical texts on traditional rounds, such as the following to be performed to 'Three Blind Mice':

> Prices rise,
> Prices rise,
> See how they mount,
> See how they mount,
> They've raised the price of your daily bread,
> And given you cruisers and guns instead,
> For they know it won't trouble you when you're dead that prices rise.

While the emphasis here was on textual innovation, Eisler's music made regular appearances in the LLCU repertoire in the mid- to late 1930s. In addition to staging the aforementioned first English performance of *Die Massnahme*, the LLCU published a number of Eisler's songs, including the 'Ballad of To-day', 'In Praise of Learning', 'Report on the Death of a Comrade', and 'The Party's in Danger'. The latter three were also performed as part of a 1935 'concert-demonstration' in Eisler's honour.

---

[29] *Twelve Labour Choruses* (London: I.L.P. Publication Department, 1930).
[30] *Labour's Song Book* (London: I.L.P. Publication Department, 1924).
[31] Alan Bush and Randall Swingler (eds.) with members of the Workers' Music Association and the Left Book Club Musicians' Group, *The Left Song Book* (London: Victor Gollancz, 1938), 3.

Ex. 2.1 Hanns Eisler, 'Solidaritätslied', bb. 5–10.

Notable too is the effect of Bush's reception of Eisler upon his own workers' songs, which may be examined via a comparison of Eisler's 'Solidaritätslied' (1931) (Solidarity Song), Bush's 'To the Men of England' (1927–8) and his 'Make Your Meaning Clear' of 1939. The 'Solidaritätslied' superficially meets conventional expectations of workers' songs in that it is brief, syllabic and suited to the capabilities of untrained singers (Ex. 2.1). Yet it is deceptively complex. Both verse and chorus are constructed from the repetition of small melodic cells, investing the song with a sense of circularity heightened by its abrupt conclusion on the dominant chord. The two-verse phrases consist of irregular units (each 3 + 3 bars). In the chorus, following an initial four-bar phrase, the first motif of the subsequent phrase is abruptly repeated and then abandoned for a contrasting figure, investing the song with momentum and rhythmic elasticity, and defying the expected regular phrasing of verse and chorus. Harmonically, the song is straightforward in that it is primarily built up of chords of D minor (the tonic), G minor, A minor and E major. The key of D minor is not, however, articulated in a conventional way. The first four bars consist of alternations of G minor and A minor. When D succeeds A minor in bar 5, Eisler adds C to suggest F major chords, while in the

Ex. 2.2 Bush, 'To the Men of England', opening (reduction).

next four bars the presence of E major suggests the dominant. In the coda of the song, Eisler again resists tonal closure by alternating bars of G minor and A major. Paralleling the melody, Eisler relies harmonically on reiteration and repetition rather than on a conventionally unfolding tonal structure. In terms of Eisler's aesthetics, the song's circularity, resistance of closure and rhythmic flexibility disrupts passive enjoyment, inviting instead a new, active response from the listener. This new function of song is, moreover, achieved through a *modern* musical language. Eisler observed with regard to efforts to reach new audiences: 'the attempt of some modern composers to reach new strata of listeners by artificially lowering standards, while retaining the old narcotic function, is no solution'.[32]

Bush's 'To the Men of England' was written for the LLCU before he discovered Eisler's music, and presents a sharp contrast with the 'Solidaritätslied'. Like the songs in *Twelve Labour Choruses*, the text – a setting of Shelley's 'Song to the Men of England' (1819) – was not topical. Rather, Bush's choice lies in a tradition of English socialist music, being a favourite inclusion in pre–First World War socialist songbooks.[33] Musically, the work is neither simplistic nor conservative. Like Eisler's song, it possesses rhythmic flexibility derived from the changing time signatures (Ex. 2.2), but this derives from the rhythms of the original text rather than the intention of energising the audience. Similar sensitivity to the text-setting is demonstrated by the subtle change of colour effected by the shift from the original

A♭ major to E major in the central section (Ex. 2.3). In the Eisler piece, however, such nuances are achieved within the framework of a song suitable for almost any level of ability and to be sung in any situation. Most striking about the Bush selection is that the song is still firmly rooted in concert practice. The length and complexity of the text and its setting and the rhythmic and contrapuntal complexities present considerable challenges for both amateur performers and audience. On the evidence of 'To the Men of England', Bush was not 'writing down' at this stage, and the work did not represent the new functions of workers' music that Bush would come to recognise in Eisler's songs.

By 1939, in contrast, Bush had expressly adopted a number of Eisler's arguments about the nature and function of workers' music. In two unpublished articles of 1936, Bush rejected an aesthetics that appealed to an abstract or static conception of beauty in music and

---

[32] Eisler, 'The Crisis in Music', 119.   [33] Waters, *British Socialists*, 110–11.

Ex. 2.3 'To the Men of England', bb. 27–31.

the notion of composition as essentially separate from life.[34] Rather, he embraced the notion of the composer as craftsman and, akin to Eisler's concept of *angewandte Musik*, a rigorously functional role for workers' music. Recalling, too, Eisler's 1930s arguments for the continued 'material' progress of music, he asserted that 'the composer is confined [...] to the material available in his time'.[35] In addition to the use of non-tonal scales, there were several ways in which the composer of workers' music could achieve this:

> [The melody] can contain prominent diminished and augmented intervals, such as were at one time carefully avoided. Chromatic semitones had better not be used. Suspensions must be used with great caution, on account of their tendency to sentimental effect. [...] In harmonising a unison song the complete major or minor common chord can be often replaced by twopart harmony, in which the third of the chord is omitted. Whole phrases can be treated in unison. Diatonic harmony is preferable to chromatic. Vigorous movements in the bass are essential. An energetic style devoid of sentimental elements is the one to aim at.[36]

---

[34] Alan Bush, 'Notes on the Problems of Workers' Music', typewritten MS for study classes delivered under the National Council of Labour Colleges, February-March 1936, ABH, 1; Alan Bush, 'Planning a Workers' Festival', typewritten MS, undat. [*c.* 1936], ABH, 2.
[35] Bush, 'Notes on the Problems of Workers' Music', 1.   [36] Ibid., 2–3.

Ex. 2.4 Bush, 'Make Your Meaning Clear' opening.

'Make Your Meaning Clear' puts several of these ideas into practice (Ex. 2.4). As in Eisler's song, the endorsement to action in the here and now is fundamental, and is propelled by a march-like bass line. Both this song and the 'Song of the Hunger Marchers' refer to contemporary events (here, the reference to the Bulgarian communist Georgi Dimitrov (1882–1949), a senior Comintern official who earned renown after he was tried for complicity in the 1933 Reichstag Fire and successfully defended himself). There is another Eisler 'fingerprint' in the alternation of major and minor to fit the text at particular points. Reflecting his own stipulations, Bush harmonises the song very sparsely and austerely, particularly avoiding the leading note and in some cases the third at cadences. Perhaps most significantly, in common with his broad musical aesthetic in the late 1930s, the intended effect of these features was an unsentimental music which encouraged engagement rather than the escapism of which Bush accused bourgeois music. The example of Eisler undoubtedly helped Bush to devise an idiom that was distinct from existing English choral repertory, that was contemporary without undue complexity.

There is, then, evidence that Bush's Eislerian aesthetic of art music informed his workers' music too. Yet qualifications are necessary. While Bush's song is unsentimental, it is certainly more conservative musically than Eisler's. Bush tends to lack Eisler's innovative construction of songs from repeated melodic cells, and is tonally unambiguous, the sparse harmonisation notwithstanding. Eisler's march-like basses, inspired in part by the jazz 'walking bass', are offset by the constantly changing time signatures and supple phrasing where Bush's retain a solid 4/4 pulse. It may also have been the case that Bush never intended to follow Eisler's model completely, despite the opportunities presented by his time in Berlin and by Eisler's periods of exile spent in London. An anonymous 1938 memorandum on the LLCU indicated that at a low point for membership in 1933 and under Bush's influence, the LLCU Executive Committee took the decision to abandon their diverse repertoire and sing only workers' songs. Although they began with songs from Germany, 'it was found that these related to political situations in those countries and the musical idiom was un-English'.[37] We have already seen in the *Left Song Book* and in Bush's exasperation with the early LLCU that there were tensions between his aesthetics and what was achievable in practice, and between his impulses towards desire for tradition and desire for innovation. So what emerges from Bush's activities circa 1930 is a degree of ambivalence about the nature of workers' music, and compromise in practice, that, as we shall see, was lasting. Finally, the most striking contrast between 'To the Men of England' and 'Make Your Meaning Clear' is perhaps not the musical complexity but the flexibility of use that this enabled. Like the 'Solidaritätslied', 'Make Your Meaning Clear' could be sung in a variety of settings, by workers of any ability, in a way that 'To the Men of England' could not. What must therefore now be considered is the extent to which Bush's reception of Eisler affected his workers' music in performance.

An Aesthetics of Performance

In 1936, Bush was becoming increasingly concerned with the bourgeois capitalist concert hall as a locus for performance due to his

---

[37] Memorandum on the Work and Aims of the London Labour Choral Union [1938], BL/ AB MS Mus. 645.

equation between capitalist and fascist aesthetics of *l'art pour l'art*. It might be assumed that in the sphere of workers' music the combination of topical socialist texts and distinctive music alone would avoid such dangers; certainly the exclusive focus on musical texts in other surveys has not challenged this assumption. In fact, the composer devoted even greater attention to elements of performance of workers' music than of art music. Just as he expressed dissatisfaction with choral repertoires indistinguishable from those of bourgeois organisations, Bush argued against the prevalence of conventional attitudes to the performance of working-class music. In 'Music and the Working-class Struggle', he noted that, in their 'methods of concertising', workers' music organisations had until recently been essentially bourgeois:

> they should seek in their methods of giving concerts and holding festivals to *depart as widely as possible from accepted middle-class standards*; in the main by stressing the fact that the concert or festival *is not to be judged on its purely musical merits alone*, but chiefly from the standpoint of how much or how little it has furthered the cause of the working-class movement as a whole.[38]

Clearly what Bush has in mind here is the avoidance of musical events that encouraged the separation of music and life, particularly politics. Yet how were 'methods of concertising' to be transformed appropriately?

One area in which Bush endorsed new practices was performance style, and again the influence of Eisler is apparent. In an article on rehearsing *Die Massnahme*, Eisler wrote that:

> it is essential to break with the 'lovely singing' typical of choral societies. [...] The aim has to be a very precise, tight, rhythmic kind of singing [...] cold, sharp and trenchant.[39]

Bush spoke similarly of the need for 'powerful and efficient' performances.[40] This might simply be realised through an energetic manner and paying particular attention to the declamation of the text. Bush

---

[38] Bush, 'Music and the Working-Class Struggle', 649.
[39] Hanns Eisler, 'Some Tips for Rehearsal of "The Decision"' in John Willett and Ralph Mannheim (eds.), *Bertolt Brecht Collected Plays*, vol. 3 pt. 2 (London: Methuen, 1997), 233.
[40] Alan Bush, '"Our Music", "Our Music"', *Red Notes* [official organ of the LLCU] 4 (January 1937), copy held in Sir Frederick Warner Collection, Albert Sloman Library, University of Essex, Colchester, National Cataloguing Unit for the Archives of Contemporary Scientists no. 144/1/06, A.80, 2.

advised an enquirer from South Africa, however, that the words of workers' songs should be 'hurled' at the audience.[41] On a recording of Bush's 1930s songs made in the 1940s or 1950s by the WMA Singers (with Bush at the piano), the performance style is indeed forceful and semi-spoken.[42] Bush actually indicated in the text of his 'Song of the Hunger Marchers' that the repeated word 'stamp' should be performed something in the manner of *Sprechstimme* (pitches are specified with crossed note-heads). Thus the avoidance of a conventional *cantabile* tone in choral singing was one means of achieving the new functions envisaged for workers' music.

More radical were Bush's ideas about the performance context of workers' songs. In his view, not only the nature of the music being performed but the kind of event it was heard in, and the context of political speeches or verbal explanation, were all crucial to the effect of workers' music. Although the concert was an established feature of working-class musical culture, Bush was particularly scathing about its possibilities because he saw it as an inferior copy of bourgeois culture's vehicle of pure entertainment:

> It generally consists of a miscellaneous string of items, the choir, solo songs, instrumental solos, recitations, dances, dramatic sketches, plays, anything in fact performed anyhow. [...] Often the solo items are of no cultural value whatever, at best a light classic, at worst a commonplace ballad or tea-shop tune, a worthless specimen of bourgeois commercialism. [...] This is stuff worker-musicians and performers should be ashamed to touch.[43]

Bush was wary of the possibilities of music in the political meeting and of the workers' music festival (the latter a longstanding preoccupation of the LLCU) for similar reasons: in the former, music could simply prove 'an irrelevant interruption'; in the latter, there was a danger again that the workers' festival would simply parallel its bourgeois equivalent. While, naturally, a crucial means of improving these events was to perform modern workers' music, Bush was also very interested in how this music could achieve the most powerful effect.

The simplest method was to select music which fitted a particular political occasion. This was particularly appropriate to political meetings or demonstrations in which music was subsidiary but could, in this way, adopt something of a 'liturgical' function in contributing to the atmosphere

---

[41] Alan Bush to E.M. Dougall, 6 June 1939, BL/AB MS Mus. 454, Miscellaneous Correspondence 1939.
[42] WMA New Topic Recordings 1 (2000) [non-commercial recording in the possession of John Jordan].
[43] Bush, 'Planning a Workers' Festival', 8.

of an event or, through choice of appropriate songs, underlining the message of the political speeches through another medium. To avoid imitating the entertainment function of bourgeois music, Bush also advocated a variety of methods of interspersing music and verbal explanation. Again, this could amount to a very simple spoken introduction to a song at a political meeting explaining its relevance to the workers' movement. Another method was montage, a favoured artistic technique of Brecht and Eisler. Bush suggested, for example, combining choral pieces or segments thereof with spoken remarks and quotations from newspapers.[44] Most elaborately in this vein, Bush suggested a means of transforming the workers' concert from its current, unsatisfactory form:

> Another method is to outrival the absurdities of the sickly love-song or religiose shop-ballad by choosing a part-song of the very worst type with a specially nauseating text. This is sung with the greatest possible technical efficiency and maximum of bourgeois decorum ... but with more than a hint of exaggeration so that the audience is not in danger of taking it too seriously. A member of the choir sitting in the audience gets up after the performance and asks the choir why they don't sing something sensible. The choir replies that some people seem to like the kind of thing they have just sung and that this is an entertainment anyhow. The interrupter says he finds it stupid not entertaining and suggests the choir should sing something that will make everyone sit up instead of sending them to sleep. Whereupon the choir sings a definitely tendencious piece ... preferably something novel in every way, *both in text and also musically*. The interrupter can then appeal to the audience to say what they think and a lively discussion could follow.[45]

Although it is debatable how effective this method would be in practice, this is the clearest indication thus far of Bush's notion of how 'methods of concertising' could be transformed. The workers' concert, it seems, was only acceptable where the pieces of music performed were a prompt for reflection and discussion rather than the kind of passive engagement Bush criticised as a feature of bourgeois listening. The theatrical performance of a 'bourgeois' item, combined with the breaking of the pattern of expected audience behaviour (heckling leading to a change of programme) provided a means of altering function in this way. As Bush remarked, substantial efforts in this direction could transform the concert into the 'concert-demonstration'. This medium aimed not at entertainment but at the illustration of an underlying idea (the need for working-class solidarity; the need to end capitalism) through a variety of artistic means. Thus, Bush's 1935

---

[44] Bush, 'Notes on the Problems of Workers' Music', 3.
[45] Bush, 'Planning a Workers' Festival', 9 (my emphasis).

concert-demonstration mounted in Eisler's honour aimed to give 'a practical demonstration of the various ways in which music could be used to further the class-struggle'.[46] *Die Massnahme*, yet again, offered a precedent in the transformation of existing conventions. Brecht and Eisler described the work as 'not a play in the normal sense. It is an event [...] which is meant to be more like a kind of demonstration'.[47] Variety of artistic media was an important means through which this was achieved: as Betz notes, the 'transformation of the concert into a political meeting' which took place in the *Lehrstück* was achieved 'by the combined effect of Agitprop groups, workers' choruses, orchestras and projected texts'.[48] Bush likewise stipulated that the conventions of concert practice and 'all hints of respectability' were to be avoided in such events in favour of an atmosphere of political demonstration.[49] The 1935 concert-demonstration was characterised by a mixture of concert and militant songs by Eisler and other composers, alongside performances by the newly formed Young Workers' Ballet and the London Labour Speaking Chorus. More than any of the other forms of workers' musical performance, the concert-demonstration enthused Bush, and it is easy to see why: in the Eisler demonstration, for example, both repertoire and the purpose of the musical activity were brought into line with his notion of a workers' music distinct from bourgeois musical endeavours.

Even these measures, however, did not completely realise Bush's ideas. Within a musical culture which embraced a new function and which aimed to energise workers to action, a final objective was to promote changed roles for both performers and audience. As with other aspects of his efforts in workers' music, this was a longstanding concern of Bush's and could have relatively straightforward implications for practice. In 1931, he became involved with *Pro Musica* (1931–3), a short-lived German journal consisting only of printed music, which aimed in the Weimar spirit to publish contemporary music ('new compositions which fulfil the requirements of the present time') for amateur performance.[50] Bush's own *Three Contrapuntal Studies* for Violin and Viola (1931) was published in the journal and is very

---

[46] Alan Bush, 'Eisler Demonstration', *Left Review* 1/8 (May 1935), 330–2.
[47] Bertolt Brecht and Hanns Eisler, 'Note to the Audience' in Willett and Mannheim (eds.), *Bertolt Brecht Collected Plays*, vol. 3 pt. 2, 232.
[48] Betz, *Hanns Eisler*, 94.
[49] This is not to say that such events were akin to public rallies; the Eisler demonstration, for example, was held in Morley College.
[50] 'Provisional Statement of the Objects of the New Music-Periodical Pro Musica and the General Lines on which its Editors will Proceed', undated typescript [c.1931], BL/AB MS Mus. 648, Correspondence relating to *Pro Musica*, vol. 1.

Ex. 2.5a Bush, *Three Contrapuntal Studies*, III (Fugue), fingering instructions.

Ex. 2.5b *Three Contrapuntal Studies*, III (Fugue), opening.

much in this vein of Weimar *Gebrauchsmusik*. As Bush indicates in a written preface to the score, he endeavoured to create a work suitable for amateurs by writing each movement in the first position, with fixed finger positions indicated at the start of each movement, as shown in Ex. 2.5. He aims at 'rational' construction and the avoidance of the sort of subjective, purely emotional content he associates with bourgeois music by turning, in a Hindemithian vein, to Baroque forms. The three movements are based on the 'Ground-bass', 'Canon' and 'Fugue' respectively (these are also the movement titles), with the last movement also incorporating inversion, stretto and a mirror canon.[51] These indications of continuity with his later 1930s ideas notwithstanding, the journal had rather limited impact in Britain and most of Bush's activity seemed to involve correspondence with fellow middle-class composers simply seeking an outlet for publication, while the high point was a concert of works from *Pro Musica* at Oxford University Press.[52] This foray on Bush's part into

---

[51] Timothy Bowers, Sleeve Notes to *Alan Bush: Chamber Music*, The London Piano Quartet (Epoch CDLX 7130, 2003), 7.

[52] BL/AB MS Mus. 648–9, Correspondence relating to *Pro Musica*, vols. 1–2.

amateur music was, however, indicative of his growing interest in increasing active participation regardless of ability. In the same year, he began to apply these ideas to workers' music at a basic level in the song 'Question and Answer' (1931), in which the choir sing a series of questions ('are the workers' badly fed?') and the audience sing a simple reply. Later, Bush would favour unison songs or those in which a unison choir could perform alongside a four-part choir, as in 'Labour's Song of Challenge' (1936). The speaking choir, too, was a means by which those with little or no musical training could participate in musical activities.

However, the relative simplicity of these means of encouraging participation should not disguise their centrality to Bush's broader aims for workers' music. In 'Planning a Workers' Music Festival', he outlined several principles regarding the roles of performers and audience in the workers' movement: music should be treated as an ordinary activity, not aloof from other concerns; performers should also participate in the political life of the movement; performers and audience should be brought into as close contact as possible, and the conductor should not be distinguished from the group as a whole.[53] While Bush did not go so far as suggesting equivalents to the Soviet experiments with conductor-less orchestras, several of these stipulations are clearly related to his rejection of elements of bourgeois musical culture in the workers' movement. Again in the Weimar spirit, Bush sought alternatives to the emphasis on professional performance, and the elevation of the conductor over the performers and the performers over the audience, which were characteristic of the bourgeois concert. Where 'worker-musicians' also took part in political work, the notion of music-making as a special and separate concern would be diminished.[54] And just as worker-musicians were, consequently, ordinary members of the movement, Bush hoped that ordinary members of the movement could become musicians. This would not only increase participation, but also raise the significance of music in the movement towards the kind of active, critical listening that Bush (after Eisler) promoted in relation to both art and workers' music. The last sentence of Bush's account of performing contrasting bourgeois and workers' songs in a workers' concert is exemplary. Bush hoped that ultimately such exercises would not only force the usually passive listener into a reflective stance, but might ultimately provoke the listener to involvement in discussion about what sort of music is suitable for the workers' movement.

[53] Bush, 'Planning a Workers' Festival', 5. [54] Ibid., 3.

Like Bush's workers' songs, his aesthetic of performance raises questions. How radical a departure were some of the practices he suggested? The communal singing of favourite socialist songs, for example, had long been a feature of the Labour movement.[55] There is also the question of how successful the measures adopted were. While evidence like the 1940s recording of workers' songs reveals Bush's success in cultivating the kind of performance practices he desired, the Eisler demonstration was clearly one event that did not fulfil his hopes. Nevertheless, the principles Bush outlined were not merely a guide to practice but were constantly informed by his experience of practical work, both its possibilities and limitations. Aside from his success in practice, the ideas behind it are also further important evidence of how far his view of workers' music as a complete endeavour went beyond simple settings of political slogans.

Paths to the Collective

If there was one element of bourgeois culture that absorbed Bush's attention more than any other, it was the primacy of individual expression. In concert works like the Piano Concerto as well as workers' songs, this element of nineteenth-century bourgeois aesthetics could, in Bush's view, be challenged via critique and through cultivating a rational, craftsman-like compositional approach.[56] Yet it was also clearly crucial to explore ways of fostering collective expression. The Soviet Union provided a vivid, although misunderstood, model of various kinds of mass participation in music that was of keen interest to the British Left.[57] Notions of unity and solidarity were equally at the heart of Bush's ideas about the 'workers' struggle' in the 1930s, and he was well aware of the possibilities of music in this regard, as he and Swingler outlined in the preface to the *Left Song Book*:

> Music has the faculty of binding together in a single emotion all those who are united by a common interest and a common purpose. Men marching in unison, riding in buses on an excursion, sitting in public bars, often are moved spontaneously to sing, in expression of their feeling of community. [...] [The *Left Song Book*] aims to do no more than provide a basis for

---

[55] Hall, 'A Pleasant Change from Politics', 13.

[56] Bush also remarked that 'There is nothing more mysterious about composing than there is about else that we do; some people can learn to do it better than others but that applies also to knocking in nails or cooking a joint'. See Bush, 'Planning a Workers' Festival', 2.

[57] See Bush, 'Music', 123–43.

a repertoire of songs which can be of use on any occasion, public or private, at which people united by a common determination to work for the sane society of socialism, may feel the impulse *to utter their unity of purpose in the traditional way of singing.*[58]

In the context of Bush's late 1930s aesthetic as a whole, however, this aim presented perhaps even more potential difficulties than his efforts to alter the material and performance of workers' music. Bush sought a new workers' culture that was new and emphatically different from bourgeois culture. His and Swingler's idealised description of spontaneous, worker-led expressions of unity through song was potentially at odds with that aim for two reasons: the necessity for a level of simplification which might preclude musical novelty, and the power of the familiar over the new in fostering such spontaneous collective musical outpourings.

Awareness of the conflict between simplicity and innovation in workers' music is clear in Bush's writings. In 'Planning a Workers' Music Festival', Bush advocates that in theory the 'worker-musician' should be a radical:

> Much of what the class-conscious worker says to his fellow workers is not at once acceptable to them, it upsets their preconceived ideas; in the same way the worker-musician will shock his public, will attack their preconceived ideas of what music ought to be like.[59]

When he describes how this might be implemented, however, Bush suggests that 'Nothing too subtle *or too radical musically* should be chosen; the attention of the audience and of the rest of the performers is best riveted on something they can fully understand'.[60] How was the balance struck between breaking preconceptions and achieving complete understanding? The example of Bush's 'Make Your Meaning Clear' suggests that this was extremely difficult to realise.

This is not to say that some means of fostering collective expression could not constitute a rejection of bourgeois culture, or represent innovation. One of the most curious of Bush's experiments of the 1930s was what might be called collective composition. Stuart Fletcher of the *Daily Herald* wrote in 1937 of witnessing one such endeavour:

> I heard a piece of music that had been composed under conditions which are probably quite unique. It was a Socialist propaganda chorus with piano accompaniment. It had a fine tune, which went with a really effective swing.

---

[58] Bush and Swingler (eds.), *The Left Song Book*, 3 (my emphasis).
[59] 'Bush, 'Planning a Workers' Festival', 2.   [60] Ibid., 9.

> *And it had been composed by nine people.* Now I know that many jazz 'numbers' are manufactured by syndicates, but – well, this was a piece of *music* which had something important to say.[61]

The work in question, 'For the People's Use', was composed under the auspices of an early endeavour of Bush's WMA, the WMA 1937 Composers' Group. According to the published score, the following method was used to compose the tune:

> A text was chosen from a number of poems suitable for the purpose. Each member of the group then composed a tune independently. All the tunes were then considered by the group and one ... was selected as the best basis. Each member of the group then worked on the tune selected and made such modifications as he or she thought desirable. The final form of the tune, incorporating various alterations, agreed by a majority of the group to be improvements, was then fixed. Each member of the group then wrote a piano accompaniment independently, one of which ... was subsequently chosen and worked on like the tune.[62]

Aside from the dazzling laboriousness of the process and the slightness of the end product, the very nature of the undertaking is fascinating. The compositional process challenged the model of bourgeois culture by eradicating the individual autonomy of the composer. Submitting each stage of the decision-making to committee vote enacted in the very compositional process the socialist understanding of democratic consensus (not to mention the excessive bureaucracy with which the British Left would become synonymous). Still more significant is the group who produced the song, an exercise in interpreting the Leninist principle of art which 'belongs to the people ... [which] must arouse and develop the artist in them'.[63] The song was not only produced for the collective mass of workers, but was also the product of what was essentially a workers' collective.[64]

On a much larger scale, a comparable experiment was Bush's efforts to involve a number of composers in the Pageant of the Festival of Music for the People, which took place from 1 to 5 April 1939. Much about the festival more generally suggested a desire for novelty and innovation. The concerts (the other two events aside from the pageant) featured

---

[61] Stuart Fletcher, 'Musical Moments: Nine Composers – One Tune', *Daily Herald* (9 April 1937), 19.

[62] Randall Swingler/Workers' Music Association 1937 Composers' Group, *For the People's Use* [Copy in ABH].

[63] Cited in Neil Edmunds, *The Soviet Proletarian Music Movement* (Oxford: Peter Lang, 2000), 11.

[64] In that it was made by the WMA Composers' Group. The identities of the composers, other than Will Sahnow, the first General Secretary of the WMA, are unknown.

Schoenberg's *Peace on Earth* and three cantatas by Eisler: *News from Vienna, 1938, Cantata of Exile*, and *Prison House Cantata*. Among the British involved were many young composers known at the time for the modernity of their music. Lutyens, Rawsthorne, Elizabeth Maconchy, and Christian Darnton, among others,[65] were involved with the pageant, while Britten composed *Ballad of Heroes* to be performed elsewhere in the festival. There was also a genuine effort to reflect in the event the new modes of participation in music that Bush associated with a workers' musical culture. Edward Clark, the organising secretary of the festival, wrote that it had the aim 'of stimulating the musical activity of the people on a mass scale . . . to break new ground in popular music-making from the standpoint of both participants and listeners'.[66] Significant in this statement is the notion that the festival aimed to foster active participation rather than a passive response, and to innovate for both *participants* and *listeners*. A preliminary memorandum on the festival boasted:

> In presenting this music to the general public, the musical forces of the British working-class musicians are enlisting the services of the most highly skilled professional musicians. In doing so they are on the one hand securing the best possible conditions of performance, on the other hand they are enabling the professional musicians to link their art directly with the progressive social forces of to-day. As a result of this the cultural development of the working-class will be stimulated – and its political power thereby increased. Moreover, the art of music will be shown once more as the medium through which the fundamental issues confronting humanity can be expressed.[67]

This involvement by professional composers meant something more than simply having works performed. Whereas Bush himself had respectively composed and arranged the music for the Pageant of Labour in 1934 and 'Towards To-morrow' in 1938, twelve composers were invited to contribute to the 1939 event.[68] Each of the pageant composers (with the exception of Vaughan Williams who provided an opening 'Flourish') was

---

[65] Christian Darnton (1905–81) was an early British experimenter with the twelve-note method, notably in his *Five Orchestral Pieces* (1938), and member of the Communist Party of Great Britain from 1941. See Andrew M. Plant, *The Life and Music of Philip Christian Darnton* (PhD diss., University of Birmingham, 2002).

[66] Edward Clark to Mrs Harry Sacher, 13 January 1939, BL/AB MS Mus. 623, Correspondence relating to the Festival of Music for the People, 1939, vol. 2.

[67] 'Preliminary Memorandum on the Festival of Music for the People' attached to letter from Alan Bush to Mr Tongue, 5 September 1938, BL/AB MS Mus. 622, Correspondence relating to the Festival of Music for the People, 1939, vol. 1.

[68] The composers who provided music were Vaughan Williams, Arnold Cooke, Elisabeth Lutyens, Victor Yates, Edmund Rubbra, Erik Chisholm, Christian Darnton, Frederic Austin, Norman Demuth, Alan Bush, Elizabeth Maconchy and Alan Rawsthorne.

required to provide music for an historical episode (with introduction and finale) in what was mostly a matter of arranging pre-existing material. The role of individual composers was further diminished by the assertions throughout the narration introducing the various episodes that the historical music being performed was the spontaneous creation of the people. Yet in all other respects the experiment is strikingly non-radical. Although showcasing original composition was not the aim of the event, an opportunity was surely missed for a more creative and far-reaching experiment, like that of the 1937 Composers' Group. Not only was there no real opportunity for collaboration given that the composers all worked via correspondence, but the records of the event show that the pageant music was intended to be even less of a collective effort than it turned out to be. Although they eventually recruited several young composers keen on modern music and left-wing politics, the organisers failed to secure many of their first choices. The fact that Walton, Bax, and Granville Bantock were asked and that Vaughan Williams was among the eventual composers suggests that there was both a concern with big names and a need to make do with the available composers rather than a sense of shared artistic sensibilities. The boast that the festival involved 'the most highly skilled professional musicians' indicates that the organisers perhaps felt a need to legitimise and promote the event through association with leading composers, over and above the artistic and political goals.

While these experiments suggested ways of encouraging the composition of new music for the workers' movement, they did not address the problem of achieving mass participation without artistic compromise, especially in the realm of singing. It was in this sphere that the second problem of fostering collective expression – the power of the familiar over the new – was particularly acute. Bush recognised that existing songs could be powerful in fostering collective feeling and expression, but they could also conflict with the aim of creating a new and distinctive workers' musical culture. Indeed, this was a persistent problem for left-wing musicians in numerous contexts in the twentieth century, as David Walls has explored.[69] On the one hand, old favourites like 'The Internationale' were powerful because the melodies and words were familiar and because they had been associated with the articulation of working-class solidarity over a long period. On the other hand, old

---

[69] David Walls, 'Billy Bragg's Revival of Aging Anthems: Radical Nostalgia or Activist Inspiration?', paper presented to the Working Class Studies Association conference, St. Paul, Minnesota, Friday, 15 June 2007, http://www.sonoma.edu/users/w/wallsd/smm-aging-anthems.shtml, accessed 4 May 2011.

favourites, especially those like the 'Bundeslied' with a problematic text, were not always ideal when attempting to achieve a political and/or aesthetic break with the past. For Bush, then, maximising participation involved addressing the issue of whether and how older music could be adapted to new purposes.

The most straightforward means of doing so was to perform songs which were already associated with the workers' movement. The *Left Song Book* contained not only unfamiliar topical and international songs but also ones 'which have become famous in revolutionary tradition and are rooted deep in the consciousness of the people'.[70] Some of these songs were unproblematically socialist: 'The Internationale' and 'The Red Flag', for instance, while the editors' appeal to the 'revolutionary tradition' explained the inclusion of songs like 'The Marseillaise' and 'Scots Wha Hae'. The corresponding tribute to Welsh nationalism in the collection, 'Cwm Rhondda', was adopted only with the addition of a completely new text by Swingler to replace the original. This was presumably primarily because of the religious content of the original, although the rounds in the book to the melodies of 'London's Burning' and 'Three Blind Mice' illustrate that setting new, topical texts to well-known tunes was a common device. The *Left Song Book*'s answer to the problem of reconciling old and new music was a mixture of appropriating familiar tunes for new texts and airing established socialist favourites as well as introducing musically modern items like Eisler's 'Einheitsfrontlied'.

Yet there were potentially more elaborate means of reconciling traditional music with the new workers' culture. 'Towards To-morrow' presents one example. The pageant – telling the story of the origins and history of the Co-operative Movement – took place at Wembley Stadium (then the Empire Stadium) on 2 July 1938. It was unarguably successful in fostering mass participation in the most literal sense – 3000 amateur performers enacted the pageant to an audience of 78,000 – yet presented corresponding artistic challenges.[71] For one, the historical pageant was a conservative, nostalgic genre, originating in late-Victorian municipal celebrations.[72] More significantly, as the Pageant Master and co-author of the libretto André van Gyseghem later recounted, the vast scale of such productions demanded a lack of subtlety. He observed that the pageant 'is not an ideal

---

[70] Bush and Swingler (eds.), *The Left Song Book*, 3.
[71] Mick Wallis, 'Heirs to the Pageant: Mass Spectacle and the Popular Front' in Croft (ed.), *A Weapon in the Struggle*, 54–5.
[72] Nicolas Bell, 'The Function of Music in the Socialist Pageant in Inter-War Britain', unpublished paper delivered at the Institute of Historical Research, London, 18 October 2004.

form, because it does not go to any great depth; it shows only the broad outlines of human development'.[73] The music at first glance reflects this state of affairs. Bush's role as composer was largely a matter of arranging a selection of English folk songs and national and international workers' songs (many of the latter also in the *Left Song Book*).

The pageant was not wholly conservative, however. It boasted a number of young, left-wing artistic talents in addition to Bush. Montagu Slater, author of the plays *Easter 1916* (1935) and *Stay Down Miner* (1936) and future librettist of *Peter Grimes*, worked on the scenario. The choreographer was Margaret Barr, interested in a form of modern dance drawing heavily on mime and drama and enabling community involvement. Van Gyseghem himself had attended the 1933 International Workers' Theatre Olympiad in Moscow and subsequently worked with the director of the Realistic Theatre, Nikolai Okhlopkov. For van Gyseghem, the distinctive feature of the pageant as a genre was the visual spectacle, the process of creating 'living pictures'. One of the most striking instances of this process was the depiction of the rise of mechanisation and industrialisation. The opening scene depicts an idyllic, pre-industrial England characterised by community Morris dancing, a maypole, and naturalistic movement. This is interrupted by a siren, whereupon a procession of figures dressed as cogs and wheels enters, succeeded by the caricatured model figure of the Capitalist and the erection of a forty-foot factory chimney in the centre of the stadium. In contrast to the opening episode, the movement in this tableau is highly artificial – 'harsh and rhythmical [...] stiffly-jointed'[74] – while the costumes show the influence of Futurism.[75] Striking in this example is not simply the use of modern influences to contrast the two scenes visually, but the economy with which capitalism and industrialisation are depicted as synonymous and essentially inhumane historical developments against the natural impulses of the working classes. This opposition is compounded in subsequent episodes, particularly when the efforts of various heroes of the co-operative movement to improve living conditions are succeeded by another tableau depicting a war engineered by capitalism (with obvious allusions to the First World War). In this way, the conventions of the pageant – the representation of a historical narrative visually – were efficiently adopted for the articulation of a central argument

---

[73] André van Gyseghem, 'British Theatre in the Thirties: An Autobiographical Record' in Jon Clark, Margot Heinemann, David Margolies, and Carole Snee (eds.), *Culture and Crisis in Britain in the Thirties* (London: Lawrence and Wishart, 1979), 217.
[74] *International Co-operative Day*, Wembley Stadium, 2 July 1938, Souvenir Programme, 20.
[75] Bell, 'The Function of Music in the Socialist Pageant in Inter-War Britain'.

of the radical Left in this period: the perpetuation of war and the dehumanisation of workers under capitalism. Although the visual dimension was at the forefront here, Bush's music played an important corresponding role. The first, pastoral episode is performed, unremarkably, to a succession of folk songs and dances. Both the tableaux depicting the rise of the machine and the war episode are, in contrast, accompanied by originally composed ballet music. Complementing the stylised, artificial movement in both scenes and unlike the folk scenes, the music is highly rhythmic, repetitive, and non-melodic. In the 'Machine Ballet', for example, the slow but insistent tempo and the cumbersome dotted rhythm of the short repeated, fanfare-like cornet phrase, enhance the visual image of the 'unsightly' procession (Ex. 2.6).[76] The music thus contributed to a means of collective expression in which older conventions and materials (both theatrical and musical) were adapted to radical new purposes.

There were ways, then, in which Bush sought to reconcile popular musical traditions with his vision of a new workers' culture. Yet what of the bourgeois musical tradition, and indeed, current practice? In theory, both the music and the primary context in which it was heard – the concert – were inappropriate for Bush's goals. Yet for several reasons, Bush was loath to exclude all art music of the past from the workers' movement. Firstly, as he revealed in relation to the LLCU's repertoire, he was committed to performing music of good quality and was aware of the current lack of specifically socialist music fitting this description. The notion among English middle-class socialists that the workers should be exposed to the 'best music available' also had a richer heritage than the idea of creating a distinctive workers' culture.[77] This was, then, another instance where Bush was working within existing practices and expectations. Secondly, with regard to more recent developments, Bush was enthusiastic about the model of the Soviet Union in promoting mass consumption of opera and concert music. Indeed, in Bush's view, the division between popular and serious music would ultimately disappear under socialism, as the Soviet Union demonstrated.[78] Thirdly, as noted in Chapter 1, Bush was worried by the use of classical works by Beethoven and Wagner at Nazi demonstrations.[79] It was 'the business of worker-musicians *as defenders of culture* to perform the best music of all periods as well as their own music'.[80] On this basis, the workers' movement had substantial claims to the bourgeois tradition. Performing works either

---

[76] *International Co-operative Day*, 20.   [77] Hall, 'A Pleasant Change from Politics', 17–21.
[78] Bush, 'Music', 142–3.   [79] Bush, 'Music and the Working-Class Struggle', 646.
[80] Bush, 'Planning a Workers' Festival', 11 (my emphasis).

Ex. 2.6 Bush, 'Machine Ballet', opening [reduction].

banned or appropriated by the Nazi regime had potential for anti-fascist statements. In addition, given the theoretical relationship between capitalism and fascism and the perception of Nazism as destructive of culture, the musical tradition could be seen as the legitimate heritage of the contemporary workers. Weimar Germany had already been the site of contested claims concerning classical composers by the extreme Left and Right, including such practices as replacing Beethoven's song texts with newly written political alternatives and accompanying concerts with written or spoken commentaries.[81] This may well also have been a factor influencing the inclusion of works by Eisler and Schoenberg in the Festival of Music for the People.

As we have seen, Bush was keen on verbal explanations to maximise the political impact of performances of workers' music. It is

---

[81] See Dennis, *Beethoven in German Politics*, 100–1.

unsurprising then that the primary examples of his performances of bourgeois music involved linking these works to working-class revolutionary history. A relatively simple exercise was the LLCU's performance of Handel's oratorio *Belshazzar* as an opera, the final chorus of which also subsequently made up part of the Pageant of the Festival of Music for the People. As the Festival programme makes clear, notwithstanding the organisers' description of a nascent commercial musical culture in eighteenth-century London, *Belshazzar* was redeemed on the basis of this final chorus depicting 'the dream of an international peace, brotherhood, and extended freedom'.[82] The programme of the concert version of *Belshazzar* provided a more detailed rationale: the story of a decaying Empire liberated by the threatened Persians was a 'prophetic' parable of contemporary politics:

> The decaying states of the twentieth century, rent with their internal conflicts, imprisoning culture and preventing its development, even destroying its products [...], these decaying states are threatened by the rising power of the internationally minded working-class movement, which they strive in vain to thwart.[83]

In order to emphasise the contemporary parallels, the original libretto was revised by Swingler. All references to God were removed, while the associations between, on the one hand, the Persians and communism and, on the other, the Babylonians and imperial interests, were enhanced. Cyrus, Leader of the Persian army, addresses a fellow soldier as 'comrade', and, as the *Musical Times* pointed out, 'All empires upon God depend/Begun by his command, at his command they end/Look up to Him in all your ways/ Begin with prayer, and end with praise' became:

> All empires upon force depend.
> Begun by greed's command, at man's demand they end.
> And those who make oppression cease
> Begin with war but end in peace.[84]

---

[82] 'The Pageant', *Festival of Music for the People*, programme, 9.
[83] 'The Meaning of the Opera', *Belshazzar*, souvenir programme, 9.
[84] 'Notes and News', *Musical Times* 80/1155 (May 1939), 373. Although the programme does not make the point, Bush and Swingler were also surely conscious of the contemporary resonances of the oppression of the Jews in the opera, particularly as they make the connection between (capitalist) imperialism and fascism explicit. The parallel is subtly highlighted in that the essay 'The Meaning of the Opera' refers to the notion that the arts and sciences of the Jews are 'mocked at or put to base uses' by the Babylonians. The essay subsequently relates this to the Nazi burning of the books as a contemporary example of 'imprisoning culture'. See 'The Meaning of the Opera', 9.

Thus in a similar manner to the use of folk songs in 'Towards To-morrow', *Belshazzar* represented a means of co-opting broadly suitable existing material for use within the new workers' culture, performed by workers and articulating a newly unambiguous political message. In the context of Bush's ideas about the use of art music within the workers' movement, this amateur performance of an 'opera' bridged the divide between popular and art music in accordance with his vision of a future socialist musical culture. In addition, the parallels drawn between the Babylonian and Nazi attacks on culture assert the role of workers as 'defenders of culture' in a period of contemporary crisis.

The inclusion of the final chorus from *Belshazzar* in the Pageant of the Festival of Music for the People reveals another level at which bourgeois music could find a role within the workers' movement. Like 'Towards To-morrow', the later event made substantial use of folk song and socialist songs as 'people's music'. In contrast to the Co-operative event, however, the Pageant of the Festival of Music for the People used excerpts from such diverse musical sources as *Fidelio* and the 'Coventry Carol' in addition to *Belshazzar*. This expansion of musical resources may be understood in the context of the contrasting role of music in each event. The music for 'Towards To-morrow' articulated bold contrasts between the feudal and capitalist epochs, thus its role was secondary and the historical narrative only implicit. In the 1939 Pageant, the central theme was the message that 'music . . . is not a drug or a world of fantasy to which men can escape from the real problems of their life. Rather it is part of the pattern of life they wish for, and a guide and inspiration to their efforts to attain it'.[85] Consequently, the Pageant was not so much a historical narrative illustrated musically, as a Marxist history of (purportedly) working-class music. The 'Cutty Wren',[86] for example, became the centrepiece of an episode depicting the English Peasants' Revolt. Both this and the next episode (depicting the Levellers and Diggers, popular radical movements of the English Civil War) end by stating the importance of the contemporary songs both in expressing unity in a current struggle and in pointing to the future when those uprisings were unsuccessful ('Your [sic] were the songs that England sang in 1649/And beaten though you were, you marked the future with a sign'). In the case of the Handel and Beethoven works, the text introduces both figures as essentially artists placing their music in the service of the principles of the people. Handel's chorus

---

[85] 'The Pageant', 7.
[86] This folk song, later used by Bush in his first opera, *Wat Tyler*, was said to have originated in the 1381 English Peasants' Revolt.

articulates 'the people's dream of liberty and peace', while, in a typical Marxist reading, *Fidelio* is associated with the ideals of the French Revolution as an essential earlier phase of the historical dialectic ultimately leading towards socialism.

As with *Belshazzar*, the use of *Fidelio* in the Pageant had a specific antifascist agenda. The excerpt – the Prisoners' Chorus – was immediately succeeded by a reference to concentration camps and a performance of 'The Peat-Bog Soldiers' ('Die Moorsoldaten'), a song said to be have been written in a Nazi concentration camp which had been adapted by Eisler and widely disseminated in the 1930s. More broadly, the Pageant is significant in illustrating the extent to which Bush's new workers' musical culture involved establishing a relationship with the past. In the Festival in contrast to *Belshazzar*, the Beethoven and Handel are not merely of value as parables. Rather, the place carved out for them in a Marxist music history identifies them as the true cultural heritage of the contemporary workers' movement. As discussed above, as an exercise in collective expression through composition, the Festival was a limited experiment. As an attempt to reconcile contemporary musical and political goals (anti-fascism in particular) with the music of the past, however, the Festival represented Bush's most sophisticated efforts at understanding the role of the bourgeois tradition in a workers' musical culture. Moreover, in its experimental involvement of such numbers of professional composers and amateur performers, and its ambition in placing the social role of music centre-stage, the Festival of Music for the People was one of the highpoints of Bush's workers' music.

A Socialist Musical Culture?

Bush's workers' music, like his 'modernism', was guided by desire for a modern material basis for composition, consciousness of the effect and context of performance, and resistance to bourgeois subjectivity. Yet the relationship between these spheres of activity goes beyond similarities of method. Both were elements of a deeper effort to transform musical culture, and the music-making individual within it. The ideal musical culture of the future state of socialism was, naturally, represented by the Soviet Union. Bush's 1944 booklet, *Music in the Soviet Union*, reveals that Soviet aesthetics and composition formed only part of his impression of music under socialism.[87] Much of his attention concerned the structures and initiatives that resulted in what Bush perceived to be overwhelming

---

[87] Alan Bush, *Music in the Soviet Union* (London: Workers' Music Association, 1944).

mass participation and state support for musical activity. In a number of his projects of the 1930s – his comprehensive analysis of the state of British musical culture in 'Music and the Working-Class Struggle', the emphasis on the history of spontaneous popular musical creation in the Festival of Music for the People, and the efforts to claim Handel and Beethoven for the people – the goal of creating a state of British musical socialism may be discerned. By questioning conventional musical articulations of bourgeois subjectivity in the Piano Concerto and by rendering himself the agitating composer-conductor of the Labour movement, Bush embarked upon the process of self-transformation into socialist musician that would become so important in subsequent decades.

In the workers' music, as in the Piano Concerto, there was an added complexity in Bush's efforts in that Britain remained a capitalist country and also faced the pressing threat of fascism. He wrote in 1937 that 'The world situation, the terrible Spanish crisis, the war preparations of the National Government and the constantly increasing dangers of fascism here in England are matters which absorb my attention increasingly [...] I do not complain as it seems of greater import and of more use to art in the long run to devote oneself to fighting against cultural night than to occupy oneself with composition'.[88] This assertion betrays the truth of Andy Croft's observation that 'the British Communist Party never made up its mind whether culture was a weapon in the struggle or the ultimate aim of that struggle'.[89] Bush undoubtedly, in his most fervent period of producing workers' music in the late 1930s, placed greater emphasis on immediate impact than on durability within a permanent socialist culture. He was also, as we have seen, hampered by financial considerations, the tastes and opinions of the (often politically more moderate) groups and individuals with which he worked, and the practical abilities of his amateur musicians. Nevertheless, the pre-war workers' music remains an extraordinary and intriguing project, with a significance beyond the immediate crises of the late 1930s and Bush's personal development. Bush's leadership of left-leaning young composers was short-lived, and yet the pre-war years were not the last moment at which a British composer sought to create modern, 'collective' works involving amateurs.[90] As Christopher Fox has noted, Britten's *Noye's Fludde* and Cornelius Cardew's *The Great Learning*:

---

[88] Alan Bush to 'Marguerite', 10 March 1937, BL/AB MS Mus. 453.
[89] Croft (ed.), *A Weapon in the Struggle*, 6.
[90] Christopher Fox, 'After the Fludde: Ambitious Music for All-comers' in Peter Wiegold and Ghislaine Kenyon (eds.), *Beyond Britten: The Composer and the Community* (Woodbridge: Boydell Press, 2015), 43.

[represent] a nexus of ideas – about the world, about humanity and about how music can represent those ideas – and it is difficult, perhaps impossible, to manufacture such a coming-together of ideas. Each also represents a moment when these wider concerns – the relationship between modernity and tradition, questions of social and spiritual order, the organisation of musical tones – flowed through a very particular set of local circumstances[.][91]

Not only is Fox's reflection an equally apt assessment of the successes and failures of Bush's efforts to fuse modern music and amateur participation, but it points to the legacy of such activities in the post-war period, the ongoing tensions between musical engagement with a notion of community, and the problematic position of modern music within national culture. How these problems were tackled by Bush himself in the post-war era shall be the focus of subsequent chapters.

---

[91] Ibid., 44.

3 Bush as Outsider: Music and Communism in Wartime

> I have found that my political activity has closed many doors of professional employment.[1]
>
> Alan Bush

One of the most memorable anecdotes of Bush's career concerns the brief ban placed on his music by the BBC during the Second World War. Bush was a signatory to the People's Convention, a short-lived wartime endeavour of 1940–1 closely linked to the CPGB, which produced a six-point manifesto calling for defence of the people's living standards; defence of the people's democratic and trade union rights; adequate protection from aerial warfare; friendship with the Soviet Union; a people's government; and a 'people's peace that gets rid of the causes of war'.[2] On 7 March 1941, Bush was called in to the BBC to be told that 'any artist who adheres to the People's Convention cannot be offered any further broadcasting engagements'.[3] The composer – always possessing an eye for publicity – instantly reported these occurrences as widely as possible, prompting Vaughan Williams to write an open letter to the Corporation withdrawing his latest commission in protest at the ban.[4] By 21 March, *The Times* was reporting from the House of Commons on Churchill's rescindment of the ban on artists.[5]

A few weeks saw the beginning and end of the ban, and yet the incident has taken on a significance beyond its relevance to Bush's biography. Bush's experience points towards renewed intolerance of communists, and of concerted institutional efforts to obstruct their careers. Bush would complain frequently in subsequent years about the impact of his communism on his career, mentioning his inability to get work composing film music, a university chair in music, or regular performances on the

---

[1] Alan Bush, 'Autobiography' completed in conjunction with a nomination to CPGB's National Cultural Committee (NCC), 29 June 1950, copy intercepted and kept by MI5 and now held by The National Archives: Public Record Office (TNA/PRO), KV 2/3518: Bush, Alan D., Item 251a.

[2] On the People's Convention, see John Callaghan and Ben Harker (eds.), *British Communism: A Documentary History* (Manchester: Manchester University Press, 2011), 154–6.

[3] N. Bush, *Alan Bush*, 40–1.

[4] 'Dr. Vaughan Williams. New Composition Withdrawn', *The Times*, 15 March 1941, 6.

[5] 'B.B.C. and People's Convention. Ban on Artists Removed', *The Times*, 21 March 1941, 4.

BBC.⁶ Nevertheless, the ban itself was brief and successfully protested. Churchill asserted as he rescinded the ban that 'Anything in the nature of persecution, victimisation or man-hunting is odious to the British people', a sensibility manifest in the response of so prominent a national figure as Vaughan Williams.⁷

At a deeper level, the ban raises questions about the place of communists in British national culture after 1939, and Bush in particular. In the 1930s, while Bush was at the extreme of the political spectrum, he was nevertheless only one of a number of young, left-leaning composers and other artists protesting against fascism and appeasement. The BBC ban, on the contrary, was prompted by Bush's opposition to Britain's war with Germany at the behest of the CPGB leadership and, ultimately, the Comintern. The incident thus raises crucial questions over Bush's personal willingness to submit to Soviet direction – with obvious pertinence to his future career – and the wider subordination of the CPGB to the international communist movement, and its true commitment to British national concerns. The wartime period was, as Andrew Thorpe has written, 'a time of unrivalled challenge, difficulty and opportunity for the CPGB'.⁸ The announcement of the Nazi-Soviet pact in 1939, the resignation and subsequent reinstatement of Harry Pollitt, the longstanding general secretary of the Party, and the shock of the Nazi invasion of the Soviet Union and subsequent alliance with Britain were tumultuous events that provoked strong internal disagreement. Yet the Party was able to treble its membership over the wartime period, with numbers increasing from 15,781 in 1938 to 45,435 in 1945, approaching 60,000 in 1942.⁹ The independence or subordination of the CPGB, its status in wartime Britain, and the relationships between the Party and individual communists, are thus still subjects of profound controversy among historians.¹⁰

---

⁶ See Alan Bush to William Glock, 23 November 1963, BBC/WAC RCONT1, Composer, Alan Bush, File 4: 1963–7; Bush, 'Autobiography'.

⁷ Cited in Angus Calder, *The Myth of the Blitz* (London: Jonathan Cape, 1991), 88.

⁸ Andrew Thorpe, *The British Communist Party and Moscow, 1920–43* (Manchester: Manchester University Press, 2000), 256.

⁹ Phillip Deery and Neil Redfern, 'No Lasting Peace? Labor, Communism and the Cominform: Australia and Great Britain, 1945–50', *Labour History* 88 (May 2005), 63.

¹⁰ While historians such as Matthew Worley, Andrew Thorpe, and Nina Fishman have argued for the autonomy of the CPGB, others, notably John McIlroy and Alan Campbell, have suggested that the Party's independence from Moscow can be overstated. See, for example, John McIlroy and Alan Campbell, 'Histories of the British Communist Party: A User's Guide', *Labour History Review* 68/1 (April 2003), 33–59; Andrew Thorpe, 'Communist Party History: A Reply to Campbell and McIlroy', *Labour History Review*, 69/3 (December 2004), 363–5; John Newsinger, 'Review: Recent Controversies in the History of British Communism', *Journal of Contemporary History* 41/3 (July 2006), 557–72.

While the experiences of a single communist can offer no comprehensive contribution to this debate, the case of Bush is significant. Due to his tendency to preserve documentation, and the recent release of his MI5 file, it is possible to trace with precision the extent of official interventions into his career and his contribution to the CPGB's cultural response to the convulsive events of wartime. As shall be demonstrated, the Party's experience of 'challenge, difficulty, and opportunity' was echoed in Bush's personal history. While the BBC ban was far from the most ignominious official act against him, the latter half of the war led to unprecedented chances for Bush to use his expertise in Soviet music and international popular song in the service of British wartime culture. Moreover, Bush's change of fortune reflected a shift in public opinion in the latter stages of the war towards admiration for the Soviet Union (as represented by the Red Army), and a sense of new social and political possibilities in the wake of a devastating war. Ultimately, it was a communist who was chosen to express the nation's victory in symphonic form, the final irony of a period in which the treatment of British communists was riven with contradictions.

The British Communist as Outsider in Wartime

The outbreak of the Second World War was undoubtedly a tumultuous time for British communists. Appendix 1 gives an overview of the policy shifts that occurred in the first two years of war.[11] At the outbreak of war, the CPGB leadership, in line with policy developed over previous months, initially welcomed the war as a necessary measure 'to secure the victory of democracy over Fascism'.[12] This support was qualified, however, by their belief in the need for a 'war on two fronts' against both fascism and the Chamberlain government. This stance was partly conditioned by the CPGB's characterisation of Chamberlain's government during the late 1930s as appeasers of Hitler and, correspondingly, communist theorisation of fascism as the most complete expression of capitalism and 'the highest expression of organisation for war'.[13] This statement had,

---

[11] For a detailed account see Francis King and George Matthews (eds.), *About Turn: The British Communist Party and the Second World War. The Verbatim Record of the Central Committee Meetings of 25 September and 2–3 October 1939* (London: Lawrence and Wishart, 1990).

[12] Cited in Callaghan and Harker (eds.), *British Communism*, 151.

[13] Rajani Palme Dutt, cited in Kevin Morgan, *Against Fascism and War: Ruptures and Continuities in British Communist Politics, 1935–41* (Manchester & New York: Manchester University Press, 1989), 22, 29.

however, second-guessed Stalin. At his behest the Comintern secretariat reclassified the war as an 'imperialist' conflict between rival states, a designation that reflected the Leninist designation of imperialism as a distinctive manifestation of late capitalism. Although it necessitated Pollitt's resignation, the CPGB complied with the change of line, until the German invasion of the Soviet Union and the forming of the Grand Alliance prompted a shift to wholesale support of the war.

While these shifts were ultimately determined by the exigencies of Soviet foreign policy, as Kevin Morgan has argued, there was confusion and disagreement at all levels, a gradual softening of anti-war rhetoric and growing interest in the war effort leading up to the invasion of the Soviet Union. To complicate matters, since 1935, the Comintern's Popular Front strategy had called upon national communist parties to work within their particular national circumstances.[14] At the Seventh Congress, the Popular Front strategy outlined by Dimitrov had necessitated working within the existing particularities of national cultures in order to build a broad front in opposition to imperialism and fascism, which in communist theory were bound together as manifestations of late-capitalism. While on the one hand, an alliance between communism and fascism was anathema, on the other hand, many communists were uneasy with supporting the British National Government in pursuing war.[15] In addition, even at this point of open conflict with the National Government, the Party's strategies were in part influenced by the desire to address concerns peculiar to Britain, and thereby attract wider support from beyond CPGB members. Thus the Party's most substantial project in these years, the People's Convention, perpetuated communist arguments about the connection between fascism and capitalism, and it channelled these arguments into demands relating to trade union rights, living and working conditions, and protection from air raids – real concerns in wartime Britain. Seen in this context, the Party's line following Operation Barbarossa was not so much a return to pre-war anti-fascism as a departure, in which the Party abandoned its characterisation of capitalism and fascism as inherently linked and supported an 'international front [...] to smash Hitler', with all that entailed in the form of patriotism, backing of Churchill's government, and the subordination of workers' interests to the war effort.[16] Equally, the Party had, throughout the early part of the conflict, been actively concerned with the domestic

---

[14] Morgan, *Against Fascism and War*, 34–5. [15] Ibid., 92ff.
[16] Harry Pollitt, cited in Morgan, *Against Fascism and War*, 304.

situation. Even at this juncture in the War, the position of the Party and communist individuals towards the nation was complex.

How did this situation affect Bush, both in terms of guiding his actions and affecting his social and professional standing? It is certain that the Security Services directly intervened in Bush's wartime career. Like other communists, Bush was the subject of increased official suspicion in this period. MI5 considered Bush to be 'probably one of the leading members of the CPGB' in this period.[17] He had first come to the attention of the Security Service (MI5) via Special Branch infiltration of left-wing cultural activities in the late 1930s, and by 1939 was under a significant amount of surveillance, including telephone checks, mail interception, and, from late 1941, regular reports from Bush's commanding officers in the Army. It was the belief of MI5 that Bush's musical activities were a front for seditious activity, rather than reflecting any genuine personal investment in culture. One especially inflammatory story concerning Bush was that while in Moscow in 1938, Bush had made a joke about wanting to '"do-in" Chamberlain'.[18] More concretely, in January 1940, the short-lived William Morris Musical Society was formed under the auspices of the Communist Party's Cultural Committee. The secretary of the society, using the name 'Ian MacKay', was in fact MI5 agent Norman Himsworth, who discovered that the headquarters of the society (also the premises of the WMA) contained a secret interview room which was being used 'to collect classified information about weapons and military operations from Communists and sympathizers in the armed forces'.[19] Himsworth also reported that Bush had admitted to him that the William Morris Musical Society was a 'cover' for the Communist Party. Once Bush joined the Royal Army Medical Corps in the autumn of 1941, MI5 also feared that he would be a bad political influence upon others in his unit. Himsworth reported that Bush audaciously requested that some Soviet songs be sent to him. It was, he added, 'obvious that BUSH wanted these songs for distribution or for actual presentation to the troops in his Unit'.[20]

[17] Activities Log, 15 March 1941, TNA/PRO KV2/3515: Bush, Alan D.
[18] Special Branch Report, 5 February 1941, TNA/PRO KV2/3515, Item 21a.
[19] Christopher Andrew, *The Defence of the Realm: the Authorized History of MI5* (London: Allen Lane, 2009), 273–4. In mitigation of Bush, later MI5 notes on the WMA describe a secret office, accessible only via password, operated by two comrades out of the WMA building 'in order to keep contact with Party members and sympathisers in the Forces'. While Bush almost certainly knew about the office, and may have been the one to offer its use to the CP, it is not clear that he or the WMA had any other involvement beyond allowing their premises to be used. See Report on Second Interview with Harold Turner, 8 July 1954, TNA/PRO KV5/132: Workers' Music Association, Item 30ab.
[20] Internal Memo, 10 December 1941, TNA/PRO KV2/3515: Bush, Alan D., Item 36d.

Consequently, a series of efforts on Bush's part to contribute to the cultural war effort were firmly obstructed. At the outset of war, he offered his specialised services 'for paid work of national importance', arguing that his experience of amateur music-making could be used in work with troops, which 'would be of tremendous significance in developing initiative, sustaining morale, and providing interesting relaxation of an educative kind which would stimulate the team spirit, and advance mutual response between the men as well as increasing their sense of individual responsibility'.[21] Bush also sought in due course to work for the Committee for the Encouragement of Music and the Arts (CEMA) and the Entertainments National Service Association (ENSA). Once a private in the Royal Army Medical Corps, he tried to transfer to the Army Education Corps. All these possibilities were quashed by MI5, who enforced blanket exclusion of communists from 1 ENSA and suspected Bush of trying to obtain such opportunities as a front for political activity. Bush was limited to directing the barracks choir and lecturing to troops under the auspices of the London Regional Committee for Education among HM Forces. Aside from this, despite his age and education, he spent four years as a private in the Royal Army Medical Corps, and narrowly avoided being shipped to the Far East in 1944.[22]

As revealing as the concrete claims against Bush is the image that emerges in the file of a particular *type* of person, in the eyes of MI5. A Special Branch report of 1941 deemed Bush 'an eccentric, arrogant and theatrical individual, who is given to violent forms of expression'. A note concerning Bush's activities in the Army asserted that he was 'a highly intelligent man likely to take advantage of any position which he may establish for himself in order to influence others on the quiet. Our record of him shows him to have been not only extremely active as a Communist but also to have *a very embittered outlook*'.[23] Central to both these accounts is the construction of Bush as an outsider. The reference to the composer as 'theatrical' evokes associations between theatricality and homosexuality that may be traced back to Wilde.[24] The statement also anticipates the construction of both communism and homosexuality as dangerous, secretive, and counter-cultural that would prove so important to the 'sexual McCarthyism' of the 1950s in the wake

---

[21] Alan Bush to Central Register, 18 September 1939, BL/AB MS Mus. 454. The Central Register aimed to meet wartime need for people with particular expertise.
[22] N. Bush, *Alan Bush*, 49–51.
[23] Johnstone to Gregory, 11 February 1942, TNA/PRO KV2/3515: Bush, Alan D., Item 46a (my emphasis).
[24] See Alan Sinfield, 'Private lives/Public Theater: Noel Coward and the Politics of Homosexual Representation', *Representations* 36 (Autumn 1991), 43–63.

of the Cambridge spies' defections.[25] The other reference, to an 'embittered outlook', seems rather to suggest something about Bush's attitude in wartime Britain, with its rhetoric of defiance, high morale, and humour in the face of adversity. Undoubtedly, Bush was also seen as possessing different and potentially threatening values because of his 'fanatical support of the Soviet Union'[26] and his ability to influence people. In short, MI5's construction of Bush is precisely a sort of Cold War, 'red under the bed' figure, engaged in subversion, able to influence people, and acting on values alien to those of wartime Britain. While their characterisation represented an extreme position, the BBC ban on artists associated with the People's Convention as a cause 'inconsistent with the national war effort' exhibits something of the same perception.[27]

Bush, Culture, and the CPGB, 1939–41

In MI5's view, culture was, for the Communist Party, a crude cloak for political activity, or (as in the case of the Soviet songs) a means of influencing the impressionable. In fact, they overestimated the degree and sophistication of coordinated Party cultural activity as it stood in 1940. Just after the outbreak of war, a Party Cultural Committee already existed and was devoting attention to the matter of cultural questions regarding 'Party Cultural Work in Wartime'.[28] The document recognised that the Party was in a 'new phase [...] of struggle to end the imperialist war in a working-class fashion'. Committee members (including Bush) were invited to consider how Party activity was being adapted to the changed 'mood, needs and opportunities of the people' in wartime and how to influence and draw into activity the thousands of 'cultural workers' believed to be interested in the Party.

Yet how the Party intended to influence even its own cultural workers, let alone those outside the Party, proved problematic. In addition to the Party Cultural Committee, there existed a London Arts Committee, which theoretically had responsibility for directing the work of amateur and professional communists in all the arts, as well as for increasing activity

---

[25] Chris Waters, 'Disorders of the Mind, Disorders of the Body Social: Peter Wildeblood and the Making of the Modern Homosexual' in Becky Conekin, Frank Mort, and Chris Waters (eds.), *Moments of Modernity: Reconstructing Britain, 1945–64* (London & New York: Rivers Oram, 1999), 134–51.
[26] Activities Log, 26 September 1941, TNA/PRO KV2/3515: Bush, Alan D.
[27] Transcript of Alan Bush's interview with the BBC, 7 March 1941, ABH.
[28] 'Questions for Consideration by Members of Party Cultural Committee in Preparation for Cultural Aggregate', 14 December 1939, ABH.

in the wider Labour movement.[29] An added complexity was that in the case of music, for example, Party members were at that time organised into the 'Musicians' Union Group', for professionals, and 'Musicians not in the Musicians' Union', and there also existed an 'Entertainment Industry Bureau' which oversaw industrial activity in the arts. The problem here was that musicians were organised into professional groups, like miners or railway workers, while most left-wing musical activity in the 1930s had involved the cooperation of amateurs and professionals. This created distinct problems in trying to create cultural policy or to influence existing cultural activity effectively.

An early attempt to address these problems was the aforementioned People's Convention. A number of communist intellectuals and artists (including, in the sphere of music, Bush and fellow composer Benjamin Frankel) became involved specifically with the Committee of Art and Entertainment Professions of the People's Convention. The movement aimed to reach a national audience by promoting people's needs and rights in wartime, with specific goals enumerated in the six points of the Convention. Given the closure of theatres upon the outbreak of war and the unemployment of musicians throughout the 1930s, the Convention was fertile ground for cultural propaganda, and the Committee's initial statement attempted to cut straight to the heart of wartime concerns:

> We stand amid the ruins not of buildings only, but of whole social activities. Theatres are closed, concert-halls empty, film-studios out of commission: thousands of professional workers in these spheres are out of work. [...] A PEOPLE'S GOVERNMENT would undertake the responsibility to make the best in theatre, music, painting and all forms of entertainment accessible to all. Only such a Government can break the stranglehold which is throttling the cultural life of the community. By removing the barriers of high prices, centralization, and of exclusive catering for a well-to-do minority, such a Government can release new sources of cultural vitality in the whole people, and by increasing the facilities for art and entertainment, thereby also increase demand.[30]

Apparent in this statement, like the manifesto of the Convention proper, is the foregrounding of specific concerns of British 'cultural workers' within the context of the CPGB's loftier long-term ambitions. The statement went on to outline vague but practical means of improving the lot of workers in the entertainment professions. The focus on the very real problem of

---

[29] London Arts Committee Memorandum, ABH.
[30] Committee of Arts and Entertainment Professions, 'Why We Support the People's Convention', *Two Concerts: People's Convention Souvenir Programme*, ABH.

sudden unemployment for artists and musicians in wartime, and the appeal to desires for better long-term opportunities, was effective. While most of the musician signatories of the Convention were communists, the Committee, through Bush, easily obtained the signatures of fellow travellers such as Lutyens, Rawsthorne, Clark, and even Professor Dent. Indeed, already in 1939, Clark had sent Bush a Manifesto of the British Musical Association (later renamed the Association of British Musicians).[31] In terms similar to those of the People's Convention, the Manifesto for the Association spoke of the need to make culture available to all, to bridge the 'gulf which at present separates producers and consumers' and to develop a strategy for promulgation of the arts that embraced 'every part of the country'.[32]

The People's Convention was, therefore, able to tap into a broader base of support, at least in music. However, its cultural efforts bore remarkably little fruit in comparison with its inflated rhetoric. One of the pressing concerns of the Committee was the approval of a suitable 'People's Convention Song'. Even following such measures as appointing a subcommittee, auditioning, and, extraordinarily, accepting contributions of words, or music, or both, the Committee was unable to find one of 'sufficiently striking character'.[33] Almost the only other effort was the production of two Christmas concerts. The first, a variety concert, consisted of miscellaneous items ranging from Shakespeare performed by Michael Redgrave to the tantalisingly named 'Paper Tearing Extraordinary', ending with Bush and Swingler's song 'Truth on the March'. The second, orchestral concert was a curious mix of English music past and present (Purcell's 'When I Am Laid in the Earth', Peter Warlock's *Capriol Suite*, and Boughton's Concerto for Flute and Strings) and works by Bach, Corelli, Bartók, and Ernest Bloch.[34] As these programmes illustrate, there was little attempt to match the content of concerts with the aims of the Convention, either in quality or programme; they relied rather on existing means and talents of committee members like Redgrave and Bush. Admittedly, the Committee was primarily concerned with 'bringing home the meaning and importance of the Convention itself to the people in the professional spheres concerned'.[35] Yet this only deferred the question of how the Party and Party-dominated movements like the

---

[31] Edward Clark to Alan Bush, 31 August 1939, BL/AB MS Mus. 453.
[32] Alan Bush to Edward Clark, 31 October 1939, BL/AB MS Mus. 453.
[33] People's Convention Committee of Arts and Entertainment Professions, Minutes of Committee Meeting, 7 January 1941, ABH.
[34] *Two Concerts: People's Convention Souvenir Programme*, ABH.
[35] People's Convention Committee of Arts and Entertainment Professions, Minutes of Committee Meeting, 26 November 1940, ABH.

People's Convention had any means of achieving an ambitious rejuvenation of national culture and what kind of rapprochement this would involve with existing cultural institutions.

Given the nascent state of cultural work in the British Party and the consequently weak basis for MI5's assessment of Bush, what exactly was his contribution to British musical culture in wartime? Certainly, he was a leading contributor to Party cultural activity, even beyond his involvement with the People's Convention. Among Bush's papers relating to the wartime Party Cultural Committee (PCC), Bush is listed as the 'comrade responsible' for music, as well as reporting on musical matters to the London Arts Committee. From this period and on into the post-war years, Bush was the person called upon to respond to party cultural policy as it pertained to music.

Bush also echoed the Party line in much of his activity beyond the Party committees. He fully supported the Party's opposition to the War, echoing their analysis of the British government in an unpublished essay of 1939, 'The National Government and Hitler'. In this piece, he argued that the Chamberlain government condoned Hitler's aggression as Hitler was to be used as 'the agent of aggression against the U.S.S.R.'. for the purposes of imperialist gain.[36] The USSR, on the other hand, was portrayed as the potential broker of an immediate peace. Evidently, this analysis reflected the Party line in late 1939, yet the reading of Hitler as an agent of imperialist, and thus capitalist, gain reflects the thinking already developed by the Party in the 1930s. Bush had certainly read a key formulation of this idea, Rajani Palme Dutt's *Fascism and Social Revolution* (1935),[37] and was already exhorting this line long before the war:

> Reason and objectivity which are the very basis of the scientific world-outlook of communism are *on principle* reviled by Nazism, and for good reason. Since the latter's whole object is to obscure its aim – the preservation of the capitalist system under another name – under the guise of pseudo scientific racial theories, which applaud the blood and ridicule the mind which enquires unbiased as far as may be into the nature of truth.[38]

Another noteworthy aspect of 'The National Government and Hitler' is Bush's reading of the war as a blow 'to the ideals of democracy and freedom for which the working-class movement stands today as always in the

---

[36] Alan Bush. 'The National Government and Hitler' [1939], unpublished typescript article, ABH, 1.
[37] Alan Bush to 'Pen', 23 April 1940, BL/AB MS Mus. 455, Miscellaneous Correspondence 1940.
[38] Alan Bush to William Busch, 19 May 1936, photocopy of typewritten letter, ABH.

past'.³⁹ Bush saw the War in terms of the ongoing aims of the Popular Front period: promoting the working-class movement in the interests of overthrowing capitalism. The article thus reveals the continuity in Bush's thinking before and after the outbreak of war, even as he was prompted to respond to the current crisis.

Most of the compositional work produced by Bush in the early part of the War consisted of the kind of agitational songs that had formed the foundation of the musical repertoire of the LLCU in the late 1930s, with texts reflecting the changed priorities of the wartime period. 'Against the People's Enemies' (1939), to a text by Swingler, is an obvious product of the Party's characterisation of the wartime government, as the following stanza illustrates:

> We hate your cynic speeches for the saving of your face,
> While mothers starve and prices rise (and profits rise apace).
> What do you care if men are killed and cities gasp for air,
> While there is plunder to be had and you will get your share?

'Unite and Be Free' (1941), written 'For the Peoples of India and Britain', is a curious song that uses a chromatically altered scale, motoric accompaniment, and syncopated rhythm to construct a clichéd Indian sound. Given the phrase in the refrain 'We call for a Peace of the peoples', alongside the condemnation of ruling-class tyranny, the song was probably directly inspired by the People's Convention's call for Indian independence. Both songs, as well as retaining something of the marching style and sparse texture of Bush's 1930s idiom, are most striking in the violence of their rhetoric against government and capitalist forces and the call for revolutionary action.

This does not mean, however, that Bush was unthinking in his engagement with Party policy and cultural work. A vignette from slightly later in Bush's career is illustrative. Pollitt wrote to Bush on his fiftieth birthday, commenting that 'in 1948 the Communist Choir was first assembled [...] Now our five London Choirs are regularly bringing colour and inspiration to our meetings and conferences'.⁴⁰ While Bush was gratified by the recognition, Pollitt's platitudes indicated how little activity was directly associated with the Party and how much was in Bush's hands. Indeed, he frequently complained of the philistinism of the Party regarding music, involving either complete failure to recognise musical contributions, or inadequate preparations leading to embarrassing musical efforts.⁴¹ The

---

³⁹ Bush, 'The National Government and Hitler', 2.
⁴⁰ Harry Pollitt to Alan Bush, 22 December 1950, photocopy of typewritten letter, ABH.
⁴¹ See, for example, Alan Bush to William Rust [Editor of the *Daily Worker*], 2 February 1946, photocopy of typewritten letter, ABH.

Ex. 3.1 Bush, 'Unite and Be Free', bb. 3–8.

William Morris Musical Society, too, was not a meaningless 'front' for political activity, but rather a concerted attempt on Bush's part to solve the organisational problems being discussed by the Party Cultural Committee in late 1940, an attempt to coordinate Party musicians by uniting amateurs and professionals beyond the unhelpful trade-union demarcations. Yet the emergence of the committee is also interesting given that Bush had been considering founding a group to consider the Marxist analysis of music back in the autumn of 1939.[42] The Society, as it emerged, was less a comprehensive coordination of musical work in the Party, and far more the foray into Marxist aesthetics envisaged by Bush. It aimed to study 'the relationship between music and social conditions in all periods and countries', and to engage with culture beyond the bounds of the Party.[43] The events the society produced were, for the most part, concerts with commentary, featuring titles such as 'Chamber Music Has Social Content' and 'The Rise of the Virtuoso'. They reflected, significantly,

---

[42] Alan Bush to Harry Hancock [contributor to *University Forward*], 13 November 1939, BL/AB MS Mus. 454 (Bush's emphasis).

[43] The William Morris Musical Society, issues by the CPGB Executive Committee, October 1940, ABH.

a style of musical event Bush had been experimenting with as early as 1936.[44] While there is much more that could be said about Bush's aesthetics in this period, this snapshot of his Party activity indicates that his involvement with cultural matters was a two-way street. Bush was prominently involved with nascent efforts to coordinate Party cultural work, yet he was also capable of shaping Party activities to reflect his own developing ideas.

Bush and National Culture

The position of both the Communist Party and individual British communists changed drastically with the German invasion of the Soviet Union on 22 June 1941. The Party went even further than might have been expected in support of the war. Following criticisms from the Executive Committee of the Comintern, they did not merely support the Soviet Union against fascism, but called for a 'united national front' against Hitler, thus supporting the Churchill government and offering outspoken support for the War effort, particularly in factory production.[45] The CPGB's cooperation was not limited to military matters; rather, communist ambitions for post-war change had much in common with ideas circulating more widely in wartime Britain, especially with regard to culture.

The Party contributed to mainstream discourse concerning the devastation caused by the War and the nature of post-war reconstruction. As Dan Stone has remarked, at a European level it was the communist characterisation of the War as an ideological struggle of civilisation against the barbarism of Fascism that 'gave the war its millenarian character', which in turn contributed to two crucial aspects of post-war life: the idea that the pre-war world was unrecoverable and the need for renewal.[46] In Britain, the 1940 pamphlet *Guilty Men* was an early attack on the inter-war systems and leaders who, in the authors' opinion, had led the country to war.[47] Similarly, the sole Communist MP of the time, William Gallacher, addressed the Arts and Entertainment Committee of the People's Convention just after Operation Barbarossa on 'Parliament To-Day':

---

[44] Programme of the William Morris Musical Society, October-December 1940, ABH.
[45] Thorpe, *The British Communist Party and Moscow*, 267.
[46] Dan Stone, 'Editor's Introduction: Postwar Europe as History' in *The Oxford Handbook of Postwar European History* ((Oxford: Oxford University Press, 2012), 3.
[47] See Tony Judt, *Postwar: A History of Europe since 1945* (London: Pimlico, 2007; Penguin, 2005), 63–4.

The old chamber was now a mass of rubble but it was no more shattered than the old policy of *appeasement* that it had sheltered. The old 'house' could not be restored – it had to be rebuilt. But there were some who wished to restore, to patch up, the old policy that it had so tragically harboured. That policy must never again be seen, for it took two forms, both of which had been disastrous in their consequences.[48]

The image of unrecoverable rubble, and something new arising from it, was one that would be invoked again and again. As to what this something new might be, there were again important parallels between communist and British thinking in the wider Left. 'Planning', a product both of the extended wartime powers of the state and the dire impact of war, was an essential ingredient in post-war reconstruction.[49] As Pollitt wrote in *How to Win the Peace* (1944), 'If the united effort of the people can be built up and all resources of the State organised for victory over fascism [...] the same can be done in peace-time, to secure social progress, provided the people are prepared to unite and fight for these things'.[50] For the Communist Party and the wider Labour movement, culture was integral to any such post-war settlement. As Heather Wiebe has described, CEMA, by then the Arts Council, was 'yoked to the vision of the new Labour government', with aspirations both of raising taste and democratising culture.[51] The Workers' Music Association in 1944 praised state endowment of the arts for generating full audiences for factory concerts, and, somewhat extraordinarily, received a subsidy for several years from the Attlee government.[52]

Still more significantly, the CPGB enjoyed an unprecedented upsurge of support based on admiration for the Red Army and a desire to promote unity and understanding among the Allied nations. For the Party, the USSR was both the deliverer of liberation and the key to regeneration of culture. To quote Gallacher again: 'If Fascism were now to be victorious, the people would be enslaved for centuries, culture would be destroyed. If the U.S.S.R. were victorious, there would be freedom for all and a rapid development in all cultural activities'.[53] Bush's enthusiasm for the role of

---

[48] Ben Frankel, Digest of Talk by William Gallacher [Communist MP], People's Convention Committee of Arts and Entertainment Professions, Minutes of Committee Meeting, 10 July 1941, ABH (Frankel's emphasis).
[49] Judt, *Postwar*, 67; Wiebe, *Britten's Unquiet Pasts*, 3, 24 ff.
[50] Harry Pollitt, *How to Win the Peace* (London: Communist Party of Great Britain, 1944), 3–4.
[51] Wiebe, *Britten's Unquiet Pasts*, 24.
[52] Callaghan and Harker (eds.), *British Communism*, 168–9.
[53] Frankel, Digest of Talk by William Gallacher.

the Soviet Union in the War was not always likely to endear him to the British public. As Jean R. Freedman, among others, has discussed, the core of the myth of wartime Britain was and is the idea that 'Britain stood, brave and united, fighting alone until joined by the Allies, never defeated, never down-hearted'.[54] In the British communist narrative, on the contrary, the Soviet Union was the liberator of Europe, and the Western allies suffered in comparison. In a talk introducing a 1946 concert, Bush's descriptions of two of his own works show this view clearly. 'The Great Red Army' (1942) is a song in which 'love and admiration for the Red Army are mingled with an uneasiness and sense of shame which our inactivity in the West engendered in the hearts of many men and women of this country'.[55] While the negative characterisation of the West was not conveyed in Swingler's text of the song, *Britain's Part* (1942), another work with a text by Bush himself, was far more explicit. Bush's later assessment of the song incorporates many facets of British communism's attitude to the War:

> the weary apathy and suspicion of the pre-war years, the shock and horror of the war itself, and lastly the growing comprehension of its inevitability as the result of Britain's past mistakes, all these are experiences which have bitten deep into the consciousness of the British people. Our unity with the people's [sic] of the United Nations gives us strength.[56]

The work itself, for speaker, mixed chorus, and orchestra, is firmly in the style of Bush's topical, agitational workers' songs, and seems far more a reaction to the urgent situation of 1942 following the invasion of the Soviet Union than a product of Bush's reflective statement in 1946. The work also has something of the dramatic quality of the finale of the Piano Concerto. Lengthy passages of didactic commentary for the speaker, accompanied only by an insistent side drum rhythm, are broken up by the choir, articulating the voice of the British people ('We British people slept while the enemies of freedom in our own land curbed our ancient freedom'), and by occasional orchestral sound effects, as with the cymbal clashes on 'Our airmen fought back!' Emerging from this, again in the spirit of the 1930s workers' music, is a slow, march-like final choral section, encompassing a call to action on the part of the British people and a large-scale shift to the major key at the prospect of winning life and freedom.

---

[54] Jean R. Freedman, *Whistling in the Dark: Memory and Culture in Wartime London* (Lexington: University Press of Kentucky, 1999), 84.

[55] Alan Bush, 'Script for Jan 6th [1945]', [Talk introducing a Concert of the Compositions of Alan Bush, Queen Mary Hall, London], ABH.

[56] Bush, 'Script for Jan 6th [1945]'.

With its verbose and simplistic text and unmemorable music, this is one of Bush's weaker works, yet it is an apt example of his belief that deliverance for Britain could only be achieved through alliance with the Soviet Union, and that Anglo-Soviet unity lay at the heart of the possibilities for a 'people's peace'. As Bush wrote in 'The Outlook for the British Composer' (1941), 'our survival depends, not in organising our affairs as we have been accustomed to do in the past, but in moving during the fight towards a far more truly democratic state of society than we have ever known in actual practice'.[57]

Such unflattering descriptions of British involvement in the War notwithstanding, it was the upsurge of public enthusiasm for the Red Army, and the circumstances of the Alliance, which gave Bush his most significant opportunities for cultural activity in wartime Britain. For the BBC, how to present Russia to audiences both at home and overseas following the entry of the Soviet Union into the War was a delicate matter, causing consternation at the highest levels over such matters as the broadcasting of the Soviet national anthem (then the 'Internationale') alongside those of other Allies.[58] However, the showcasing of Russian 'cultural achievements' was safer ground than politics, and members of the BBC Music Department did not necessarily share the squeamishness of their senior colleagues. The Music Department did face the problem of a lack of expertise and recordings, particularly of popular music. Bush was not only an acknowledged expert on Soviet music, but in possession of a number of gramophone recordings sent by Grigori Shneerson of the Soviet organisation VOKS (the All-Union Society for Cultural Ties Abroad), whom Bush had met in the 1930s and with whom he maintained a lively correspondence and exchange of sheet music and records. From September 1941 onwards, Bush wrote and introduced a wealth of programmes for Home, Overseas, and Forces audiences, presenting examples of Soviet popular, folk, and art music. In some of the scripts, Bush had free rein to present highly favourable accounts of Soviet musical life. For one programme broadcast on the Overseas Service, Bush countered suggestions that there was no jazz in Russia and gave an account of the varieties of Soviet 'light music'.[59] Following one talk, Bush received listeners' letters stating their enthusiasm for the Russian recordings and

---

[57] Alan Bush, 'The Outlook for the British Composer', *The Author, Playwright and Composer* LII/1 (Spring 1941), 65.

[58] Asa Briggs, *The History of Broadcasting in the United Kingdom: Volume III: The War of Words* (London: Oxford University Press: 1970), 389.

[59] Alan Bush, Typewritten script for BBC programme 'Your Questions Answered', General Overseas Service, 17 August 1945, ABH.

asking where they could obtain copies.[60] Bush's expertise was in demand in official circles beyond the BBC. In 1942, the British Council sought Bush's advice in responding to a letter from Soviet composers which commented on the joint fight against fascism and expressed the desire to hear about British music in wartime.[61] The Ministry of Information later commissioned an article on 'Russian Music in Britain' from Bush for the Ministry's Russian-language Moscow paper, *British Ally*.[62]

This upsurge of interest in Soviet music also had consequences for Bush's career as a composer. Appendix 2 provides an overview of Bush's works of the period covered by this chapter. As it reveals, his main patron in the war years was the BBC. Bush received two commissions for military band, both of which were woven from Soviet songs. *Russian Glory* is based on Dunayevsky's *Song of the Motherland* and Khachaturian's *Poem about Stalin*. The *Fantasia on Soviet Themes* incorporates melodies by Zacherov, Sedoi, and Dunayevsky. Enquiring after the progress of the *Fantasia on Soviet Themes*, Hubert Clifford, Empire Music Adviser, wrote to Bush that 'in view of the magnificent efforts of the Red Army, this music becomes more topical than ever!'[63] Even more extraordinary was the inclusion of Bush's song, 'The Great Red Army' (1942), in an overseas programme. This amateur song, in Bush's 1930s agitprop style, would normally have been anathema to the BBC's score reading committee, yet proved of keen interest to Clifford who praised the quality of Dunayevsky's songs and remarked to Bush: 'It is lamentable if we ourselves cannot produce a few popular songs of this type'.[64]

It would be wrong to conclude that Bush's enjoyment of BBC patronage in wartime was simply about showcasing a sample of Soviet popular music. As a conductor, Bush enjoyed regular employment with the organisation directing two ensembles he had founded: the London String Orchestra and the WMA Singers. The former won favour with the BBC for the quality of their playing and for their novel mixed programmes, including works by Bartók and Berg, and selections of

---

[60] Alan Bush, Typewritten script for 'A Connoisseur Programme of Russian Gramophone Records presented by Alan Bush', 3 March 1942; photocopies of original letters from the public, ABH.
[61] Pamela Henn-Collins [British Council] to Alan Bush, 30 July 1942, photocopy of original, ABH.
[62] Raymond Broad [Ministry of Information] to Alan Bush, 27 November 1945, photocopy of original, ABH.
[63] Hubert Clifford, Empire Music Supervisor, to Alan Bush, 27 January 1942, BBC/WAC RCONT 1: Artist, Alan Bush, File II, 1942–62.
[64] Hubert Clifford to Alan Bush, 10 August 1942, BBC/WAC RCONT1: Artist, Workers' Music Association Singers, 1942–61.

eighteenth-century English music.⁶⁵ Part of the purpose of this ensemble was to provide employment for musicians suffering reduced opportunities in wartime, yet Bush also wrote intriguingly to the BBC in 1940 that 'It really is important to keep some first-class music in existence as long as possible, *in case* Hitler gets beaten'.⁶⁶ Arguably, the selection of such *entartete Musik* as Berg's *Lyric Suite* as an example of 'first-class music' was a product of Bush's desire to fight fascism through culture by preserving music banned under Nazism. The WMA Singers, too, with their specialist repertoire of international folk and popular song, were useful in fulfilling certain aspects of wartime cultural propaganda. They were able, for example, to contribute a programme of old and modern Dutch songs, broadcast on the European Service on the day after VE Day, and to provide programmes of Soviet songs for the Home and Forces radio.⁶⁷ Their most regular engagement was for the Overseas Transmission programme 'Britain Sings!', for which they broadcast themes selections including 'Songs of Battle' and 'The Soviet Sings' to North America and the Pacific regions. In each case, it is notable that the sort of repertory that formed part of Bush's decidedly anti-bourgeois socialist musical endeavours in the 1930s, was now acceptable as part of BBC efforts to promote examples of Allied music being sung by British people. Naturally, the singing of Soviet songs had taken on new meanings in the context of wartime alliances, but the singing of a range of international repertory, undertaken by an amateur, ostensibly working-class choir, suggests a more powerful symbolism of solidarity between the people of nations opposing Hitler. In this, at least, Bush's work with the BBC involved a more complex engagement with British cultural priorities than simply providing expertise in Soviet music.

This possibility is also suggested by Bush's *Symphony in C*. Although performed in the Proms during wartime, it was not a BBC commission. Rather, it was a product of Bush's preoccupation with British capitalist complicity with fascism in the early part of the war. Although not revealed at the time of the first performance, Bush had given the three movements the place-names 'Cliveden', 'Dowlais' and 'Harworth', referring respectively to the 'Cliveden set' of 'pro-Hitler monopoly capitalists', a Welsh village that had suffered acutely in the 1930s, and a site of working-class protest in 1938/9.⁶⁸ Nevertheless, there is reason to associate it in the same

---

⁶⁵ See BBC/WAC RCONT1: Artist, London String Orchestra, 1939–62.
⁶⁶ Alan Bush to Kenneth Wright, BBC/WAC RCONT1: Artist, London String Orchestra.
⁶⁷ BBC/WAC RCONT1: Artist: Workers Music Association Singers.
⁶⁸ O'Higgins (ed.), *The Correspondence of Alan Bush and John Ireland*, 116.

way with the consensus that had arisen between Bush's vision of wartime and wider currents in Britain. Firstly, the Prom performance was conducted by the composer in uniform. This was only one of a number of wartime concerts in which composers in the forces conducted their own works, a visual spectacle that would enhance the connection between cultural expression and the fight against fascism.[69] Secondly, while the composer's programme was summarised in Edwin Evans' programme notes simply as 'aspiration' (in the Prologue preceding the three main movements), followed by 'greed, frustration, and liberation' the movement titles bear a strong similarity to fellow-communist Stevens' *Symphony of Liberation*.[70] This work, begun in 1940, with movements entitled 'Enslavement', 'Resistance' and 'Liberation' won the *Daily Express* 1946 competition for a victory symphony, and was performed as part of a victory concert at the Royal Albert Hall on 7 June 1946. For the *Daily Express*, the occasion was redolent with symbolism. Like Bush conducting his symphony, 'Private Stevens' was wearing 'the battle-dress he has worn for six years'.[71] Not only that, but the newspaper was eager to connect the symphony with the civilian experience of war:

> [Stevens] began it during blitz nights when he was billeted in Bloomsbury [...] with radio dance music to blanket London's ack-ack noise. The sunny, spirited third movement he added when the war ended in Europe.[72]

Shoring up this connection between the civilians' war and military victory, the *Express* commented on the 'thousands' of Londoners who came to hear the music, civilians and men and women in uniform, from throughout the Empire. This was music that had 'much that is experimental', but the composer also faced '*a new audience*'.[73] Even making allowance for the boasting of newspapers regarding their own initiatives, it is clear that the symphony and the composer were being placed in a position of strong cultural importance, to which, indeed, Stevens contributed with statements like 'I felt the necessity of writing something to sum up my feelings about a wonderful episode'.[74] Stevens, the soldier-composer, forged a link between London's struggle and Britain's victory, one which the symphonic trajectory of struggle overcome in victory could easily support.

---

[69] Personal communication from Lewis Foreman to the author.
[70] Edwin Evans, 'Analytical Notes', BBC Promenade Concerts Programme, 24 July 1942.
[71] Roy Johnson, 'Thousands Acclaim New Symphonies', *Daily Express*, 10 June 1946, 3.
[72] '£250 Symphony Written in the Blitz', *Daily Express*, 29 March 1946, 1.
[73] Johnson, 'Thousands Acclaim New Symphonies', 3.
[74] '£250 Symphony Written in the Blitz', 1.

In addition, the perceived novelty of Stevens' symphony, and the grandeur of the occasion, touched upon the impulses towards cultural renewal and democratisation in post-war Britain. The notion that the symphony was inspired by radio dance music and the sounds of gunfire, like a British 'Leningrad' Symphony, is a compelling image of the post-war British public hopes and sympathy with Soviet Russia that communists were able to share and even direct.

Any construction of Bush – such as that of MI5 – as an outsider in British society, or as a straightforward, ultimately political agent of Moscow – must be rejected. While the interest of British communists in national concerns in this period may be traced back to Comintern policy, it is clear that the CPGB had only the beginnings of a cultural policy, and small collective cultural impact at this stage. Bush's relationship to this developing cultural work was complex. He was, alongside others, an architect of CPGB cultural work, and yet also used Party resources to develop his own ideas, as in the case of the William Morris Musical Society, a product of reflections on the relationship between music and society going back to the 1930s. With the German invasion of the Soviet Union, Bush's ideas about state sponsorship of the arts and his enthusiasm for the Red Army invested his work with greater relevance to British culture than ever before, and the result was an unprecedented period of career success. In the peculiar circumstances of the Anglo-Soviet Alliance, a communist's Fantasia on Soviet popular song could sound the keynote of the moment. In spite of the suspicions of the Security Services, in the 1940s Bush was an insider in British culture as never before.

4 Building in the Rubble: *The Winter Journey* and *Lidiče*

> Let us create and perform works which will express the great tasks now confronting the people of Britain and the world, and let us learn to perform them as though we meant every word of them. In this way, and in this way only, the vivid outlook for the British composer, which the present situation opens to us, may be realised in a new musical renaissance.[1]
>
> Alan Bush

Bush's compositional activity in wartime was almost entirely limited to topical mass songs and choral works, or specific commissions for Soviet-inspired instrumental music like the *Fantasia on Soviet Themes*. A striking exception was *Lyric Interlude* for violin solo and piano accompaniment dedicated to Nancy Bush and written, according to Bush's daughter Rachel O'Higgins, as consolation following the death of their seven-year-old daughter Alice in a traffic accident.[2] Despite being one of a trio of pieces specially written for the émigré virtuoso violinist Max Rostal, *Lyric Interlude* studiously avoids brilliant technical display.[3] It is a work of restraint and intimacy. The *unlyrical* ascending melodic gesture in the first bar, the sparse, imitative accompanying phrases and the effect of the Mixolydian flattened seventh invest the opening with a quality of bleakness and expectation that characterises much of the work (Ex. 4.1). The lyricism indicated by the title is rather present in fleeting moments like bar 8, in which the music briefly takes on a tender, lilting, waltz-like quality, which is almost immediately lost again. The effect of this all-too-brief moment of joy is comparable to what Rupprecht has called the 'warmth without issue' of the 'Lacrimosa' in Britten's *War Requiem*.[4] Yet while the *War Requiem*, in the 'Lacrimosa' and throughout the work, juxtaposes public and intimate expressions of grief, *Lyric Interlude* may be seen as a purely personal expression of grief in itself.

In addition to the work's articulation of private grief and personal loss, it is worth considering its place in Bush's artistic response to the experience of war. *Lyric Interlude* featured in a concert of the composer's works in

---

[1] Bush, 'The Outlook for the British Composer', 65.
[2] O'Higgins (ed.), *The Correspondence of Alan Bush and John Ireland*, 106.
[3] Bush apologised in a letter to Rostal for being unable to incorporate his suggestion of passages of triple-stopping, because this would injure the character of the work. Alan Bush to Max Rostal, 14 September 1944, photocopy of original, ABH.
[4] Cited in Wiebe, *Britten's Unquiet Pasts*, 213.

Ex. 4.1 Bush, *Lyric Interlude*, bb. 1–11.

January 1945, providing a sharp contrast to the voluble and bombastic public call to action of *Britain's Part*. Where most of Bush's works in wartime took up the objective, didactic aesthetic of his pre-war workers' music, *Lyric Interlude* is private, preoccupied with loss, and gives no directives. It resonates with Bush's observation, in his commentary on the 1945 concert, of a need to deal with the 'shock and horror of war', and to the wider dichotomy in British culture between a positive desire for post-war change and the negative sense that this need had been created by the utter destruction of the pre-war world. By exploring Bush's creative response to wartime loss, it is possible to identify a small number of works which articulate the private experience of war, lyrical miniatures that stand in contrast to the public political statements that preoccupied Bush in the immediate post-war period. Not only do these point to a more ambivalent engagement with war than might be suggested by the music surveyed in the last chapter, but they allow Bush's music of the 1940s to be properly situated in a wider British cultural effort to deal with the legacy of war.

The Winter Journey

Bush's *The Winter Journey*, op. 29 (1946), a cantata retelling the Nativity story for soprano and baritone soloists, mixed chorus, string quintet, and harp, is a curiosity in the output of the fiercely atheistic Bush. The work was a commission, first performed in Alnwick Parish Church, Northumberland, on 14 December 1946, and broadcast live on the BBC Third Programme. It was in fact a product of initial efforts towards post-war democratisation, localism, and renewal of the arts under the new Labour government. The Council for the Arts, Music and Drama in Northumberland had created a festival 'where a massed choir from surrounding towns and villages [around Alnwick] come together to perform something of a religious character, and includes in the programme a new or newish work by a British composer'.[5] Having staged a performance of Britten's *Ceremony of Carols* in 1945 ('a sort of neo-mediaeval collection of Christmas songs, of varying degrees of religiosity, very takingly set with a pretty harp accompaniment'),[6] the organisers proposed to Bush that he compose a Christmas cantata. The religious dimension of the commissioned work caused Bush some uneasiness, but he accepted by reasoning that it would be possible to create something both secular and appropriate to the occasion. It was Swingler, Bush's frequent collaborator and fellow communist, who provided a solution when the composer approached him regarding a suitable text:

> I began writing, a little time ago, with a vague general idea of musical setting, a sort of secular mass – that is to say a sequence of very short poems based roughly on the form of the mass, being a sort of examination of the emotions activating a post-war world – Pity and Guilt in the Kyrie, Triumph in the Gloria, a statement of conviction in the unity of the people and history in the Credo, and so on. Do you think there is any possibility in the idea? Or do you think it would be too shocking to Christians? Otherwise I could write a short Christmas cantata on the general theme of what new-born world will rise out of this chaos, very simple, very traditional in form.[7]

---

[5] Alan Bush to Randall Swingler, 25 April 1946, photocopy of original, ABH.   [6] Ibid.
[7] Randall Swingler to Alan Bush, 16 May 1946, photocopy of original, ABH.

It is clear from the result that poet and composer pursued the latter suggestion, rather than Swingler's intriguing idea for something along the lines of the *War Requiem* (Fig. 4.1). *The Winter Journey* is 'a materialist retelling of the Christmas story', omitting any reference to Christian salvation and focusing on the inequality and pursuit of wealth that permits the impoverished family to be denied room.[8] The final stanza ('And all in vain they made/That journey through the waste and wild/Unless we make some place to lay the child') places salvation firmly in human hands. The image of the Christ child's birth as the inversion of wealth and power is also invoked in hopes for the future in 'Mary's Song', in a clear allusion to the Magnificat.

Nevertheless, Swingler's modest proposal for a traditional cantata dealing with universal questions belies the distinctive, almost puzzling features of the text that emerged. Rather than make recourse to conventional Christmas imagery of a natural, snow-filled landscape, Swingler evokes the disorienting experience of traversing the city in winter. Yet the second movement, 'The Journey', is another departure, describing 'the yawning heat of the desert, the crags of terror,/The nights of exhaustion, the days without water'. 'The Journey' reflects something of Swingler's own wartime service, which in 1943 saw him travel over three thousand miles in a month through Iraq, Syria, and North Africa.[9] At a deeper level, the juxtaposition of the boiling desert and the freezing city bespeaks a desire to unite, like the rhetoric surrounding Stevens's *Symphony of Liberation*, both military and civilian experiences of war. As Tony Judt has noted, the War embraced civilians as well as soldiers and indeed for those occupied nations of Europe was *primarily* a civilian experience.[10] Moreover, ruined cities 'were the most obvious – and photogenic – evidence of the devastation, and they came to serve as a universal visual shorthand for the pity of war'.[11]

The wartime city was an image with specific connotations in Britain. As Freedman has discussed, London had a crucial role in wartime British narratives, as chief protagonist, both sufferer and resister, in the fight against fascism.[12] Moreover, Leo Mellor has argued that the *bombed* city in particular was an image of extraordinary cultural impact for British writers and artists in the middle decades of the twentieth century.[13] While images of ruins and fragments were part of the language of British literary

---

[8] Croft, *Comrade Heart*, 179.   [9] Ibid., 135, 179.   [10] Judt, *Postwar*, 13.   [11] Ibid., 16.
[12] Freedman, *Whistling in the Dark*, 84.
[13] Leo Mellor, *Reading the Ruins: Modernism, Bombsites and British Culture* (Cambridge: Cambridge University Press, 2011).

> Introduction
> No. 1: The City – chorus, soprano and baritone soli
> No. 2: The Journey – baritone solo
> No. 3: The Sleepers in the City – chorus
> No. 4: Mary's Song – soprano solo
> No. 5: Final Chorale – chorus and semi-chorus

Fig. 4.1 Schema of Bush, *The Winter Journey*.

modernism long before aerial bombing became a reality, not least in T.S. Eliot's *The Waste Land*, in the Second World War and afterwards they took on particular resonance in literature examining the profound changes to people's lives. Swingler's Eliotic text is emphatically in this vein. The disconcerting abrupt shifts in narrative of 'The City' are superficially reminiscent of Eliot. Equally indicative of the experience of bombing is the description in 'The Journey' of how 'the very sky exploded upon us'. Significant too in the context of wartime literature is Swingler's preoccupation with ghosts, part of the 'generic language for representations of London's inhabitants in the Blitz'.[14] He evokes a 'haunted city', swirling with fog, and refers to the 'sleepers' of the city, meriting comparison with the opposition of sleep and death explored in Wilfrid Owen's poem 'Futility', which itself would be so resonantly associated with British experience of war in the *War Requiem*.[15] As Mellor describes, part of the fascination of the bombsite for Graham Greene, for example, was the images it threw up of the 'permeable boundaries between the living and the dead'.[16] In Swingler's hands, these boundaries not only evoke the bombed city, but connect the contemporary situation with the Christian narrative. As Wiebe has noted, the sacred, and the Nativity in particular, was a powerful trope in the English experience of wartime destruction, evoking the notion of a sacred English past being preserved for the future, despite the proximity to death.[17] Following the description of the sky exploding in 'The Journey', Joseph states that 'we could not have endured it, but for the new life already quick and stirring in the womb'. At the crux of *The Winter Journey*, Mary asks:

> What is the price of life in your market now?
> And when my child shall stretch out arms to me,
> Which shadow shall I see along the floor,
> The cross of death, or blossoming tree?

---

[14] Ibid., 139. [15] Wiebe, *Britten's Unquiet Pasts*, 213ff.
[16] Mellor, *Reading the Ruins*, 141. [17] Wiebe, *Britten's Unquiet Pasts*, 46.

Again drawing on Eliot, in this case 'The Journey of the Magi', the question of the Nativity being 'Birth or Death' is thus posed. While many commentators have found the work's references to capitalism, as in this stanza, off-putting, the text is more than a demand for new economic conditions. The permeability of life and death in the bombed city symbolised both the alienating experience of war and the precarious possibilities of post-war regeneration.

Given Bush's admiration for *A Ceremony of Carols* and the parallels already identified with the *War Requiem*, it is worth considering the extent to which his music, like Swingler's text, may be situated within a broader British cultural response to the experience of war. In fact, Bush's music warrants extensive comparison with two significant British musical articulations of wartime suffering: *A Ceremony of Carols* and Tippett's oratorio *A Child of Our Time*. Tippett wrote the text of the latter with advice from Eliot, also informed by his own reading of Owen. As Kemp describes, Tippett based the opening chorus on lines from Owen's poem 'The Seed':

> OWEN: War broke. And now the winter of the world
>   With perishing great darkness closes in.
> TIPPETT: The world turns on its dark side.
>   It is winter.[18]

The parallels between Tippett and Swingler's texts are apparent not only in this instance, but throughout Tippett's verses, with their blending of natural and urban imagery and musings on the significance of Christ's sacrifice. Musically, aspects of Bush's work bear comparison with Tippett's. Bush's 'The City' shares with Tippett's 'Double Chorus of Persecutors and Persecuted' the juxtaposition of the words of oppressors and oppressed and the sardonic, jocular musical setting of the callous statements of the oppressors. Both are also strongly reminiscent of the 'Dance of Death' from Britten's *Ballad of Heroes*, with its juxtaposition of the civilised drawing room with 'gas and bomb' set to a macabre scherzo. In Tippett's movement, the initial interjections of the persecuted (Chorus II) into the statements of the persecutors (Chorus I) give way to a shift of texture, time signature and harmony to a pedal on F♯ to articulate the final lament of the persecuted, 'We have no refuge'. In Bush's movement, the texture of the writing for the chorus, representing unfriendly and mercenary voices in the city, bears much resemblance to Tippett, while again, a shift of texture and the introduction of a pedal (G♭) accompanies the pleas for help of Mary and Joseph (Ex. 4.2).

A further comparison may be made in Bush's use of the chorus. He expressed his perplexity after the premiere of *A Child of Our Time* that

---

[18] Kemp, *Tippett*, 152–4.

Ex. 4.2 *The Winter Journey*, 'The City', bb. 75–84.

Tippett should think that 'the solution of the world's ills (or even of the individual's sufferings) is to be found in stealing away to Jesus', and that he should 'present [this solution] in the most seductive possible light with all the emotional panoply at your command'.[19] Nevertheless, Tippett's decision to use the spirituals as a contemporary substitute for the chorales of Bach's Passions had some effect on Bush, judging by his creation of a 'Final Chorale'. In contrast to Tippett's spirituals, Bush's intended effect is not so much the expression of 'common emotions at a common level', but the inducement to collective action. Writing rehearsal notes for a 1981 performance, Bush indicated that stress must be placed on 'we' in the phrase 'Unless we make some place to lay the child', to avoid an effect of 'sentimental resignation, the exact opposite of what the composer intended'.[20] Bush learned from Tippett musical possibilities for articulating a contemporary message via the medium of a quasi-religious text, but was unable to fully discount his own Eislerian preference for extolling collective action over collective emotion. Bush's 'Final Chorale' should not, however, be viewed as another musical sacrifice for propagandistic effect. In order to fully understand the impact of the finale, we must turn to the other important parallel work to *The Winter Journey*.

Britten's *Ceremony of Carols* was, as discussed previously, the inspiration behind the commission of *The Winter Journey*, and was also performed again as a companion item at the premiere of Bush's work. Like *The Winter Journey*, it is a product of the experience of wartime, a work that posits the sacred as a source of renewal. The musical parallels are also striking. Like Britten, and probably directly inspired by him, Bush made the unusual choice of the harp for accompaniment. He also followed Britten's precedent by employing medieval procedures in the service of an 'interpenetration of distant ideals and embodied and immediate realities'.[21] While Bush introduced *organum*-like motion in parallel fourths and fifths and pervasive false relations in the instrumental 'Introduction' to the work, it is in 'The Sleepers in the City' that they are brought to the fore. The allusions to *organum*, the circular, almost palindromic short melodic phrases invest the music at the outset of the movement with an empty, searching quality, evoking the 'haunted city',

---

[19] Alan Bush to Michael Tippett, 14 September 1944, BL/AB MS Mus. 449, Correspondence with Sir Michael Tippett.
[20] Alan Bush, typewritten notes on interpretation of *The Winter Journey*, 24 March 1981, ABH.
[21] Wiebe, *Britten's Unquiet Pasts*, 46.

the permeability between life and death, that so fascinated Greene (Ex. 4.3). In conjunction with the text, the movement specifically evokes the figure of the sleeper who, like the ghost, represents something lost or unreachable. Yet Swingler's sleepers are also those unwilling or unable to take action, to participate in renewal:

> A wind stirs in the city like a reminder
> Of something we must do, but have forgotten.
> The starlight on the sleeper's face
> Disturbs his dreams, and when he wakes,
> Knowing that something has happened, something is born
> To-night, but where and what he cannot tell.

In the initial choral phrase, the observation of the stirring wind is in contrast to the complete stasis of the phrase, circling above a G pedal, again with the use of parallel motion and consequent false relations investing the music with archaism. The one moment in the movement where the circling, contrapuntal patterns are abandoned is revelatory. A shift to homophonic texture, the introduction of the harp, and the Mixolydian cadence into G major on 'something is born tonight' all provide a transient moment of clarity – the sleepers' wakefulness – that instantly disappears on the resumption of the opening music (Ex. 4.4). In sum, musically and textually the movement expresses the alienating experience of the wartime experience, but also the fleeting hope of rebirth.

What is hinted at in 'The Sleepers in the City' is fully realised in the 'Final Chorale'. The choral writing recalls the archaism of 'The Sleepers' through the unaccompanied homophony and parallel fifths. As in 'The City', chorus and semi-chorus are placed in a dramatic relationship. While the semi-chorus' austere music on 'Winter it may be' recalls the condition of sleep, of lack of awareness, the chorus declaims the words 'Unless we make some place to lay the child'. While Bush's large-scale transitions from minor to major in workers' songs could be crude, the effect of this technique on 'in the season of the heart' is luminous (Ex. 4.5):

> Winter it may be in the streets of time,
> And all in vain they made
> That journey through the waste and wild,
> Unless we make some place to lay the child
> That will be born this Christmas
> In the season of the heart.

Ex. 4.3 *The Winter Journey*, 'The Sleepers in the City', bb. 1–22.

Ex. 4.4 *The Winter Journey*, 'The Sleepers in the City', bb. 38–40.

The arrival of E♭ major, as in 'The Sleepers', immediately gives way to the seven-note, circling motif, yet it is transformed in the new harmonic context, now above a pedal tonic chord and enriched by the full resources of the string quintet and harp. Thus, whereas 'The Sleepers in the City' presented a fleeting hope of rebirth in the midst of suffering, the 'Final Chorale' offers a more substantial vision of the future if collective action ('we make some place to lay the child') is taken. Nevertheless, the ending of the movement remains ambiguous. The seven-note figure retains its original motivic profile and archaic open parallel fifths, and the repeated invocations of the chorus are overlaid with the semi-chorus' insistent reminder of the opening sentiments of the movement, and original motif. Thus, in the final choral phrase of the work, the call to 'make some place to lay the child' and the statement 'And all in vain they made/That journey through the waste and wild' are juxtaposed. Wiebe argues that Britten's *Ceremony of Carols* uses an archaic idiom to evoke 'intermingled real and imagined worlds', reflecting something of the situation of the very situation of post-war Britain.[22] *A Child of Our Time*, too, is in many ways an interplay of real and emotional worlds, of the horrors of the present and the possibility of future healing.

[22] Ibid., 71.

At this point in their relationship, Tippett's Jungian solutions were anathema to the materialist Bush. Yet the mingling of ancient and modern music, religious and secular themes, past suffering and future hope in each of the works discussed reveals a common

Ex. 4.5 *The Winter Journey*, 'Final Chorale', bb. 40–9.

Ex. 4.5 (cont.)

cultural obsession – and set of aural symbols – for responding to the experience of war. In Bush's 'Final Chorale', belonging and distance, action and inaction, are overlaid in a way that presents a more ambiguous picture of post-war recovery than might be expected from the force of Bush's public rhetoric. Bush and Swingler's work is very far from the crude and voluble political statements of their weakest collaborations of the period in the field of political song. It engages deeply with major trends in mid-century British culture: adaptations of literary modernism to the bombsite, and the early efforts of Britten and Tippett to synthesise artistic and political goals after their rejection of the aesthetics of the 1930s. *The Winter Journey* indicates too, that far from clinging anachronistically to the values of that decade, Bush also sought new musical means for new times.

Lidiče: Memory and Loss in a New Europe

Perhaps no work of Bush's underscores more the transformation of his workers' music aesthetic in the 1940s than the brief unaccompanied choral work *Lidiče*. On 10 June 1942, the Czech mining village of Lidiče was the site of a Nazi atrocity that would earn worldwide notoriety. Following the assassination of Reinhard Heydrich, the 'Butcher of Prague', by a Czechoslovak team of parachutists trained in Britain, the village was falsely suspected of having aided the parachutists. In reprisal, the men of the village were shot immediately, and the women and children were deported, with the majority of the latter gassed at Chełmno on the orders of Adolf Eichmann. The village itself was razed to the ground, the space it had occupied renamed 'Vorwerk' [outlying estate], in an effort to obliterate the town from existence.[23] The village has since formed a special symbol both of memory and resistance. Given that Hitler intended the town to be forgotten, the very *act* of remembering constitutes resistance to Nazism. In the immediate aftermath of international condemnation, towns across the world were renamed Lidiče, and works of literature and music commemorating the village were composed, such as Edna St. Vincent Millay's *The Murder of Lidice* (1942) and Bohuslav Martinů's *Memorial to Lidice* (1943).

In Britain, the wartime home of the Czechoslovak Government-in-Exile, the atrocity prompted a variety of actions at all levels of society. Lidiče could be invoked as a symbol of the need for resistance and solidarity in countries fighting against fascism, with Pollitt mentioning the village in calls for miners to give their all to the war effort.[24] Humphrey Jennings created the 1943 film *The Silent Village*. Made

---

[23] Eduard Stehlík, *Lidice: The Story of a Czech Village*, trans. Peter Kurfürst (Praha: For the Lidice memorial by Jitka Kejřová, 2004), 96–7.
[24] Kevin Morgan, *Harry Pollitt* (Manchester: Manchester University Press, 1993), 135.

for the Ministry of Information, and with the collaboration of the Czechoslovak Ministry of Foreign Affairs in Exile, the film depicted the events of the massacre enacted by the people of the Welsh village of Cwmgiedd. There is no attempt to pretend that the Welsh villagers are the people of Lidiče. Rather, the film's message concerned the horrors that could occur as easily in Wales as in Czechoslovakia, should Hitler win the war. The ending of the film – depicting the men being led away to be shot while singing 'Land of My Fathers' – also highlighted courage and resistance. Such efforts in solidarity, however, could also be concerned with the survival of life. A local councillor in Stoke-on-Trent, Barnett Stross, enlisted local miners' help and founded the 'Lidice Shall Live' campaign in September 1942 to raise funds for the rebuilding of the village.[25] Invoking the same imagery of wartime loss and recovery imagined in sacred terms and explored in *The Winter Journey*, the campaign's posters showed the word 'Lidice' in flames juxtaposed with an image of the new village and church, bathed in light from above. Images of international solidarity in the face of suffering under Nazism, such as those suggested by the WMA's BBC performances, also informed the campaign for years after the cessation of the war. As well as contributing financially to the building of a new village next to the old in 1947, Stross was responsible for the planting of a rose garden between the old and new villages in 1955. Rawsthorne was commissioned to write the choral work *A Rose for Lidiče*, with words by Swingler, which was first performed simultaneously at the opening of the rose garden in 1956 and at a service in Thaxted.[26] The positioning of the rose garden as a bridge between old and new, both a memorial and symbol of life arising from destruction, and the simultaneous Czech and English performances, constituted a complex and powerful gesture of sharing both suffering and healing across international borders.

Bush's *Lidiče* (1947), written to a text by Nancy Bush, is in many respects a piece of workers' music. It is suited to the abilities of an amateur choir, it was published, like most of the composers' workers' songs, by the WMA, and first performed by the WMA Singers on the site of the ruined village.[27] It complemented the WMA's existing expertise in the field of internationalist popular song, and as an expression of hope in

---

[25] See Jessica Rapson, 'Mobilising Lidice: Cosmopolitan Memory between Theory and Practice', *Culture, Theory and Critique* 53/2 (2012), 134–5.

[26] See John McCabe, *Alan Rawsthorne: Portrait of a Composer* (Oxford: Oxford University Press, 1999), 148–9.

[27] The performance, in August 1947, was conducted by Bush and recorded and broadcast by Prague Radio.

the face of fascist destruction, it was topical in the immediate aftermath of war. The introduction to the published score of the work underlined the significance of the composition:

> The crime of Lidice [sic] committed by the German occupying forces on 10th June 1942 is something unprecedented in the history of enlightened humanity [...] The Germans were successful in removing all traces of Lidice, but by that very act they built in the hearts of the peoples of all free nations a new Lidice, an immortal Lidice, a Lidice which shall live![28]

Yet just as *The Winter Journey* transcended the topical wartime accompanied choral works that preceded it, Bush's *Lidiče* went far beyond the austere musical style and calls to political action of his pre-war workers' music.

On the cover of the published score accompanying the introductory text are two photographs. The first, taken from a distance, is of the houses and church of the village prior to the massacre. The second photograph shows all that remained of the village after the war, a scene of rubble and empty fields. It is bold visual expression of emptiness and loss, of what had been utterly destroyed by the 'transformative violence' of the Nazi regime.[29] As Brent J. Steele has argued, the empty space of Lidiče, the 'absence' that the changed landscape bears witness to, is in itself a powerful account of Nazi action.[30] Part of the power of the monument to the children of Lidiče created by Marie Uchytilová is as 'a representation of that which exists no more' in the midst of the 'nothingness' of the landscape.[31] While the text and photographs on the cover of the score of *Lidiče* thus frame the work as dealing with the dichotomy of absence and presence as a mode of resistance, how could this be conveyed by the music in performance? Music is by its very nature an aural *presence*. The solution created by Alan and Nancy Bush encompassed the text, music and first performance of *Lidiče*. In the tripartite structure of Nancy Bush's text, a central section, concerned with the moment of destruction, is framed by two brief outer sections projecting the present silence of Lidiče:

> When the last marching step has gone,
> And the outstretched hands, clenched in agony, were motionless.
> Silence returned to Lidiče.

---

[28] *Lidiče* for mixed voices by Alan Bush, words by Nancy Bush (London: Workers' Music Association, 1947).

[29] Judt, *Postwar*, 40.

[30] Brent J. Steele, *Alternative Accountabilities in Global Politics: The Scars of Violence* (London & New York: Routledge, 2013), 129.

[31] Ibid., 130.

> Voiceless, the threads of smoke crept up
> From smould'ring wood and shattered stone.
> The charred beam falling to the ground
> Alone disturbed the empty noon.
> Men and women, friends and lovers,
> Now had left the valley lonely,
> And the despairing child's last cry,
> As he looked back, an echo only.
> Here ranged along this shallow pit
> The men of Lidiče once stood,
> And here their last glimpse of the world
> Was this green curve of field and wood.
> From the frail cavern of the skull
> Their sightless eyes confront the sky.
> A stare undaunted from the dust,
> Proud men who did not fear to die.
> Man's priceless treasure here lies spilt;
> But from this bitter ash of pain
> An unquenched spirit stirs and springs,
> Renewed to live and burn again.
>
> Now silent Lidiče lies still,
> And stirs not, yet its stones proclaim, ravaged and mute, to all the earth,
> A matchless and immortal fame.

The text thus not only juxtaposes past and present, presence and absence, but dwells on the sounds that connote these two states. Nancy evokes not the visual images of the town but the sounds of destruction – the falling beam, the child's cry – that contrast with the silence of the present. While beginning and ending in silence, the poem is also transformative. In the course of the central section, the images of fire as destructive – another element that formed part of the language of dealing with British wartime experience[32] – is transmuted into a burning spirit. At the same time, the silence of the rocks that, at the opening of the poem, denotes what has been destroyed, becomes a proclamation of the fame of the village: in other words, the resistance of memory to destruction.

Musically, this poetic dialogue of past, present and future, of memory and action, is expressed through a fusion of the intimate language of *The Winter Journey* and *Lyric Interlude* with the aesthetics of the workers' song. *Lidiče* retains many features of Bush's Eislerian songs of the

---

[32] See Mellor, *Reading the Ruins*, 47ff.

1930s: the accessibility of the work for amateur singers, the alternation of major and minor, the marching rhythm, underlined by the first line of text, the simplicity and austerity of harmonic idiom via the frequent avoidance of the third and leading note, and the cell-like melodic units that unify the whole and form the basis of melodic phrases. Yet here they are put to new purposes. Rather than using the minor-major shift as the basis of a crude structural progression from suffering to hope, Bush constantly moves between major and parallel minor, particularly at cadence points. Combined with his established techniques of avoiding root-position chords and the third, and flattening of the leading note, these procedures render the music unsentimental and austere, thus evoking the silence of the present in Lidiče (Ex. 4.6). In a further departure from many of the 1930s workers' songs, Bush avoids a verse and chorus structure, instead matching the text by creating two outer sections which frame a through-composed middle section, producing an A B B^1 B^2 A^1 structure in which the music at each point is sensitive to the character of the poem. At B^1 ('Here ranged along this shallow pit'), for example, the faster tempo and rhythmic character of the section emphasise the marching character of the work, expressing the resolution of the men of Lidiče.

The relationship of past and present is also achieved through the use of procedures seen in *The Winter Journey*. The importance of the subdominant throughout, culminating in the final plagal cadence of the work, give the work an archaic quality shared by the earlier work. Combined with Nancy Bush's biblical allusion in the final section of text – 'its stones proclaim, ravaged and mute' – this also invests the work with the religious quality noted in *The Winter Journey*.[33] In the central 'B' sections, moreover, Bush introduces the parallel fourths and fifths, false relations, and open fifths that invested *The Winter Journey* with its archaic and sacred quality. It is notable that these procedures occur first on 'The charred beam falling'; even as the aural presence of the past is recalled, the music articulates our separation from it. Like the sleepers and ghosts of the bombed city, the lives in Lidiče are absent and unreachable. Most significantly, as in the 'Final Chorale' of *The Winter Journey*, a revelatory cadence occurs at a moment of textual importance, in this case in the final bars of the work as the choir describe 'A matchless and immortal fame' immediately following the resumption of the opening material and musical

---

[33] 'And some of the Pharisees in the multitude said to him, "Teacher, rebuke your disciples." He answered, "I tell you, if these were silent, the very stones would cry out"'. Luke 19:40, Revised Standard Version. I am indebted to Jordan Summers Young for this observation.

Ex. 4.6 Bush, *Lidiče*, opening.

Ex. 4.7 *Lidiče*, closing bars.

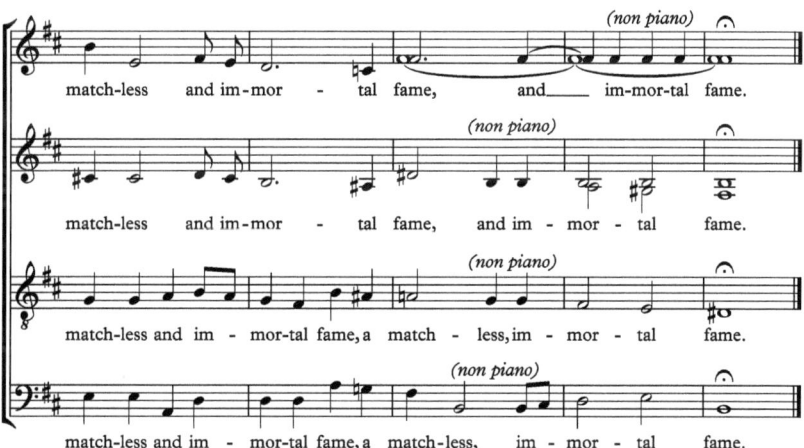

'silence' of Section A[1] ('Now silent Lidiče lies still') (Ex. 4.7). Against the backdrop of the distance of the past and silence of the present, this palpable moment of arrival heralds a future in which Lidiče is remembered and thus still present, reflecting the rhetoric with which the Nazis' attempts to eradicate the village from memory were resisted. Thus, like *The Winter Journey*, *Lidiče* ultimately reveals an ambivalent sense of loss and hope in the face of destruction.

It is no coincidence that *Lidiče* contains so much in literary allusion and musical procedure that bears comparison with the earlier work. The musical construction of the sacred and archaic as a distancing technique, the allusions to fire as both destructive and transformative, and the central juxtaposition of past, present and future – all of these techniques place *Lidiče* firmly within British efforts to deal with the past and the possibilities of the future in the aftermath of war. As British wartime interest in the Lidiče tragedy indicates, the notion of international solidarity, of overcoming the past through shared experience, was not incompatible with this British cultural project. Such sentiments must have been palpable at the first performance of the work, on the site of the old village, without audience and before the project of building the new village had begun.[34] In the performance, the aural presence of the past in the silent space of Lidiče, conjured up by Nancy Bush's poem, was made real. *Lidiče* was and remains a moving act of remembrance, one which mediates European post-war hopes and memory through complex and subtle means.

'Things fall apart'

The Winter Journey and *Lidiče* place Bush within a British cultural moment at the end of the Second World War, in which cultural figures articulated both the suffering of war and the tentative hopes for renewal. This moment encompassed a sense of solidarity among international victims of fascism that prompted the many acts of commemoration for Lidiče, culminating in the twinning of Lidiče and the heavily damaged city of Coventry in 1947. Yet Bush's *Lidiče* is also symbolic of the fragile nature of this solidarity amid the realities of the nascent Cold War. The first performance of *Lidiče* took place during the WMA Singers' participation in the inaugural 1947 World Festival of Youth and Students. This, in turn, came in the midst of two lengthy conducting tours of Eastern Europe undertaken by Bush that year.

Bush had brought about the initial tour, in January 1947, through connections with the Czech Embassy in London, and on the back of a concert of Czechoslovak music he organised at the Wigmore Hall in November 1946. The concert programmes for the tour – in contrast to those pageants and concerts in Britain which constructed narratives of progressive English music or articulated topical messages – were designed with the idea of acquainting audiences with English music, and consisted of Purcell, Boyce, Elgar, and Ireland. While in some concerts, Bush's own *Fantasia on Soviet Themes* and *Overture: Resolution* were included, this was as much a product of his desire to have his own most recent orchestral works performed as an

---

[34] Personal communication from Dr Rachel O'Higgins to the author.

ideological choice; *Lyric Interlude* was also suggested for a chamber concert. In his reflections on the journey, Bush focused on the desirability of friendship and cultural exchange between Britain and Czechoslovakia, especially – in terms reminiscent of British cultural debate – using cultural renewal as an expression of liberation from the oppression of the recent past.

Yet there was also already a political dimension to Bush's rhetoric. Bush spoke of the Czech people's 'dual liberation, both from foreign domination and from the oppression of their own reactionary propertied classes'[35] and the fact that 'the people [of Czechoslovakia, Yugoslavia and Bulgaria] are well on the way to achieving the freedom from care and want which the British people have been fighting for throughout their history'.[36] Liberation in Eastern Europe, in Bush's eyes, was the advent of socialism at the hands of the Red Army. Although, as we have seen, British communists would adapt their ideas to national circumstances, renewal for Bush ultimately meant a socialist Britain on the model he uncritically perceived in Eastern Europe. In the period of the Grand Alliance, Bush had real hopes that international solidarity would produce such an outcome. As he wrote in February 1945:

> The historic Yalta Declaration, with its firm re-statement of solidarity among the United Nations, brings new hope of betterment and peace than [*sic*] one would have thought possible even two years ago. Of course, the reactionary forces in Britain and the USA will work unremittingly for the non-fulfilment of this policy, they will try to sow the seeds of discord between the United Nations, and as far as this country is concerned they are even at this moment trying to tear asunder the comradely unity between ourselves and the Soviet Union. Later these same interests will stir up suspicion of the United States' sincerity in implementing the latter's declaration of intended participation in world affairs. And in this support of fascism all over the world these forces will be helped by their isolationist counterparts in the USA. The situation therefore can only develop its most beneficial potentialities through the active work of everyone in every country. And what a prospect of progress then opens up before us![37]

The naivety of Bush's call for mass popular support for socialism led by the Soviet Union is obvious. In October 1947, when Bush made his second

---

[35] Alan Bush, 'A Musician in Eastern Europe' (undat.), ABH, 1.
[36] Alan Bush, 'A Musical Journey through the Balkans', *Changing Epoch* 1 (1947), copy held in ABH, 22.
[37] Alan Bush to 'Lydia, Dick and Dickie' [relatives], 1 March 1945, photocopy of original, ABH.

visit, Czechoslovakia was already in the grip of the increasing Sovietisation that would culminate in the coup of February 1948. Czech efforts to commemorate Lidiče would be misappropriated by the ruling Communist Party in coming years. In 1952, for example, the platform built in Lidiče for prominent figures to speak at the annual memorial bore a portrait of Stalin and protests against West German re-armament and the Korean War.[38] Yet Bush, oblivious to the enforced nature of the change, continued to adumbrate a narrative of international friendship and a 'bottom-up' transition to socialism. In a programme he selected for Prague Radio, he created a narrative of historical and contemporary progressive action: his own work *Piers Plowman's Day*, depicting the Peasant's Revolt, Ireland's *These Things Shall Be* and Khatchaturian's *Song of Stalin*.[39]

In Britain, too, the disparity between Bush's communist vision of post-war reconstruction and the circumstances of the Cold War became increasingly marked. The year 1948 was marked by a curtailing of the most significant facet of his wartime career: his work with the BBC. In the midst of a crackdown on communists working for the corporation in March and April 1948,[40] the BBC wrote to MI5 requesting a report on Bush's political views, and consequently placed a restriction on his employment as a speaker, although not as a musician.[41] Bush's work for the BBC had been, ultimately, a marriage of convenience prompted by wartime alliances, and unsurprisingly ended when those alliances collapsed into open hostility. Nevertheless, in the first few uncertain, hopeful post-war years, Bush's two works of mourning and expectation evoked an image of a European future that was profoundly of its time, and through which the composer transformed the rhetoric and techniques of his 1930s songs. By reinventing the language of his most political works in the service of more ambiguous statements about suffering and renewal, Bush placed himself, however briefly, at the centre of British culture in the aftermath of war.

---

[38] Stehlík, *Lidice*, 128.

[39] 'Talk by Alan Bush' [typescript with handwritten note: 'Given 16 October 1947 from Czech Radio, Prague and broadcast to England'], ABH.

[40] See John Jenks, *British Propaganda and News Media in the Cold War* (Edinburgh: Edinburgh University Press, 2006), 44ff.

[41] N.E. Wadsley (BBC) to Major Badham (MI5), 2 April 1948, TNA/ PRO KV2/3516: Bush, Alan D., Item 125a.

5 Bush as Stalinist: The Year 1948

SCHAFER: Who accused you of formalism?
BUSH: I accused myself.[1]

It is impossible to pinpoint the moment at which the cultural Cold War began. In hot spots like Germany, rival visions of post-war culture were being laid out before the end of the Second World War, and concert life in competing zones resumed almost as soon as the conflict was over.[2] Frances Stonor Saunders has pointed to the key role in promoting the American vision of culture of the Congress for Cultural Freedom, a CIA-led initiative that started to be formed in 1947.[3] In the sphere of music, no events of the 1940s were more decisive and notorious than the actions taken against Soviet musicians in 1947–8. In November 1947, the Party leadership attended a performance of Vano Muradeli's opera *The Great Friendship*. Their displeasure at the performance occurred in the midst of the *Zhdanovshchina*, a series of cultural purges undertaken by Stalin's close associate Andrei Zhdanov in response to the former's post-war reassertion of ideological opposition to the capitalist world. After convening a meeting with leading figures of Soviet music in January 1948, Zhdanov prepared the notorious Central Committee resolution of 10 February 1948. Focusing on the 'defects' of Muradeli's opera, the document mounted a broader attack on the 'formalistic, anti-national school' of Shostakovich, Prokofiev, Khachaturian and others, whose music was purportedly characterised by:

> the negation of basic principles of classical music; the preachment of atonality, dissonances and disharmony, supposedly representative of 'progress' and 'modernism' in the development of musical forms; the rejection of such all-important concepts of musical composition as melody, and the infatuation with the confused, neuropathological combinations which transform music into cacophony, into a chaotic agglomeration of sounds. This music is strongly reminiscent of the spirit of contemporary modernistic bourgeois music of

---

[1] Schafer, *British Composers in Interview*, 58.
[2] See Toby Thacker, *Music after Hitler, 1945–1955* (Aldershot: Ashgate, 2007), 17ff.
[3] Frances Stonor Saunders, *Who Paid the Piper? The CIA and the Cultural Cold War*, 2nd edn (London: Granta, 2000), 1–2.

Europe and America, reflecting the dissolution of bourgeois culture, a complete negation of musical art, its impasse.[4]

In the Soviet Union, the immediate consequences of the document were the reorganisation of the leadership of the Composers' Union and an intensifying series of attacks on the 'formalists'. The longer-term effect was the lasting reassertion of 'realism' and – in light of the vagueness of the characterisation of formalism – the stifling of musical creativity. Internationally, and not least in Britain, the Soviet crisis was profoundly significant for the international reputation of Soviet music and composers of other nations who identified therewith.[5] During formal discussion between Zhdanov and Soviet composers in February 1948, Tikhon Khrennikov condemned the 'universal dissolution and spiritual impoverishment of bourgeois culture', mentioning Stravinsky, Messiaen, Hindemith, Krenek, Berg, and Britten.[6] Thus, months after a British choir performed *Lidiče* as a gesture of anti-fascist solidarity within the emerging Communist Bloc, the leading composer of post-war Britain was named in an assertion of ideological and musical opposition.

In certain respects, Bush is easy to situate within this changed situation. While slow to respond publicly to the Soviet crisis, he became irrevocably convinced of the rectitude of both the attacks on composers and the aesthetic recommendations of the Resolution, even following the partial rescindment of the latter in 1958.[7] Even more notoriously, Bush spoke passionately in later years of the changes the Soviet crisis had engendered in his music, prompting a new determination to 'bring out a national character in my music'.[8] Nor were critics slow to connect Bush's support of the *Zhdanovshchina* with the musical and ideological content of his works. The *Daily Telegraph* critic Martin Cooper undertook what would become a sustained critique of Bush's major works after 1948. He commented that the popular fair depicted in the finale of Bush's 1949 'Nottingham' Symphony was 'attended by those same Stakhanovites and Heroes of the Soviet Union who haunt the finales of modern Russian

---

[4] Cited in Nicolas Slonimsky, *Music since 1900* (London: Cassell, 1972), 1359–1360.
[5] For extensive accounts see Alexander Werth, *Musical Uproar in Moscow* (London: Turnstile Press, 1949), and Kiril Tomoff, *Creative Union: The Professional Organization of Soviet Composers, 1939–1953* (Ithaca, N.Y.: Cornell University Press, 2006), chs. 4 and 5.
[6] Cited in Slonimsky, *Music since 1900*, 1366.
[7] The resolution 'On Rectifying Errors in the Evaluation of the Operas *Great Friendship, Bogdan Khmelnitzky*, and *From All One's Heart*' was adopted on 28 May 1958, although it merely admitted errors and excesses in the denunciation of certain composers, without rescinding any of the aesthetic principles expressed. See Boris Schwarz, *Music and Musical Life in Soviet Russia, 1917–1970* (London: Barry & Jenkins, 1972), 311–12.
[8] Schafer, *British Composers in Interview*, 59.

symphonies'.[9] Reviewing Bush's second opera, *Men of Blackmoor*, in 1960, Cooper implicitly compared Bush himself to the puppet-like characters in his opera, 'whose behaviour depends not on the ordinary principles of human motivation, but on the political labels arbitrarily attached to them [by their creator]'.[10] In Cooper's view Bush's music, like Soviet opera, consisted of an uneasy alliance of folk song and late-romantic melody; only where folk song was abandoned did the music gain 'individuality'. As he opined at the end of his review of the 'Nottingham' Symphony: 'Alas for the composer of *Dialectic!*'[11]

While Cooper's reviews are an egregious example of negative criticism, they are indicative of the binary oppositions that have characterised discussion of Bush's relationship to the Soviet crisis, oppositions with a much wider currency. Underlying Cooper's critique are two accusations: firstly, that Bush regressed stylistically, and secondly, that such a willingly undertaken, politically motivated action was tantamount to a rejection of artistic integrity, the very loss of musical self. With regard to the former, numerous commentators both condemnatory and sympathetic have identified similarly a sharp stylistic distinction between early works that were 'modernist', 'Central European', 'chromatic', or 'intellectual' and the later products of Bush's 'accessible' or 'simple and direct' national style.[12] With regard to the latter, the claim that Bush's turn to nationalism after 1948 was tantamount to a forced or voluntary relinquishment of artistic integrity is bound up with accusations of stylistic regression. Schafer, for example, challenged Bush on the accusation that his own post-1948 works were 'less interesting' than the previous ones, as a result of the incursion of politics into artistic conscience.[13] In this way, dichotomies of progression/regression, freedom/control, and national/cosmopolitan have become bound up with Bush's broader allegiance to Soviet ideology.

---

[9] Martin Cooper, 'Music: The Politically Purposeful Symphony', *Spectator*, 19 December 1952, 843.

[10] Martin Cooper, 'Puppets in the Cause of Realism', *Daily Telegraph and Morning Post*, 3 December 1960, 11.

[11] Cooper, 'Music: The Politically Purposeful Symphony', 843.

[12] Arthur Hutchings, for example, although sympathetic to Bush, wrote: 'Why, since he admired Schoenberg and actually used twelve-note themes in two movements of his C major Symphony, did Bush decline to join the radical serialists? Plainly for reasons which are bound up with his acceptance of Soviet composers' manifestos concerning proletarian understanding of ambitious music'. See Arthur Hutchings, 'Music in Britain: 1918–1960' in Martin Cooper (ed.), *New Oxford History of Music: The Modern Age, 1890–1960*, vol. X (London: Oxford University Press, 1974), 523.

[13] Schafer, *British Composers in Interview*, 63.

Despite the force of his own rhetoric, there are significant reasons to doubt the veracity of this model of Bush's response to the events of 1948. Given the discussion of the previous chapter, how did Bush reach this position of enmity to Western values from his eager vision of British socialism and solidarity with the East a few months earlier? Stonor Saunders has described:

> an assorted group of former radicals and leftist intellectuals whose faith in Marxism and Communism had been shattered by evidence of Stalinist totalitarianism [...] their disillusionment was attended by a readiness to join in a new consensus, to affirm a new order which would substitute for the spent forces of the past. The tradition of radical dissenter, where intellectuals took it upon themselves to probe myths, interrogate institutional prerogative, and disturb the complacency of power, was suspended in favour of supporting "the American proposition".[14]

Perhaps Bush, around 1948, may be seen as the photographic negative of such figures, similarly moving from the experiments of the 1930s to the hardened aesthetics of the 1940s on the Soviet side. And yet the Red Army generated genuine enthusiasm in wartime Britain, and the CPGB trebled its membership, retaining large numbers of its intellectuals. Bush himself remained loyal to the Party throughout the wartime challenges. Furthermore, in that period, the composer developed communist musical policy for Britain with a high degree of autonomy. If, after 1948, Bush abdicated his intellectual individuality for a 'Soviet proposition', how did this marry with his work in a peculiar national climate? At the heart of assessments like Cooper's lies an uneasy conflation of (collectivist) nationalism and Marxism as categories in opposition to Western cosmopolitanism, individual autonomy, and modernity. As Benedict Anderson has cogently observed, 'nationalism has proved an uncomfortable *anomaly* for Marxist theory, and precisely for that reason, has been largely elided, rather than confronted. How else to explain Marx's failure to explicate the crucial adjective in his memorable formulation of 1848: "The proletariat of each country must, of course, first of all settle matters within *its own* bourgeoisie"?'[15]

Bush's situation as a communist intellectual able to act with relative freedom, working within the peculiar cultural priorities of post-war Britain, was unique. Rather than being shoehorned into the broad divisions of the incipient Cold War, his actions around 1948 demand comprehensive

---

[14] Stonor Saunders, *Who Paid the Piper?*, 2.
[15] Benedict Anderson, *Imagined Communities: Reflections on the Origin and Spread of Nationalism*, rev. ed. (London & New York: Verso: 2006), 3–4 (Anderson's emphases).

reassessment; the meaning of such key terms as 'national' and 'modern' must be newly interrogated in his case. This chapter examines the events of 1948 and situates them in the context of Bush's ongoing development as composer and communist. Rather than arguing for either loyalty or independence on his part, this chapter employs new research on communist subjectivity to interpret Bush's choices as part of his developing communist *selfhood*. In contrast to previous accounts, this unfolding political self-consciousness is not examined as an abrupt change in 1948, but traced backwards in Bush's political and musical thought from the late 1930s onwards. Indeed, what becomes apparent is the impossibility of separating Bush's growing political and musical ideas, as both were bound up with his sense of his musical and moral responsibilities in an era of crisis.

Bush and the Soviet Union in 1948

Assessing the immediate impact of the Soviet crisis on Bush, or even the quality of his information regarding it, is difficult. Although Bush visited the Soviet Union in 1938 and 1939, carried out an energetic wartime correspondence with Shneerson, and met a number of Soviet musicians including Shostakovich in Prague in 1947, Shneerson's letters abruptly ceased that same year until 1958, and it was only during the Prague Congress in May 1948 that Bush would meet any Soviet colleagues again. Nevertheless, Bush had links with both the Soviet Embassy and the 'Society for Cultural Relations with the USSR' (hereafter, SCR), and through these channels had detailed access to official accounts of the Soviet events distributed by VOKS.[16] With these tools in hand, Bush became a voluble defender of the CPSU's actions.[17]

There is no reason to suppose any coercion or immediate obligation upon Bush to change his style, either from the Soviet Union or through the CPGB. It was Bush himself who suggested discussion of the events at a Musicians' Branch meeting in March 1948, and this resulted in no immediate action.[18] In 1949, the Party was embroiled in the 'Battle of

---

[16] Bush refers to the 'official V.O.K.S. translation' in his review of Werth's book. See Alan Bush, 'A Remarkable Document', *Anglo-Soviet Journal* 10/3 (Autumn 1949), 20.

[17] In addition to the review of Werth, Bush wrote several articles on the controversy and planned a pamphlet presenting the documents with commentary. See Alan Bush, 'Soviet Music', *Anglo-Soviet Journal*, vol. 10, No. 1 (Spring 1949), 32–4; Alan Bush, 'Problems of Soviet Musical Theory', *Modern Quarterly* 5/1 (1949–50), 38–47; Alan Bush to Maurice Cornforth, 23 March 1950, BL/AB MS Mus. 467, Miscellaneous Correspondence January–June 1950, vol. 1.

[18] Alan Bush to ? ['Dear Comrade'], 18 March 1948, ABH.

Ideas', a new post-war phase of CPGB politics which characterised the world as divided into two ideological camps and proposed to defend national culture and Soviet-led aims for world peace against 'the violent struggle of Wall Street for world domination'.[19] By May, the Party's National Cultural Committee (NCC) was becoming keener on helping its cultural workers work out 'a Communist line of advance to help them fight reactionary ideas', and convened a 'Special Closed Meeting for Party Musicians on The Battle of Ideas in the Musical World' that would report back to the NCC.[20] Yet it was left to Bush to determine the substance of the meeting, and it was he who decided that the Soviet criticisms must be the main topic of discussion.[21] When he published a pamphlet on 'Marxism and the Battle of Ideas, with Special Reference to the World of Music' in 1950, it consisted substantially of a Marxist reading of the origins and social function of music in terms Bush had been developing since the mid-1940s. While Zhdanov's actions were defended and the principle of art being 'directed along the lines of national tradition' reasserted, Bush had remarkably little to say about how such a directive might be addressed by British musicians. It was only with the formation of the CPGB Music Group in 1955 that a new formal plan of action for Party musicians was drawn up by Bush, and even here no directives were aimed at composers.[22]

This evidence immediately suggests a more gradual, thoughtful response to the Soviet Resolution. Embracing this view, Julie Waters has argued that a far more influential event was the Second International Congress of Composers and Musicologists, held in Prague in May 1948. Having already attended the lesser-known First Congress the previous year, Bush was invited by the organising Syndikat Ceskych Skladatelu (Syndicate of Czech Composers) to 'help us [...] to build up the constant tradition of these Congresses contributing not only to the development of music but also forwarding the deeper understanding among the nations and fortifying the World's peace'.[23] Under the Congress title 'Tendencies in the Development of Music', delegates were asked to choose from a selection of pre-ordained

---

[19] James Gardner, 'The Battle of Ideas and the Importance of Theory', *Communist Policy to Meet the Crisis*, Report of the 21st National Congress of the Communist Party, November 1949, Marxists Internet Archive, accessed 5 February 2014, https://www.marxists.org/history/international/comintern/sections/britain/congresses/21/05.htm

[20] Alan Bush to Benjamin Frankel, 23 May 1949, ABH.

[21] Alan Bush to Sam Aaronovitch, 17 May 1949, ABH.

[22] See 'Music Group of the Communist Party', *Music and Life* [Journal of the CPGB Music Group] I/1 (April 1956), n.p.

[23] Syndikat Ceskych Skladatelu [Syndicate of Czech Composers] to Alan Bush, 24 January 1948, BL/AB MS Mus. 655, Correspondence with the Society for the Promotion of New Music and the Syndikat Ceskych Skladatelu.

titles on which to lecture, including modern music, national traditions, and methodology of music criticism. Following a gruelling ten days of discussions, including Bush's paper on 'The Structure and Expression of Modern Music', a written Declaration was produced, signed by a Praesidium of delegates including Bush, Stevens, Eisler, and Khrennikov, Yarutovsky and Shaporin from the Soviet Union.[24] The document identified a 'profound crisis' in contemporary music, characterised by a conflict between 'serious' and 'light' music.[25] It advocated a series of measures to be undertaken by composers, including renouncing 'the tendencies of extreme subjectivism', turning towards 'national culture' against the 'cosmopolitan tendencies of contemporary life', showing preference for "concrete" musical forms such as opera, oratorio, cantata and song, and becoming 'active and practical workers in the musical education of their peoples'.

There are clear shades of the Soviet Resolution here, and the Declaration was said to have been effectively prepared in Moscow. Yet, as Waters argues, the turmoil in Moscow may actually have reduced the Soviet role: the CPSU initially refused the Soviet composers permission to attend, and their departure was delayed.[26] Nor did delegates report the overweening influence of the Soviet contingent in preparing the Proclamation. Bush himself, never reluctant to credit the Soviet Union, claimed that Eisler drafted the document, while a number of others ascribed an important role to the Western delegates in general, and Bush in particular. Waters suggests that because his paper addressed issues of music theory rather than nationalism, with respectful mentions of Schoenberg and Hindemith, he was not 'seeking to fall in line' with the Soviet Resolution in every respect.[27] Certainly, the Prague document, written by composers, not Party officials, was less prescriptive regarding new musical styles and more idealistic than the Soviet Resolution. Bush and Stevens were enthusiastic upon their return regarding the spirit of free and open exchange between composers at the conference, and for the possibilities for shared action that could profoundly influence musical life.

Reasons for Nationalism

Waters' account of Bush's involvement in the Prague Congress is persuasive in its argument for Bush's active participation in the process rather

---

[24] 'Declaration of the Second International Congress of Composers and Musicologists in Prague', 29 May 1948, reproduced in Slonimsky, *Music since 1900*, 1378–9.
[25] Slonimsky, *Music since 1900*, 1378.   [26] Waters, 'Against the Stream', 158–62.
[27] Ibid., 153.

than unthinking acceptance of Soviet aesthetic doctrine. However, with regard to the central claims surrounding Bush and 1948 – regression of style and relinquishment of self – her account leaves questions remaining. While Waters argues that the watershed event was Prague, not Moscow, and that Bush did not simply seek obeisance to Soviet policy, the essential stylistic dichotomy between pre-1948 modernism and a post-1948 'more direct', 'national and accessible' idiom remains intact.[28] This reading is in part a product of Waters' case studies of the first three symphonies, and in particular the contrast between the *Symphony in C* (1939–40) with its palpably 'modernist' use of a twelve-note row in the first two movements, and the 'Nottingham' Symphony that attracted Cooper's condemnation for its socialist realist qualities. A passage indicative of the broader sweep of Waters' argument is her interpretation of the start of the second movement of the *Symphony in C*, in which a modal theme is combined with a version of the tone row:

> By juxtaposing English and romantic style elements with a twelve-tone row, Bush created a situation whereby the tone row effectively provides an ironic comment, albeit subtle, on the modal melody. Bush's strategy was arguably to undercut the English pastoralism implied in the modal idiom, and to prevent an audience from being lulled into escapist modes of listening.[29]

By conflating the use of a modal idiom with 'English pastoralism', she thus interprets the twelve-note element as an ironic, distancing commentary on a bourgeois musical topic. More widely, the passage reinforces the division of features associated with a national style and those associated with modernism in Bush's music.

Yet even at the stage of writing the *Symphony in C*, his attitude to the use of folk song and modes in composition was far from clear cut. In a 1936 article, for example, Bush was particularly scathing about using folk song because of its 'romantic associations of an idyllic pre-capitalist era'.[30] Yet he used a modal idiom throughout his piece of Gebrauchsmusik, the *Three Contrapuntal Studies* of 1931. Again in 1936, he was discussing the possibility of programmes of workers' music which contrasted 'the usual (sentimental, sweet) type of folk songs, part songs, etc. with a type of more aggressive revolutionary folk songs and part songs'.[31] In a 1942 essay, Bush went much further in his assertion of the 'immense importance' of folk music:

---

[28] Ibid., 220, 153.   [29] Ibid., 105–6.
[30] Bush, 'Music and the Working-Class Struggle', 650.
[31] Bush, 'Notes on the Problems of Workers' Music', 3.

It is the basis, and must be the basis of all vigorous and stimulating art – has it not been the saviour of music during a good many crises of "official art", flowing on quietly underneath and keeping alive great traditions where the art of the rulers failed to further inspire its rulers.[32]

On the basis of a historical survey ranging from the catacombs of Rome to modern-day working-class movements, he went on to argue that 'all progressive movements in particular have developed their own folk songs' and to point out the importance of folk song for composers ranging from Mozart to Mussorgsky.[33] Bush directly acted on this belief in the music he chose for pageants of the late 1930s. The pageant of the 1939 Festival of Music for the People, for example, included songs of the Chartists and Diggers, and the 'Cutty Wren', which was associated with the Peasants' Revolt. Even more curiously, in his notes for a set of lectures on English music, almost certainly from 1938,[34] he remarked on the use of English folk music by his much-admired teacher, John Ireland and even characterised his own music as 'Folksong/Central Europe'. To return briefly to the *Symphony in C*, given that Bush already considered folk song especially characteristic of the working classes, and that the second movement was a programmatic representation of the 'suffering' working class,[35] one may question the idea that the modal melody was supposed to be debunked. On the contrary, his 1942 essay suggested that his theoretical commitment to the revolutionary character of folk song, and its potential to bridge art and popular music, was already in place. Moreover, this evidence as a whole reveals the difficulty of applying the term 'national' to Bush's music in a uniform manner. English folk song, depending on the type, could prop up bourgeois culture or sound the keynote of popular resistance.

Further problems surround the question of how far Bush's post-1948 national style was the product of acquiescence to the Soviet decrees or a response moderated by an abiding interest in modern composers. Firstly, what did fidelity to the Resolution mean for a British composer living, however reluctantly, under capitalism? In Marxist theory at least, Britain in 1948 was still in the death throes of capitalism, with a nascent revolutionary

---

[32] Bush, 'Marxism and Music', 7–8. [33] Ibid., 7–8.
[34] Alan Bush, 'Handwritten Notes for a Lecture on English Music', undat. [?1938], ABH. While the notes are undated, some of the material is written on the notepaper of a New York hotel, Bush having visited the USA only once, in 1938. In addition, his survey of younger composers is notable for the lack of mention of Tippett, and for the subsidiary position allotted to Britten, which surely would not have been the case were the notes from the post-war period.
[35] Bush, cited in Waters, 'Against the Stream', 80.

popular socialist movement which Bush was duty-bound (as an individual communist) to use his skills to support. In the Communist Bloc, on the contrary, culture *in practice* then consisted of the subjugation of the intelligentsia for the preservation of Soviet power and influence against the West. Frolova-Walker has spoken of the 'art of boredom', that is, the aptness of crushingly dull Socialist Realist ceremonial music of the 1940s for a society of actually existing socialism that cultivated unthinking obedience over creative participation.[36] Bush tacitly acknowledged the distinction between conditions of capitalism and socialism in his response to the Resolution:

> Bourgeois civilization is now in its last stages. Hence its art can be no other than an art which expresses 'the decay of bourgeois culture'. In socialist society, on the other hand, the art will be the art of socialist realism. To create this art the Soviet composers must search for new ways of expression, since this is a new art.[37]

There is strong evidence that Bush perceived a distinction between the condemnation of composers within a functioning socialist state, and musical practice in those nations either newly communist or, like Britain, potentially so. Bush's tours of Eastern Europe in the immediate post-war years were highly influential in this regard. A particularly revealing anecdote occurs in Bush's account of his arrival in Yugoslavia, published early in 1948. During a stopover at a railway station, Yugoslavs spontaneously engaged in folk dancing, and subsequently:

> a young soldier came forward and sang for us the folk-songs and partisan songs of his district to his own accordion accompaniment. In a most dignified way he refused any remuneration – though he accepted a drink – he wished only to introduce us to the songs of his country as we were his country's guests. [...] I wish I could convey the happiness I felt during the two months I was away. Unless you have experienced it, it is difficult to imagine what it is like to see men and women creating societies where richer opportunities for all are unfolding every day, where greater material welfare is being made available to all, and where an uncomplicated but noble outlook informs a whole community. It is not only that the people of these three countries are free from the unspeakable horrors of Nazi domination and are therefore enjoying the opportunity to live as they were living before. In the process of liberation they have all overcome [...] the contradictions of their own pre-war social conditions, contradictions inherent both in the unfettered

---

[36] Marina Frolova-Walker, 'Stalin and the Art of Boredom', *Twentieth-Century Music* I/1 (March 2004), 101–24.

[37] Bush, 'A Remarkable Document', 19.

capitalism of Czechoslovakia and in the semi-feudal dictatorships of Yugoslavia and Bulgaria.[38]

What this instance of spontaneous popular musical expression represented for Bush can scarcely be overstated. It was the cultural promises of socialism made manifest, the very process of history in action in the triumph of Soviet-inspired socialism over the most extreme form of capitalism in Nazism.

This was exactly the kind of cultural future which Bush envisaged in post-war Britain. Another facet of life witnessed on his tour was the foregrounding of native art music through state planning of concert life, a subject Bush had been canvassing on vociferously throughout the wartime period. At this juncture, he was still optimistic for a socialist post-war Britain based not only on the fact of the Anglo-Soviet wartime alliance, but also on the progress made towards greater state planning through the foundation of ENSA, CEMA, and, subsequently, the Arts Council. Where, in the 1930s and early part of the war, Bush situated his artistic efforts within a highly oppositional working-class culture, in the 1940s his model of socialist culture had changed. In 1945 the Workers' Music Association published a document after the manner of the Beveridge Report, *A Policy for Music in Post War Britain*, and while Bush was not identified as the author, his dominant position in the organisation and close association with the organisers make it highly likely that he influenced and approved the booklet at the very least. In the course of a comprehensive survey of British musical life, calling for state support and fostering of music-making at every level, the document makes two highly pertinent assertions. Firstly, quoting Elie Siegmeister's *Music and Society* regarding the ideal role of the composer in a post-war, democratic Britain:

> The composer of the people's movement and of the collective society will utilize all the skills and techniques he has inherited from the past to write not luxury music for the few, but music which shall be of, for, and about the many. His is the task of *breaking down the age-old division between learned or art music on the one hand, and folk or popular music on the other.* In doing so he will be helping to break down the class division which these musical divisions have symbolised and helped to perpetuate. It will also be his task to unite learning and popularity into an art which must become a broad instrument of social enlightenment and change.[39]

---

[38] Bush, 'A Musician in Eastern Europe'.
[39] *A Policy for Music in Post War Britain* (London: Workers' Music Association, 1945), 12 (my emphasis).

And in the concluding remarks:

> The free peoples stood up to Fascism and they beat it. To do so they had to get together, nationally and internationally, whatever their class, whatever the colour of their ideas. [...] certainly this getting together, this national unity, led to a great reawakening of pride in the traditions and the national culture of the free nations. And it led also to a keen thirst for knowledge of the culture and traditions of other people too, the people one was fighting alongside. As we see it, this is something to encourage. We need to work with other nations no less closely in peacetime than in war. The more we understand of our friends the better chances we have of lasting peace.[40]

The assertions here – the identification of a breach between serious and popular music, the call to embrace national traditions in the wake of war, and the identification of internationalism as a route to peace – would all prove to be important elements of the Prague Congress and Resolution. Three years before the Congress, therefore, Bush already envisaged a new nationalist musical culture in Britain, embracing the principles the Congress would promulgate. It is noteworthy that in the opinion of the WMA as expressed in the *Policy*, while national music may foster accessibility in the sense of popularity, the call to 'unite learning and popularity' suggests the opposite of simplification, at least in principle. Moreover, the cultivation of national music was part and parcel of global cultural exchange. In the years leading up to 1948, then, Bush already viewed folk song as an element of his own style. He was also invested in the cultivation of national musical culture as a union of art and popular music that was called for by the Soviet Resolution and, in Bush's opinion, was already being created in the new socialist nations of Eastern Europe.

The idea that Bush actively cultivated an individual response to the Resolution, that he did not seek to fully fall into line, must, however, be treated with caution. Those actions that appear to show a less-than-full acceptance of the Resolution – his speech on theory to the Prague Congress, his previous interest in nationalism – may be put down to his perception of the document as primarily a critique of musical culture unfolding under the conditions of socialism. While, due to his unique circumstances and personal interpretation of Marxist theory and Soviet policy in his own situation, an individual response is what occurred, it is important not to view this as an assertion of independence on the part of the composer. After all, he never disavowed the Resolution publicly, and this was entirely in keeping with his concept of personal freedom.

---

[40] Ibid., 20.

Writing to Rajani Palme Dutt (at the time another aging hardliner in the CPGB) in the wake of the 1968 Soviet invasion of Czechoslovakia, Bush stated that he was:

> rather cynical about the demands for freedom under socialism which are fashionable at the moment, even [...] in our British Party. I agree with Gus Hall, who was quoted as having said: 'We are for the defence of socialism. We are for the development of a democratic structure that is in keeping with the advancement of socialism. We are for freedom. But we are not for the freedom of those who endanger socialism'.[41]

Even when other CPGB members left the Party in droves, in no instance among the crises of the post-war period would Bush criticise the Soviet Union's actions. At the CPGB's 25th Congress in April 1957, Alan Bush was one of a minority to vociferously defend the Soviet intervention in Hungary. He was the only member of the Party's NCC to vote in support of the Executive Committee's policy on Hungary, and, in the face of some ambivalence among his British comrades, he used his contacts in East Germany to present an Eastern European perspective – and apologia – for the Soviet intervention in the communist publication *World News and Views*.[42] Bush's unshakeable belief that he had witnessed socialism in action in Eastern Europe led him to argue consistently that the uprising of 1956, for example, could be laid at the door of 'fascist' elements. To raise Bush's most shocking political opinions at this juncture is not to evoke the image of Bush as unthinkingly supportive of any caprice of Soviet policy, but it does reveal the care that must be taken over his conception of concepts of 'freedom' and 'independence', as with his views on 'nationalism'. What is needed is a conception of Bush's actions that make sense both of the freedom of individual action he enjoyed and his sense of collective responsibility towards the ideals of socialism.

Forging an Identity

Addressing precisely this difficulty of navigating traditional and revisionist conceptions of individual agency, Hellbeck has constructed a productive model of communist selfhood through his study of Stalin-era personal diaries.[43] Hellbeck charts the surprising extent to which, even in private

---

[41] Alan Bush to Rajani Palme Dutt, 28 September 1968, ABH.
[42] Copy of F.4/KAFH Report on The Cultural Committee of the British Communist Party, mentioning Alan BUSH, 14 December 1956, TNA/PRO KV 2/3519: Bush, Alan D., Item 277z.
[43] Hellbeck, *Revolution on My Mind*.

diaries, Soviet citizens reflected on such topics as their own inadequacy as socialists, and their efforts to conquer personal feelings and priorities so as to embrace Soviet life more fully. Rather than escaping into a private sphere through diaries, Soviet writers 'revealed an urge to write themselves into their social and political order'.[44] As Hellbeck describes, in the communist state, not only humanity and society as a whole, but individuals were to be transformed. The Stalinist dream transformed the passive, oppressed workers of capitalism 'into conscious producers of their own "fate," into real architects of their own future'.[45] Yet this future, of course, was the collective, ideological goal of bringing about socialism. Thus the individual was not merely a social subject, but raised 'to the level of a historical subject who in his daily life helped implement history's progression toward the perfect future'.[46] Autobiography represented a potent means through which one's progress towards this future collective state of perfection could be charted on a daily basis, through which one could identify and change the self.

While caution is necessary in applying this assessment of Soviet diarists to a British communist composer, there are nevertheless parallels that may be fruitfully pursued. Bush's admission to Schafer, 'I accused myself', is revealing. He went on to describe a 'subconscious' nationalism dating back to his studies with Ireland, which he determined to bring out consciously.[47] In essence, Bush, like Hellbeck's diarists, described his dedication to improving his individual socialist consciousness and realising it through (musical) labour. As important to the parallel as Bush's socialist consciousness is the fact of his *narration* of his own transformation. As Hellbeck argues, the process of viewing oneself as the creator of one's own biography, as a self-determining 'subject over one's own life', was profoundly modern.[48] Rather than regressing from Western individualism, Soviet diarists 'conceived of an ideal form of existence in opposition to the capitalist West, which they perceived as individualist, selfish, narrow-minded, in a word, bourgeois'.[49] Bush not only articulated this journey of rejection of individual habits for collective goals verbally to Schafer, but also in notable works in the decade prior to the Soviet Resolution: the Piano Concerto, *Symphony in C*, and the Violin Concerto, op. 32 (1946–8). In each of these works, Bush used generic, topical and intertextual references to articulate a struggle with bourgeois subjectivity that eventually gives way to the victory of an active, revolutionary collective. In the two

---

[44] Ibid., 4. [45] Lydia Chukovskaya, cited in Hellbeck, *Revolution on my Mind*, 7.
[46] Ibid., 14. [47] Schafer, *British Composers in Interview*, 59.
[48] Hellbeck, *Revolution on my Mind*, 9. [49] Ibid., 9.

concertos, this is suggested by the resolution of conflict between solo instrument and orchestra (and the choral finale in the Piano Concerto). In both the Violin Concerto and *Symphony in C*, Bush associates a twelve-note row with the bourgeoisie and their social influence in the first two movements, before abandoning it for the final movement's evocation of the revolutionary working class. This is not to suggest that Bush etched his own life crudely into any of the works, but certainly in the years leading up to 1948, he had a marked interest in musical narratives of individual transformation towards collective existence.

The idea of Bush as a modern, self-determining *musical* subject can enable a new and more complete understanding of his actions around 1948. It immediately makes sense of his reaction to the Soviet controversies and his neglect of nationalism during his Prague paper. Notably, in his first article defending the Resolution, in 1949, Bush had far more to say about the avoidance of formalism than the specifics of how one might cultivate nationalism, and his definition was surprisingly devoid of the thinly veiled attacks on modernism that characterised the original:

> If in the music there is such an extreme emphasis on rhythm that melody, harmonic progression, and form are at a discount, if there is too rich a development of the harmony at the expense of the other details of the music, or so strong a dictation by formal construction that the other elements suffer, then in all those cases the composer falls into the danger of formalism and will not produce a work of art which throughout conveys what it was intended by its composer originally to convey.[50]

The most important issue, for Bush, was the notion that such formalism was both the result of a too-distant relationship to the people on the part of the composer, and produced further distance through its (supposed) inability to convey the composer's intentions. He portrayed Soviet composers, supported by State salaries, as 'cushioned', living in a world of professional music and almost never encountering 'the people' except at performances. Nevertheless, Bush also denied that composers were in any way less than impeccably socialist in their *intentions*, and also emphasised that the entire purpose of the Resolution was to make Soviet music even better within an already flourishing musical culture. While Bush's critique was, it hardly need be said, fundamentally misguided about the true nature of the attacks on composers, the basis for it was his sense of the need for composers to engage in individual transformation in the collective interest. Given his emphasis on the luxuries of musical life in the Soviet Union,

---

[50] Bush, 'Soviet Music', 32.

a frequent refrain, it is likely that he saw the controversies as a specifically Soviet problem. Considering, too, his own commitment to national musical culture leading up to 1948 – evident in a slew of works, writings, and performance activities – it was not necessarily immediately obvious to Bush that he had cause for self-criticism.

Bush's commitment to his own musical self-transformation suggests a further means of understanding the composer's aesthetic trajectory in the years around 1948: it suggests the possibility of reading his move towards nationalism not as an abrupt departure, but as a process of rethinking and altering his interests in modern music, which had since the 1930s existed in a complex relationship with his experiments in political music-making. The WMA *Policy* had already identified the need to bridge the gap between serious and popular music in the interests of national culture, but gave no indication as to how composers could achieve this. As his 1949 article on Soviet events makes clear, Bush was keenly aware that socialist goals of allying individual artistic intentions with those of the people involved specific questions of musical style and technique. Consequently, to form a complete picture of his actions in 1948, it is necessary to turn to a consideration of a neglected plank of Bush's interests in the 1940s: his contributions to music theory. Here his brief but cogent efforts indicate a process of rationalising and transforming his own practice that is profoundly relevant to his progress as musical socialist.

Marxist Music Theory

Bush's conclusions on music theory were first fully articulated in a 1946 article on 'The Crisis of Modern Music':

> in this period of increasing human control of the forces of nature and of human society itself to a point of approximately complete humanisation of the world, the adequate and therefore correct musical style must be one which approximates to the complete humanisation of the musical tones, *it must contain in principle only musical tones which are organised thematically.*[51]

These principles – sometimes referred to as 'total thematicization' but more commonly called 'the thematic method' by Bush – have been outlined frequently by commentators, yet their relationship with Bush's emergent interests in nationalism and socialist realism have remained

---

[51] Alan Bush, 'The Crisis of Modern Music', *Keynote* 1/4 (Summer 1946), 6 (Bush's emphasis).

obscure. Indeed, at first glance, even on a purely technical level, Bush's method appears rigid and arbitrary. However, by examining the development of the theory alongside Bush's cultivation of his socialist self, it is possible to trace his efforts to fuse his priorities as a modern composer with his commitment to Marxism.

Bush's creation of a system of composing was the product of his long-standing interest in the nature of modern music. His earliest exposition of his ideas, a 1936 talk delivered to the Musical Association on 'What is Modern Music?' was a radical formulation by the standards of 1930s Britain. There were premonitions of the Prague Congress in Bush's identification of a 'crisis' in modern music manifest in the 'bewilderment' of audiences, the proliferation of modern styles and techniques, and the lack of objective standards of criticism.[52] Yet rather than simply condemning modern music, Bush united modern composers from Berg to Vaughan Williams, observing that 'a modern period is in process of development, that it will be based on scales other than the major and minor, and that it will be polyphonic rather than harmonic'. The pervasiveness of non-tonal scales was apparent not only in the twelve-note method but through the use of 'scales on which the national folk songs of the particular composer are based'. The definition of modern music as 'polyphonic' reflected the Schoenbergian practice of having the same theme provide 'both the horizontal and the vertical structure'. Bush rejected arguments for the continuation of the tonal system based on instant emotional reaction or assumptions about the 'psychological' basis of particular intervals like the fifth or major third. Both the tonal scales and the twelve-note method were, Bush argued, compromises, and therefore arbitrary. Turning to the question of why modern music had arisen at the current time, Bush used a nascent analysis of the social function of music to argue that, aesthetically, what he perceived to be the psychologically escapist music of Schoenberg and Stravinsky belonged to 'decadent romanticism'. The most truly modern music would be new music that was 'conscious of its progressive function in society'.

It is apparent from this that Bush harboured considerable uncertainty regarding the path of modern composition and the future of tonality at this juncture. His most radical pronouncement in the eyes of the assembled Musical Association members was the claim that tonality was an arbitrary, not a natural phenomenon. In spite of this belief, Bush was unwilling to fully endorse Schoenberg's method, on the grounds that it was 'arid and

---

[52] Bush, 'What is Modern Music?' Quotations in this paragraph are from pp. 25 and 29.

Ex. 5.1 Schoenberg, *Klavierstück*, op. 33a, Bush's analysis of the opening chord.

hysterical', revealing both personal taste and an anxiety about a breach between modern composer and public. What his lecture reveals, too, is that it was no impartial critique of major contemporary composers, but one in which Bush's own choices as a composer were already influential. It is clear from his references to his own music in lectures from the 1930s onwards, and above all in his desire to establish himself as modern composer-theorist alongside Schoenberg and Hindemith in 1946, that Bush viewed debate over methods of modern composition as a guide to personal action as much as analysis. The 'non-tonal scales' and polyphonic methods, which he identifies in music ranging from Berg to Vaughan Williams, may be discerned in Bush's own works. In 1934, writing to his pupil Herbert Murrill, Bush enthused about Schoenberg's op. 33a (1929), which he had just analysed:

> I looked into the Klavierstueck, Op 33a (what a fantastic numbering, I suspect that we may look forward to a further piece built up on the same Grundgestalt). You will see that the chords 4, 5 & 6 are the chords 3, 2 & 1 inverted; 1, 2 & 3 form the Grundgestalt, covering all the twelve semitones. The first one is a typical Schoenberg "achtklang" [*sic*], derived from a successive building up in perfect fourths from the bass B, the other three notes being the three highest of the chord, four being left out; (I am writing this without the copy, but believe the first chord to be B, C, F and B flat). The rest of the piece is an unusually obvious development from these three chords.[53]

Notably, Bush analyzes the first chord as an incomplete quartal collection (Ex. 5.1). It is worth recalling Bush's string quartet *Dialectic* (1929) here, which Bush would later identify as his first essay in the thematic method.[54] The initial, unison theme is based around the alternation of stepwise movements and perfect fourths, with the rhythmically stressed notes of the first two bars outlining a four-note quartal collection (Ex. 5.2). The entire work is subsequently woven from Bush's various chromatic alterations, re-orderings and contrapuntal combinations of this basic material to achieve different harmonic and expressive effects. For example, the first

---

[53] Alan Bush to Herbert Murrill, 6 May 1934, BL/AB MS Mus. 651, Correspondence relating to the Royal Academy of Music.

[54] Bush, 'The Crisis of Modern Music', 7.

Ex. 5.2 *Dialectic*, first and second subjects as quartal collections.

Ex. 5.3 *Dialectic*, closing bars.

three notes of the quartal collection are arranged in bar 31, as shown in Ex. 5.2, which in the context of B Phrygian and the string writing creates a lyricism that contrasts with the opening material. To very different effect, at the end of the movement, the three dissonant chords preceding the final unison E delineate the motif of the seventh built up of two perfect fourths both vertically and horizontally (Ex. 5.3).

This brief discussion of Bush's thematic techniques raises similar questions to the discussion of the *Concert Piece* in Chapter 1. It is debatable whether his appreciation of Schoenberg's ideas about serial organisation and motivic permutation achieved a result in his own thematic method that was distinctly different from the modally influenced, expanded harmonic palette employed by composers like Vaughan Williams or Holst. Indeed, when expounding the method Bush mentioned Vaughan Williams as a composer who employed modal scales in an otherwise tonal framework. He had also written regarding the composition of modern workers' songs that scales used should either differ from the major and minor *or* 'the use of the intervals of those scales must be such as to contradict the practice of this previous music'.[55] The quartal collections of *Dialectic* should be interpreted in this context. Nevertheless, this discussion of the string quartet does reveal something about how Bush understood and rationalised his own compositional

---

[55] Bush, 'Music and the Working-Class Struggle', 650.

processes. Within his own broad technical definition, *Dialectic* may be considered modern on the basis that the thematic material dictates both vertical and horizontal dimensions of the work. Moreover, when considering Bush's nationalism and his change of style, it is striking that in *Dialectic*, what is modern by Bush's definition – the use of the quartal collections – could produce more or less dissonance and be put to very different expressive purposes. Bush's concept of the modern in 1936 had the potential to encompass both 'emancipated dissonance' and national musical material.

Hindemith and Caudwell

Against this background of practical and theoretical work, Bush's 'thematic method' as expounded in 1946 was both a proffered solution to the perceived crisis of modern music and a validation of his compositional methods. In reaching this solution in the mid-1940s, two theorists were of unquestionable importance to Bush: Paul Hindemith and Christopher Caudwell. Caudwell was a British communist who had been killed at age twenty-nine while fighting in the Spanish Civil War, but not before he had completed a prolific body of Marxist theory that would prove influential in the CPGB. While Caudwell primarily discussed poetry, Bush applied his ideas to music. Of overwhelming importance to Bush was Caudwell's interpretation of the social function of poetry based on theories of the role of art under 'tribal communism'. Bush, following Caudwell, argued that because human society may be understood in origin as a technique of human survival, man's freedom was therefore defined as 'the extent by which his control of hostile nature exceeds the bare necessity required to preserve his existence'.[56] Sustaining life in the face of nature was the collective goal of tribal society and required collective effort. In Caudwell's argument, art provides a 'social mechanism' to achieve such collective effort, as it enables man to imagine the real world in changed or idealised form, and to articulate such changes emotionally. Thus 'the function of art is to adapt man's emotions to the necessities of social co-operation'[57] and the 'bourgeois' notion of individual freedom in opposition to society is an illusion.[58]

---

[56] Alan Bush, 'The Structure and Expression of Modern Music' [1948], ABH, 1 [photocopy of original typescript article held by National Library of Scotland, Ronald Stevenson Musicological Correspondence, Inventory Acc. 11567].
[57] Ibid., 3.   [58] Ibid., 4.

Caudwell's theory offered a sophisticated Marxist conception of art at a time when Bush was seeking to undertake a more robust social analysis of music. While many of the ideas which Bush openly attributed to Caudwell in his paper for the Prague Congress – the connection between music and labour in tribal music, the concept of music as organising emotional life – were nascent in his article 'Marxism and Music' (1942), Caudwell's writings helped Bush to refine his ideas substantially. In earlier essays, Bush had struggled to apply his assertion of the twofold function of art – as both shaped by society and exercising a formative influence thereon – to concrete examples. His rather crude description of the progressive content of Beethoven's *Missa Solemnis*, and his only partial success in combining a call to revolutionary action with generic conventions in the Piano Concerto are cases in point. By arguing that art drew on man's emotional life and presented it back in an idealised form that could inspire change, Caudwell suggested a means by which Bush could go beyond the creation of works with ostensible political content such as a topical text, without sacrificing the goal of influencing society through his music. As Bush wrote in his Prague paper:

> Man can thus practise or rehearse the changing of the real world in imagination, can live differently in his thoughts and desires, and thus instigate himself to make further changes in the real world, changes which will give him a greater control over the real world. These imaginative creations make up the world of art.[59]

Implicit in this passage is not only the ability of the artist to influence the contemporary world, but his very role in historical change. Caudwell's ideas model the artist as an ideal socialist like those imagined by Hellbeck's diarists: the historical subject who in his daily activity helps to bring about socialism.

Caudwell's books could not answer questions specific to music. Given Bush's beliefs about the social nature of music, cultivating music that was technically modern was still important. Yet how was modern music to inspire collective action, particularly in view of the division between modern composers and audiences, and the proliferation of compositional techniques? It is regarding this quandary that Hindemith's theoretical work *The Craft of Musical Composition* assumed importance for Bush.[60] It is easy to see why Hindemith's work proved attractive. Like Bush, Hindemith was a modern composer

---

[59] Bush, 'The Structure and Expression of Modern Music', 3.
[60] Bush read Hindemith's *Unterweisung im Tonsatz* (published in English as *The Craft of Musical Composition* in 1941) during the war, and studied the theory in some depth with

concerned by the proliferation of techniques and seeking to establish a single legitimate theoretical system. Hindemith's ideas also had an affinity with those of Caudwell, in that he legitimised his system with reference to its basis in Nature and 'primitive music'.[61] At the same time, because he rejected modal scales, for example, as inherently suited only to monody, Hindemith's system was ostensibly a modern progression from ancient practices.

Overturning his 1936 assertion that both tonality and the twelve-note method were arbitrary systems, Bush in 'The Crisis of Modern Music' embraced Hindemith's arguments concerning the natural origins and primacy of the tonal system. Yet he still deemed Hindemith not to have answered the problem of how to compose in the present day. The argument he presented was, consequently, a curious synthesis of the theories of Caudwell, Hindemith and Schoenberg. Following Hindemith, he argued that the interval was a product of nature. The origins of human music, however, lay in the combination of two or more rhythmic and pitched utterances, used by a group in order to organise manual labour.[62] Such basic combinations of stressed and unstressed tones, Bush argued, were the earliest equivalents of 'the basic element of music, the theme'. This act of organisation of musical tones into the theme thus constituted the *humanisation* of musical 'nature'. Given that Bush, following Caudwell, defined human freedom – the ultimate goal of socialism – as collective control of nature, it follows that the method of composition fit for Marxism was one that was tonal and involved complete thematic organisation.

Compared with Schoenberg and Hindemith, this was an under-developed theory, remaining vague concerning implications of the method for harmony. Schoenberg wrote in *Theory of Harmony*:

> Whenever all chords of a complete piece of music appear in progressions that can be related to a common fundamental tone, one can say that the idea of the musical sound (*Klang*) (which is conceived as vertical) is extended to the

---

Hindemith's pupil Franz Reizenstein. See Alan Bush, 'Obituary: Franz Reizenstein, 1911–68'. *The Royal Academy of Music Magazine* 196 (Midsummer 1969), 24–5.

[61] Paul Hindemith, *The Craft of Musical Composition*, Book I: Theoretical Part, trans. Arthur Mendel (New York: Associated Music Publishers, 1941), 14–15.

[62] It is interesting that as early as 1945, the folk-song expert and sometime collaborator with Bush, A.L. Lloyd, rejected the work-song theory of musical origins, writing in the journal of the Workers' Music Association, *Vox Pop* (see A.L. Lloyd, 'Prehistoric Music', *Vox Pop* 2/5 (May 1945), 7–8). Bush nevertheless doggedly espoused the theory for many years, supported not only by Caudwell but also by reading Curt Sachs' *The Rise of Music in the Ancient World* (1943; London: J.M. Dent & Sons, 1944) and his CPGB colleague Professor George Thomson's pamphlet, *Marxism and Poetry* (London: Lawrence & Wishart, 1945).

horizontal plane. [...] It is likewise doubtful whether the aggregate of events in a piece of music must inevitably refer to the fundamental postulate, to the fundamental chord, just because – as I have said – such reference assures good results through formal completeness and agrees with the simplest attributes of the material. It is doubtful, once the question is raised, whether such reference does not agree *just with the simpler* attributes, and especially, whether it still agrees with the more complicated.[63]

Bush never delved into this sort of theoretical question, and as such his theory remained incomplete. Yet for his purposes it was an elegant solution on a number of counts. By reinforcing the principle of complete thematic organisation, it perpetuated his 1936 admiration for Schoenberg as the composer who 'carries out to the completest degree the tendencies of the period',[64] while also permitting him to pursue a preference for tonality that was apparent even then. It was a solution that answered his concerns for addressing both the material and social progress of music; it was a suitably Marxist method which gave concrete instruction that could be adapted to any style of composition. Finally, considering the accusations of regression surrounding Bush's change of style in 1948, it should be emphasised that the thematic method, while conservative in reinforcing a tonal basis, was in no sense a rejection of Bush's previous practice. Rather, like Hindemith's theories in relation to his own music, it represented an attempt to rationalise and justify his existing methods, an effort further demonstrated by his retrospective list of compositions employing the thematic method (including *Dialectic*) in 'The Crisis of Modern Music' (Fig. 5.1).[65] The extent to which Bush pursued his method in the works of the 1940s will be considered presently. It is, however, worth noting already that Bush's Marxist music theory – developed as he pondered both the future of modern music and how to promote national culture – had deep roots in his period of purported 'modernism'.

The Place of the National: The *English Suite*

It remains to be seen how Bush envisaged the place of national music within his compositional method. He did not discuss it in 'The Crisis of Modern

---

[63] There is no evidence beyond his familiarity with the term *Klang* that Bush was acquainted with Schoenberg's pedagogical texts at this stage; he rather based his theoretical assessment on his knowledge of Schoenberg's works. See Arnold Schoenberg, *Theory of Harmony*, trans. Roy E. Carter (Berkeley: University of California Press, 1978), 28.
[64] Bush, 'What is Modern Music?', 26.
[65] See Simon Desbruslais, *The Identity, Application and Legacy of Paul Hindemith's Theory of Music*, DPhil diss., University of Oxford, 2013, 3.

> *Dialectic* for string quartet (1929).
> *Symphony in C* (1939–40)
> *Meditation on a German Song of 1848* (1941)
> *Lyric Interlude* (1944)
> *20 Songs* (1945)
> *English Suite* for string orchestra (1945–6)

Fig. 5.1 Compositions employing the thematic method.

Music' beyond noting the legitimacy of 'modal as well as major or minor forms of tonality' and making the curious assertion that his method was 'available equally to composers of all countries and national peculiarities'.[66] Some enlightening evidence on this subject exists among his preparatory notes for the 1948 compositional textbook, *Strict Counterpoint in Palestrina Style*. In his introduction, Bush remarked that, in tandem with a study of the common-practice era, a study of sixteenth-century polyphony 'makes familiar the freer tonal relations of the ecclesiastical modes, thus opening up possibilities of diatonic chordal progression, of which those available in the harmonic system of the major and minor scales form only a restricted proportion'.[67] This judgement does not necessarily incorporate the modes of folk song, yet his sketch material for *Strict Counterpoint* includes juxtaposed examples of the use of the ecclesiastical modes in both Gregorian chant and English folk song. The notion that sixteenth-century modes may offer the modern composer an expanded harmonic vocabulary was not a precept of Hindemith's, but did reflect influential strands of English music theory and composition of the time.[68] It is no coincidence that Bush had obtained Vaughan Williams's *National Music* in 1946, in which Vaughan Williams argues for an evolutionary connection between folk song and plainsong.[69] In a 1950 talk Bush described Gregorian chant as a form of folk song which had fertilised the tradition of art music due to its origins (he claimed) as music of popular resistance in the early church.[70] R.O. Morris, who taught Tippett, also wrote in his influential study of sixteenth-century counterpoint of the possibilities of music of this period as a modern source of inspiration. Recalling Stravinsky's famous phrase, he described the 'rhythmic freedom and subtlety' of Palestrina and Byrd, of practical interest to composers who

[66] Bush, 'The Crisis of Modern Music', 6–7.   [67] Bush, *Strict Counterpoint*, 3.
[68] Hindemith, *The Craft of Musical Composition*, 49.
[69] On this subject see Anthony Pople, 'Vaughan Williams, Tallis and the Phantasy Principle' in Alain Frogley (ed.), *Vaughan Williams Studies* (Cambridge: Cambridge University Press, 1996), 60.
[70] Alan Bush, 'Tasks of Cultural Workers', *Communist Review*, February 1951, 53.

have been 'slaves of the bar line'.[71] He also suggested the advantage to the composer of studying the modal system due to the contemporary 'outcry against the shackles of the major and minor scale' and their implications for form.[72] All of this not only suggests that the possibility of using national musical material was already implicit in Bush's theory in 1946, but it also suggests that he was already considering such material as a route to enhanced, not restricted, compositional possibilities. Bush's comment about Gregorian chant reveals another possibility: that modal musical material furnished a bridge between the serious and popular, already, as we have noted, a major goal of Bush's post-war musical work and a belief implicit in his comments on folk song in 1942.

The appearance of Vaughan Williams as an influence in this period raises an additional, important observation regarding the place of nationalism in Bush's theory. His theory was expounded just as Bush was achieving unprecedented recognition in national musical life. As discussed in Chapter 3, whereas Bush had engaged with a radical, oppositional, working-class culture in the 1930s, he entered the mainstream in the mid-1940s. This was also a juncture in which other composers of his generation – notably Britten – sought a deeper rapprochement with national culture. In a later article on his teacher and Vaughan Williams' contemporary, Ireland, Bush described learning the contrapuntal techniques of Palestrina and being introduced to English folk song.[73] Arguably, then, Bush's interests in nationalism combined a reconnection with his musical education, consolidation of previous practice through his theoretical work, and renewed commitment to national culture, as well as exploiting the Marxist potential of folk song.

In order to explore these possibilities, an exemplary case for enquiry is Bush's *English Suite* for String Orchestra, op. 28 (1945-6). One of a number of compositions and arrangements produced by Bush for the London String Orchestra, it fits into Bush's wartime and post-war programme of cultivating British musical life. Mellers, who considered the work a 'masterpiece', wrote that 'when Bush was consciously trying to make his toughly thematic idiom more accessible because more

---

[71] R.O. Morris, *Contrapuntal Technique in the Sixteenth Century* (London: Oxford University Press, 1922), 3. The interview in which Stravinsky made his pronouncement is reproduced in F. Lesure, *Le Sacre du Printemps: Dossier de Presse* (Geneva: Minkoff, 1990), 76-7.

[72] Ibid., 5.

[73] Alan Bush, 'My Studies and Friendship with John Ireland' [article written for a John Ireland Centenary Programme broadcast by the BBC in October 1979], ABH.

tonally concordant, and therefore presumptively more congenial to the people'.[74] Given this assertion, and the fact that the work was written just as Bush made the first comprehensive articulation of the thematic method, it is an ideal focus for considering the relationship between Bush's nationalism and his compositional theory leading up to 1948.

The work engages with English musical traditions on a number of levels. It consists of three movements: 'Fantasia', 'Soliloquy on a Sailor's Song' and 'Passacaglia'. The first movement is based on the 'In Nomine', an antiphon of the Sarum rite, which was used as a cantus firmus and first associated with the 'In Nomine' text in John Taverner's mass *Gloria tibi Trinitas* (1530), sparking a rich tradition of English instrumental music of the sixteenth and seventeenth centuries. The second and third are based on folk songs, respectively 'Lowlands, my lowlands' and 'The Cutty Wren', the latter a folk song associated with the English Peasants' Revolt that would have an integral place in *Wat Tyler*.

The 'Fantasia' shows abundant evidence of the thematic procedures witnessed in *Dialectic*. The thematic material is entirely derived from Taverner's cantus firmus, although with considerable freedom. Bush juxtaposes melodic cells drawn from different parts of the cantus firmus, subjecting them to rhythmic and melodic alteration and inversion in counterpoint. There is an intriguing parallel with two of Peter Maxwell Davies's works inspired by the 'In Nomine' twenty years later: *Seven in Nomine* (1965) and *First Fantasia on an* In Nomine *of John Taverner* (1962). As Rupprecht argues, the latter work marked a shift in Davies's music from open questioning of 'national feeling' in art towards a rapprochement with English tradition.[75] Davies disavowed any patriotic motive, emphasising a 'purely musical interest in national forbears'. Nevertheless, like Bush, he weaves the cantus firmus into the contrapuntal texture rather than presenting it as a melody and, his assertions notwithstanding, betrayed a similarly complex relationship to national identity in taking up this particular melodic fragment. In Bush's treatment of the cantus firmus, his stipulation to make every note of every voice part thematically significant is aided by the contrapuntal nature of the writing. For example, the opening four voice entries combine (i) the cantus firmus, (ii) a variation in inversion, (iii) a violin counter-melody freely derived from motif x and (iv) a phrase derived from motif y (Ex. 5.4). In each subsequent section of the movement, the theme and subsidiary material are likewise ultimately derived from the 'In Nomine'.

[74] Wilfrid Mellers, 'Review', *Musical Times* 136/1824 (February 1995), 108.
[75] Rupprecht, *British Musical Modernism*, 264–7.

Ex. 5.4a Bush, *English Suite*, 'Fantasia', cantus firmus.

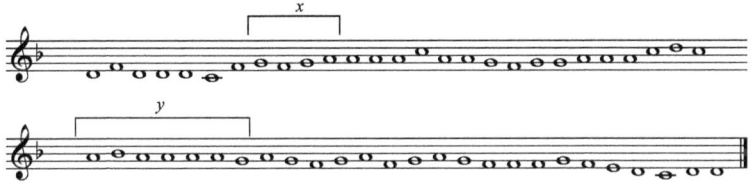

Ex. 5.4b *English Suite*, 'Fantasia', opening.

Recalling Morris's arguments and Bush's own comments about the 'freer tonal relations' of the ecclesiastical modes, the melodic range of the opening of the cantus firmus – a tonal centre of D descending to C and ascending to G – determines the chief harmonic relations of the movement (Fig. 5.2).

Anticipating Davies's works, Bush's choice of source material was not only musically motivated, but evidence of a multifaceted engagement with the national past. The 'In Nomine' was the basis of an exclusively English tradition of instrumental works during the Tudor and Stuart periods. Of particular salience are Purcell's two 'In Nomines' – in six and seven parts respectively – which are essentially fantasias and rich in techniques of

Section	Description	Tonal centre/modality
(i) Opening	Complete declamation of the 'In Nomine' as 'tenor' within contrapuntal texture, leading to invocatory folk-like theme on cello.	D Aeolian – CAeolian
(ii) Fig. 3	Dance-like version of cello invocation, derived from the cantus firmus (motif z), gradually displaced by 'In Nomine' variant in lower strings.	G Aeolian
(iii) Third bar of Fig. 5	Contrasting folk-like section, based on modified inversion of cantus firmus.	G Mixolydian
(iv) Fig. 7	Ecstatic declamation of Fig. 5 material.	C – transitional
(v) Fig. 9	Reprise of invocatory theme, with elements of (iii)	G Dorian
(vi) Fig. 10	Varied reprise of opening section with final statement of 'In Nomine'.	D Mixolydian with plagal conclusion.

Fig. 5.2   Structure and tonality in 'Fantasia'.

contrapuntal elaboration.[76] As well as employing techniques recognisable to the earlier tradition such as inversion and imitation, in Section (i) of his 'Fantasia', Bush employs five solo players only, with the 'In Nomine' part hidden in the texture on second viola, thus evoking Purcell's viol consorts with a cantus firmus tenor. The Fantasia or Phantasy, of course, also enjoyed a resurgence in the early part of the twentieth century under the auspices of W.W. Cobbett's competitions and in the context of Tudor rediscovery. Bush himself was part of this tradition, having dedicated the early Phantasy for Violin and Piano, op. 3 (1923) to Cobbett, although *Dialectic* betrays a problematic relationship with the genre. As a one-movement work for string quartet in modified sonata form, with an allusive title and episodic elements in the development section, it shows affinities with the phantasy genre. On the other hand, the specific choice of title, and the work's logic, energy, and rigour, seem a pointed dissociation from the rhapsodic qualities of the phantasy.[77]

---

[76] Bush also arranged Purcell fantasias for concerts and broadcasts of the London String Orchestra, although none are extant.

[77] See David Maw, '"Phantasy Mania:" Quest for a National Style' in Emma Hornby and David Maw (eds.), *Essays on the History of English Music in Honour of John Caudwell: Sources, Style, Performance, Historiography* (Woodbridge: Boydell, 2010), 97–121.

Ex. 5.5 *English Suite*, 'Fantasia', 5 before Fig. 3.

Ex. 5.5 (cont.)

In his return to the genre here, the most meaningful influence from more recent English music was undoubtedly Vaughan Williams's *Fantasia on a Theme of Thomas Tallis*, and specifically the conscious combination of elements of Tudor music and folk song. Following the Purcellian opening, Bush introduces a folk-like, invocatory theme in the cello immediately before Fig. 3. With its oscillating melody, rhythmic fluidity and improvised quality in the midst of static surrounding harmony, this section is arcadian in the manner of the opening of Vaughan Williams' 'Pastoral' Symphony, as described by Grimley (Ex. 5.5).[78] At Fig. 3 (the tempo change in Ex. 5.5) however, the invocation is immediately fused with Tudor elements. It is extended into a melody derived, again, from the 'In Nomine' and played in parallel fourths in first and second violins. Nevertheless, the folk-like character is retained, not only in boisterous, dance-like rhythmic character, but due to Bush's choice of a melodic fragment of the cantus firmus which outlines the pentatonic substructure of the overall G Aeolian. As Elliot Antokoletz has noted, the preponderance of the Dorian, Aeolian, and Mixolydian modes, often with emphasis on their pentatonic substructures, was a feature of English folk song noted by Cecil Sharp and Vaughan

---

[78] Grimley, 'Landscape and Distance', 153.

Williams.⁷⁹ By utilising that specific fragment of the cantus firmus at this juncture, Bush forged musically the connection he was researching: that between folk music and plainchant. The fact that Bush at the outset adopted a syncopated rhythm for the setting of the 'In Nomine' is a further connection with Vaughan Williams' Tallis theme, while Bush's Section (iii), with the faster-paced syncopated folk-like theme heard in imitation between solo instruments, is particularly reminiscent of the section of the *Tallis* Fantasia that begins with the viola solo. Above all, the climax of both sections in an ecstatic, *largamente* statement of the theme, underpinned by chords a third apart and involving false relations: a characteristic Vaughan Williams musical fingerprint adopted by Bush.⁸⁰

These affinities with Vaughan Williams' practices again raise the question of whether Bush's turn to nationalism in the 1940s was tantamount to stylistic regression or deliberate simplification. The 'Fantasia' points to a more complex reality. Thematically and harmonically, the movement is as complex in construction as *Dialectic* and similarly avoids conventional tonal practice, yet with emphasis on an expanded tonal vocabulary in the direction of English tradition rather than the new sonorities of modernism. Bush's overt adoption of some of Vaughan Williams' most characteristic procedures suggests not so much a conservative step as a conscious assertion of the truth of the older composer's synthesis of folk song and Tudor influences. As *Dialectic* may be seen as a conscious distancing from the Phantasy genre, so the 'Fantasia' proclaims Bush's intention to situate himself within English music. Moreover, in the context of the work as a whole, it becomes clear that the 'Fantasia' illustrates only one expressive possibility for Bush's personal vision of English music.

The 'Soliloquy on a Sailor's Song', like the 'Fantasia', makes pervasive use of the initial thematic material in all parts and incorporates folk song, in this instance using a single, pre-existing melody – 'Lowlands, my Lowlands', a lament which tells of the death of a lover by drowning in the 'Lowland sea' (Ex. 5.6). This was a melody of particular interest to Bush. As well as comparing it with pieces of plainchant as examples of the

---

[79] Elliott Antokoletz, *A History of Twentieth-Century Music in a Theoretic-Analytical Context* (New York: Routledge, 2013), 133.
[80] Hugh Ottaway and Alain Frogley, 'Vaughan Williams, Ralph.' *Grove Music Online. Oxford Music Online.* Oxford University Press, http://www.oxfordmusiconline.com/subscriber/article/grove/music/42507, accessed 27 May 2014.

Ex. 5.6 Bush's transcription of 'Lowlands, my Lowlands'.

Ionian mode in his research material, Bush also arranged 'Lowlands' for inclusion in *20 Songs* (another of his stated examples of his thematic method).[81] Where, in the 'Fantasia', the pre-existing English material produced a contrapuntal movement blending influences from folk song and Tudor music, in the 'Soliloquy', the product is an atmospheric, impressionistic seascape (Ex. 5.7). The final 'Passacaglia' on the 'Cutty Wren' promises the deepest parallels with Vaughan Williams's *Tallis Fantasia*, combining the use of folk song with another seventeenth-century form, although not a typically English one. As a finale employing a buoyant folk song with implicit revolutionary content,[82] it is also the movement most open to accusations of politically

---

[81] *20 Songs* for three part accompanied or unaccompanied singing, selected by A. L. Lloyd, arranged by Alan Bush (London: Workers' Music Association, [194?]). Bush embarked on this project, considering Cecil Sharp's arrangements of folk song 'appalling', and arranging in three parts to aid performance by amateur choirs lacking tenors. See Alan Bush to Will Sahnow, 30 July 1944, BL/AB MS Mus. 656, Correspondence with the WMA, 1939–59.

[82] While definitive proof that the 'Cutty Wren' actually dates from the Peasants' Revolt is lacking, the song is purported to be a veiled narrative of those events, depicting the intention to depose Richard II ('shoot the Cutty Wren') and divide wealth more equitably among the poor.

Ex. 5.7 *English Suite*, 'Soliloquy on a Sailor's Song', opening.

Ex. 5.7 (cont.)

motivated simplification. However, this was certainly one instance in which Bush did not play up political connotations, describing the 'Cutty Wren' simply as an 'English peasant song [...] from the war of 1381' in his prefatory description in the score.[83] Not only do Bush's choices in the movement reflect primarily musical considerations, but the movement also reveals that the composer had by no means abandoned the expansive harmonic possibilities of the thematic method witnessed in *Dialectic*.

The folk-song source material, the 'Cutty Wren', has obvious melodic parallels with the 'In Nomine', thus adding to the overall thematic cohesion of the work (Ex. 5.8). The folk song is also a complete harmonic structure, and thus the passacaglia is an apt structure for both retaining its internal cohesion and allowing for infinite variation. Finally, the folk song may have been attractive in view of its affinities with *Dialectic*. Like *Dialectic* from the first note, the melody traces two rising fourths, B-E and E-A, combining to form a minor seventh. Thus, as well as providing opportunity for the harmonisation via fourths that Bush favoured as a means of avoiding conventional tonal progressions, the melody offers the possibility of establishing an ambiguity between

---

[83] Alan Bush, *English Suite for String Orchestra*, op. 28 (London: Joseph Williams, 1950).

Ex. 5.8 *English Suite*, 'Passacaglia', 'Cutty Wren' ground bass.

D Mixolydian, the modality on which the theme concludes, and B Phrygian. In the brief introduction that precedes the first full declamation of the folk song as ground-bass, Bush exploits both possibilities. Harmonies, as in Bars 3–4, consist of strings of parallel fourths compounded into sevenths (Ex. 5.9), while the overall harmonic direction creates the expectation of resolution to, successively, C, A, and E immediately preceding the ground-bass beginning on B♮. This opening up of harmonic possibilities at the outset has implications later in the movement.

Following the introduction, the movement is a broad ternary structure. Throughout the prolonged first section (Fig. 1 to Fig. 10a) the ground bass and the harmonic foundation it provides remain essentially intact, variety deriving from the successive contrapuntal entry of instruments and rhythmic variation from Fig. 7. Following a brief transition, the start of the middle section at Fig. 11 features what has emerged as a pervasive technique of the *Suite*: the juxtaposition of chords a third apart involving false relations. These chords are subsequently broken down into a single melodic line, emerging in an improvisatory solo violin melody underscored by chains of first-inversion chords characterised by parallel fourths and false relations. The middle section is thus, essentially, the distillation of the folk song into its most characteristic elements, and those most conducive to an expanded – and English – tonal vocabulary. While the perpetual shifting of thirds with chromatic alteration leads to a sustained section in Bb in the middle section, it also ultimately provides the solution to the ambiguity set up in the introduction. Bush establishes a descending chain from B♭-G-E, with the initial B upbeat of the ground-bass in the reprised and truncated A^1 section now conceived as the fifth of a dominant minor ninth on E, resolving to a now unambiguous D Mixolydian.

Ex. 5.9 *English Suite*, 'Passacaglia', introduction.

Neither *Dialectic* nor the *English Suite* constitute the sort of musical progress implied by Bush's rhetorical claims for a perfect synthesis of the theories of Hindemith and Schoenberg. As the foregoing analysis demonstrates, the thematic method in many ways tells us little about what makes these works distinctive. However, the *English Suite* does, crucially, reveal the continuity of Bush's practice between a work (*Dialectic*) lauded as the high watermark of his modernism and one which consciously and pervasively engages with national musical tradition. While Bush's thematic method resulted in a more or less dissonant or English sonority in each work, his compositional principles had not essentially altered. Moreover, the *Suite* highlights the connections between Bush's nascent theorising of national music at this time as both rooted in popular practice and a theoretically legitimate manifestation of modern compositional practice. Encompassing his desire to establish a rigorously Marxist method of composition within existing modern developments, his concern to heal the breach between serious and popular music to create a unified national culture, and constituting a reconnection with his personal musical development, the *English Suite* was a landmark in solving Bush's dilemmas in the mid-1940s. In these years, Bush was navigating a complex set of priorities as Marxist and musician: his commitment to personal growth in the cause of socialism; his interests in modern music and his theoretical ideas; his notions regarding the cultivation of a new English musical culture; and the pressure of absorbing external events in the Soviet Union. It is clear that in this context, it is not possible either to assert Bush's independence from Soviet events of 1948 or to portray him as blindly and crudely altering his style in line with official doctrine. Bush's turn to nationalism was affirmed by the Soviet controversy, and his continued defence of national music and efforts to practice it were motivated by a desire to ally himself with the collective path of world socialism. Yet Soviet events did not engender his interest in nationalism, which had long been a concern, and had become a particular priority through Bush's wartime work and the calls for renewal of English culture that rang through post-war Britain. Truly, he accused himself.

The way in which Bush cultivated nationalism in the *English Suite* was highly personal, and it exhibited deep continuities with his practices as a self-proclaimed modern. It is for this reason that Hellbeck's model of selfhood provides such an apt point of comparison; the *English Suite* constitutes the very act of self-transformation towards collective goals. While this sets him apart from major strands of the high modernist musical tradition, it importantly affirms his modernity in the broad terms outlined at the start of this study: as a self-aware subject attempting to situate himself within the historical and social circumstances of modernity, rather than an unreflective puppet reflecting the Soviet Union's iron grip on world communism. It is, finally, testament to the personal nature of Bush's commitment to nationalism that even while he embraced the new generic and aesthetic challenges of opera, he never abandoned his commitment to 'theoretical' instrumental works. The zenith of this enterprise was Bush's *24 Preludes* for piano, op. 84 (1977), a compendious exploration of Bush's tonal and modal landscape, which ascends the circle of fifths from F♯ to B not alternating major and minor but exploring the range of 'English' modes (Dorian, Lydian, Phrygian, Mixolydian, Aeolian, Ionian, and the pentatonic scale) in both 'diatonic' and 'chromatic' versions. Indeed, the *Preludes* demonstrate that in his sense of musical self, Bush remained a modern seeking to establish a consensus on the future of musical practice, by presenting an encyclopaedic account of the tonal system he had created comparable to Shostakovitch's *24 Preludes and Fugues* and Hindemith's *Ludus Tonalis*. Ultimately, rather than relinquishing his modern musical self in favour of politically prescribed nationalism, as suggested by Cooper, the modern and the national, the progressive and the accessible, were entwined halves of Bush's compositional practice throughout his career.

6 Bush and the Self: *Wat Tyler*'s Rituals of Becoming

None of Bush's works has generated more praise, opprobrium, and soul-searching than *Wat Tyler* (1948–51). The work, on an ostensibly populist English historical subject, won a prize under the 1951 Festival of Britain opera-commissioning scheme.[1] It nevertheless had to wait until 1956 for a BBC broadcast and until 1974 for a semi-professional production under the auspices of the WMA. In the meantime, the work launched Bush's career as an opera composer within the GDR. It was succeeded by three commissions for East German opera houses: *Men of Blackmoor* (1954–5), *The Sugar Reapers* (1962–5), and *Joe Hill: The Man Who Never Died* (1966–8).[2] In sum, the four operas enjoyed eleven productions in the Communist Bloc between 1953 and 1973.[3] By contrast, in Britain *Blackmoor* received two student productions – in Oxford and Bristol – and *The Sugar Reapers* and *Joe Hill* were performed only in truncated broadcast versions.[4] Despite this relative dearth of performances in Britain, *Wat Tyler* and *Blackmoor* in particular generated an enormous amount of criticism and reflection, both in public and behind the closed doors of cultural institutions such as the Arts Council and the BBC.

The reasons for this disproportionate amount of critical reflection are complex. In a 1960 article on the Oxford production of *Blackmoor*, David Drew insightfully identified three phases of 'free world' critical response: first, resentment that the work of a senior British composer should have been produced in a foreign country; second, embarrassment that said country 'is on the wrong side of the Iron Curtain'; and third, 'ill-disguised satisfaction' at the poor reception of the works in this country.[5] Undoubtedly, the fact of Bush's patronage in the GDR provoked a variety of reflections. A major cause of concern among British critics and

---

[1] See Lew, 'A New and Glorious Age', 429ff.
[2] The first three operas were all composed to libretti by Nancy Bush, while *Joe Hill* was adapted by the American playwright Barrie Stavis from his play, *The Man Who Never Died*.
[3] These productions were all in East Germany, with the exception of two productions of *The Sugar Reapers* in Tartu (1969) and Odessa (1973). See Lewis Foreman, 'Spanning the Century: The Music of Alan Bush' in N. Bush, *Alan Bush*, 127–8.
[4] Ibid., 127–8.
[5] David Drew, 'Man and People', *New Statesman*, 10 December 1960, 920 and 922.

promoters was the operas' intimate relationship with an oppressive regime, made worse by the fact that some major performances coincided with some of the most notorious incidents in the Soviet domination of Eastern Europe. *Wat Tyler* was performed in Leipzig in the September following the brutally suppressed demonstrations in East Germany in June 1953; it was first broadcast on the BBC shortly after the conclusion of the Hungarian Uprising of 1956. As late as 1981, Paul Griffiths condemned this state of affairs, calling Bush's operas: 'all studies of the rise of oppressed peoples and all allowed, even encouraged, by their composer to commit the perversion of being used by that shining light of liberty the German Democratic Republic'.[6] Yet to emphasise the ideological freedom enjoyed by citizens of Britain over those of the GDR created problems in turn. Was Bush's opera ignored in Britain because of the composer's political affiliations, thus stifling his freedom of expression?[7] There was also the matter of state sponsorship. The establishment of the Arts Council and state funding for culture was a central pillar of the post-war settlement.[8] In addition, as Toby Thacker has shown, modern British music (including *Peter Grimes*) formed part of a programme of re-education for Germany based on British values.[9] Thus, East Germany's promptness in staging a prizewinning British opera ahead of its native country was potentially embarrassing in exposing the failures of state sponsorship and Britain's desire to become a modern cultural leader. On the other hand, the oppressive nature of the sponsoring state in the case of *Wat Tyler* could prompt reflections of a different sort on the value of art under the auspices of government.

Bound up with these questions of impartiality in patronage were those concerning musical and dramatic content of both *Wat Tyler* and its successor, *Men of Blackmoor*. Many commentators criticised Bush's characterisation in the former, considering the heroes and villains of the piece to be too sharply distinguished and one-dimensional, and the peasant chorus to be unconvincing; they associated these attributes with the perceived political content of the work. One BBC score reader, Norman Fulton, commented that 'I could not find musical justification for the melodramatic use of harsh discords and brassy scoring on each entry of the presumably "capitalist" characters!'[10] Critics such as Drew endeavoured to evaluate the operas on a musical, not political, basis. Yet Drew

---

[6] Paul Griffiths, 'Review: 80+', *Musical Times* 122/1660 (June 1981), 380.
[7] See, for example, Desmond Shawe-Taylor, 'Public and Private: Desmond Shawe-Taylor on Bush and Strauss', *Sunday Times*, 23 June 1974, 27.
[8] See Wiebe, *Britten's Unquiet Pasts*, 2ff. [9] Thacker, *Music after Hitler*, 89–92.
[10] Norman Fulton to Assistant Head of Music, 10 April 1952, BBC/WAC RCONT1, Composer, Alan Bush, File 2: 1948–1952.

revealed another unconscious critical prejudice in his observation that it was 'rather hard' on *Blackmoor* to receive its British premiere in the same week as Covent Garden's revival of *Wozzeck*.[11] Drew considered the work 'home-spun', 'folk-like', and 'curiously mild' in comparison to the 'naked fury' of *Wozzeck*, surprising in the context of Bush's political radicalism and revolutionary subject.[12] Other critics felt that Bush's creative instincts had been hijacked by political considerations, complaining of a lack of inspiration and affinity for operatic writing on the part of the composer.[13]

In part, these criticisms and unflattering comparisons with *Wozzeck* reinforce Bush's position in the Cold War dichotomy of music as modern or national, individual or collective, progressive or regressive. In situating his opera in the latter category, his critics expressed revulsion at the presence of what were perceived to be crude, even naïve, Soviet conventions in a British opera, recalling Cooper's Stakhanovites attending the Nottingham Goose Fair (discussed in Chapter 5). As usual, Bush's own uncompromising rhetoric came into play. In a 1974 essay, for example, he disavowed any aesthetic parallel with trends in modern opera in the West:

> At the moment in the West pathological states of mind and guilt are fashionable subjects. [...] I avoid in my subjects unrelieved murky pessimism and triumphant corruption, and aim to represent objective pictures of human life, past and present.[14]

By his own account it seems, as in those of the critics, Bush's very construction of humanity in his operas was at odds with prevailing attitudes in his own country. In Bush's hands, the national became, paradoxically, un-British. In one of the few efforts at serious musicological appraisal of *Wat Tyler*, Nathaniel Lew has made a persuasive case for greater appreciation of Bush's adaptation of the conventions of socialist realism, and for the significance of the opera in post-war cultural reconstruction. Yet even there, the conception of Bush's work as essentially un-modern comes into play, with Lew noting that 'The kind of moral ambiguity which makes *Peter Grimes* so endlessly fascinating is completely lacking in *Wat Tyler*' and that *Grimes*' moral complexity is 'a mark of its modernity'.[15]

---

[11] Drew, 'Man and People', 920.
[12] Such criticisms were pervasive in responses to the 1974 production of *Wat Tyler* too, for example in Bayan Northcott's perception of the 'spectre of the English Folk Dance and Song Society'. Bayan Northcott, 'Notes on Marx', *New Statesman*, 28 June 1974, 932.
[13] See, for example, Anon., 'In Honour of Alan Bush', *The Times*, 20 November 1961, 14.
[14] Alan Bush, '"Wat Tyler" and the Purpose of Opera', *Opera* 25/6 (June 1974), 490.
[15] Lew, 'A New and Glorious Age', 513, 169.

A wholesale reappraisal of the opera and its relationship to competing Cold War aesthetic positions is urgently needed, for several reasons. In light of the foregoing analysis of Bush's complex relationship to modernism, nationalism, and individual identity, it is necessary to look again at the manifestation of these themes in his *Wat Tyler*. The fact that an opera with so few British performances could generate such an impassioned and prolonged response is significant in itself. Critics devoted huge energy to the question of what made *Wat Tyler* un-modern or un-British, in the same post-war period in which *Peter Grimes* and *Gloriana* engaged with the national past and future and provoked similar soul-searching. This raises the question of whether Bush's opera really lacked those essential qualities of British opera in the 1940s and 1950s, or whether it amounts to an alternative, unpalatable projection of British modernity. This chapter considers these questions through a detailed analysis of *Wat Tyler*. It considers Bush's own conception of modernity and the modern subject, as well as ideas circulating along these lines within Bush's British communist milieu. *Wat Tyler* was not a crude transplantation of Soviet aesthetic principles onto an English subject, but was rooted in radical communist conceptions of English history emerging in the immediate post-war period, and articulated these conceptions in musically sophisticated ways. The chapter also pursues the comparison with *Peter Grimes*, not to denigrate Bush's opera, but to suggest enlightening affinities between the two. Both works were conceived in the depths of the war years, both are parable-like commentaries on modern society, and both, in the central figure, reveal something about the composer's view of the artist and his relationship with society. Ultimately, while Bush's operatic vision of modern Britain could never have been acceptable, like Britten's, it opened up trenchant issues in post-war British musical culture.

Origins of an Opera

Let us first of all examine the genesis and content of *Wat Tyler*, as a prelude to discussing its complex interactions with Soviet aesthetics and English culture. Its subject is, of course, the English Peasants' Revolt of 1381. Nancy Bush indicated that she endeavoured in her libretto to follow history exactly, except where the necessities of the drama demanded alteration.[16] In fact, in addition to inventing Tyler's family life (as almost nothing is

---

[16] Nancy Bush, 'Preface', *Wat Tyler: Opera in Two Acts with a Prologue* [Libretto] (Richmond: R.W. Simpson, 1956), 1. Subsequent citations from the libretto are taken from this source.

known about the historical figure), she does not include notable incidents of violence on the part of the peasants. Simon Sudbury, Archbishop of Canterbury, for example, appears among Richard II's advisors, but the opera does not depict his murder at the hands of the peasants in June 1381. Nancy's sources were the Anominal Chronicle of St Mary's, York, the chronicles of Stowe and Froissart, and the writings of such figures as J.J. Jusserand and G.M. Trevelyan.[17] A final influence, upon which Alan Bush placed much stress, was Hyman Fagan's 1938 account, *Nine Days That Shook England*, provocatively titled to recall John Reed's famous account of the October Revolution.[18] Appendix 3 gives an overview of the *dramatis personae* and a detailed synopsis slightly adapted from Nancy Bush's own.

The music of the opera had a long gestation. One of Bush's protégés, the conductor David Ellenberg, referred to it as early as March 1944. Having just read the text of *A Child of Our Time*, Ellenberg recommended that Bush 'set out to write a work in "Cantata" form about some topical episode. The time is ripe for it, and it would be a good precedent for your opera'.[19] By June 1945 Nancy Bush had completed her historical research and started writing the libretto, and Bush was excited about an operatic subject which 'lends itself very well to a spectacular and exciting opera with good opportunities for chorus, which has always been a feature of English opera'.[20] With inevitable delays, it was 1948 before Bush was able to undertake substantial work on the opera[21] and mid-1950 before he had completed the vocal score.[22] Much of the process of composition was conducted during the Arts Council's lengthy consideration of the opera for the Festival of Britain opera-commissioning scheme, during which the judges requested ever more portions of the score and full orchestral segments before reaching a decision.[23] *Wat Tyler* eventually won a prize, alongside Arthur Benjamin's *A Tale of Two Cities*, Karl Rankl's *Deirdre*

---

[17] Ibid., 1.
[18] Hyman Fagan, *Nine Days That Shook England: An Account of the English People's Uprising in 1381* (London: Victor Gollancz, 1938).
[19] David Ellenberg to Alan Bush, 21 March 1944, BL/AB MS Mus. 431: Correspondence with David and Diana Ellenberg.
[20] Alan Bush to Vilmos Palotai, 1 June 1945, BL/AB MS Mus. 457: Chronological correspondence, 1945. Note that this evidence contradicts Nancy's later, published recollections of the timescale. See Nancy Bush, 'Writing for Music' in Stevenson (ed.), *Time Remembered*, 142.
[21] Alan Bush to Grigori Shneerson, 24 December 1948, BL/AB MS Mus. 440: Correspondence with Grigori Shneerson.
[22] Alan Bush to David Ellenberg, 12 June 1950, BL/AB MS Mus. 431.
[23] See BL/AB MS Mus. 662: Correspondence with Amnesty; Arts Council, and Victoria and Albert Museum Archives, Arts Council of Great Britain records, EL6/70, Festival of

of the Sorrows, and Berthold Goldschmidt's *Beatrice Cenci*. All four prize-winners were disappointed that the Arts Council did not secure professional productions, or even guaranteed broadcasts, of their works.[24] Bush seized the initiative and arranged a 'play-through' concert performance, paid for by the Arts Council, which took place on 26 November 1950. Despite the attendance of BBC staff, the opera was not picked up for broadcast. In 1951, Bush played excerpts of the opera at the piano for a selection of musical dignitaries in the GDR, and the opera was broadcast the following year on Berlin Radio. This was followed by a full stage performance at the Municipal Theatre, Leipzig, in September 1953, and subsequent productions in Rostock (1955) and Magdeburg (1959). By contrast, in Britain, in addition to the delay in achieving the 1974 stage production, wranglings with the BBC over their initial rejection of the work delayed broadcast until December 1956.

A Soviet Transplant?

To what extent were Alan and Nancy Bush guided by Soviet aesthetics? In Lew's opinion, Bush aimed to achieve three essential qualities of socialist realism: *narodnost* ('national character'), *partiynost* ('party-mindedness') and *ideynost* ('ideological commitment').[25] Several features of the opera identified by critics support this judgment: characters who are sharply delineated good and bad ciphers for their social position, rather than psychological portraits; the prominence of the chorus; the use of folk song; and the preponderance of diatonic over chromatic writing. In addition, the plot is a typically utopian socialist realist narrative, presenting not only the grim reality of 'what is' but also the hopeful future 'what may be'.[26] However, Lew argues that Bush adapts socialist realism in several important regards. The treatment of Christianity, the focus on Tyler's family life, the tragedy of the opera's conclusion, and the peasants' deference to the King are instances where historical accuracy and consciousness of the

---

Britain Opera Commissions: Alan Bush's "Wat Tyler" and EL6/75, Festival of Britain Opera Commissions: Alan Bush's "Wat Tyler" Audition, 26 November 1950.

[24] As the late John Lowerson discussed, the fact that three prizewinners were not British and the fourth was a communist may have caused embarrassment to the Arts Council, but much store may also be placed upon the 'cock-up' theory that insufficient funds and planning led to the works not being staged. Certainly, this is borne out by the Arts Council's efforts on *Wat Tyler*'s behalf. John Lowerson, 'The Wrong Sort of History? The Problems and Productions of Alan Bush's *Wat Tyler*', paper delivered at the Institute of Historical Research, London, 11 May 2009.

[25] Lew, 'A New and Glorious Age', 489.   [26] Ibid., 489.

characters as human beings (and not merely representatives of social forces) trumped the demands of socialist realism.

The difficulty with this reading is that it implies a clear conception of socialist realism on the part of Alan and Nancy Bush, which they chose to embrace or adapt. Yet it is clear from the correspondence cited above that the subject was chosen before the end of the war, and the libretto completed before 1948. Much planning of the opera, then, occurred in a period of flux for Soviet aesthetics. Furthermore, while Bush did not begin serious work on the music until that year, he was developing material for the opera in the finale of the *English Suite* and the symphonic suite *Piers Plowman's Day* (1946–7). The latter is based on William Langland's fourteenth-century allegorical poem, in which the narrator, Will, experiences a series of visions featuring Piers Plowman, a peasant figure representing Christ. Avoiding these allegorical figures entirely, Bush composed three movements, 'The Keep', 'The Bower' and 'The Forest', which depict respectively the home of the feudal landlord in the era of his decline, the courtly world of the lady entertained by troubadours, and the growth of the peasant rebellion. The stylised pastiche of the second movement foreshadows the minstrel's songs in *Wat Tyler*, while the third movement, like the opera's Prologue, uses a forest setting and incorporates fragments of the 'Cutty Wren'. Ellenberg's proposal in 1944 that Bush write a topical cantata to prepare for the opera is also suggestive. If the planned opera were in Bush's mind as he composed *Lidiče* and *The Winter Journey*, it suggests that *Wat Tyler* was less a musical response to the events of 1948 and more a culmination of the process of aesthetic reflection the composer had been engaged in throughout the mid-1940s.

The libretto, too, reveals a complex reception of Soviet aesthetics, especially in the depiction of Wat Tyler himself. The positive hero is a Russian literary trope with a rich prehistory in fields as different as hagiography and nineteenth-century radical literature. In the Soviet era, this exemplary figure was not limited to literature: men such as the legendarily productive miner Alexey Stakhanov, cosmonaut Yuri Gagarin, and above all, Lenin and Stalin themselves were held up as models of how to live a socialist life.[27] Within literature, as Katerina Clark has argued, the positive hero had a precise function within the ritualised plot of the Soviet novel.[28] One of the prototypical versions of the positive hero was to be found in Gorky's

---

[27] See Sheila Fitzpatrick, *Everyday Stalinism: Ordinary Life in Extraordinary Times: Soviet Russia in the 1930s* (New York and Oxford: Oxford University Press, 1999), 71ff.

[28] Katerina Clark, *The Soviet Novel: History as Ritual* (Chicago: University of Chicago Press, 1981), 9–10.

Mother. Gorky's novel is a fictionalised account of a workers' uprising in an early-twentieth-century industrial Russian town. The 'mother' of the title is an initially ignorant and humble woman who is inspired by her revolutionary son. Eventually, she is beaten to death by police while trying to carry out revolutionary work. As Clark indicates, it is a precursor of the socialist realist novel in several regards: the focus on the relationship between the nuclear family and the socialist cause, the mother's transformation and eventual martyrdom via a ritualised plot, the lack of psychological depth in the characters, and what Clark calls the spontaneity/consciousness dialectic played out in the roles of 'mentor' and 'disciple'. Thus, in Gorky's work, the love of mother and son becomes a microcosm of social commitment, and indeed, the latter transcends the former. The mother acts as disciple to her better-informed son, a workers' leader. Through his example, she is transformed from responding to personal instincts ('spontaneity') to actions guided by political awareness ('consciousness'). The plot is teleological, leading to the martyrdom of the mother. However, the ending is not tragic because she has become, as an individual, at one with the cause, which will continue.

It is not clear whether Alan or Nancy knew Gorky's novel, but they certainly knew Brecht and Eisler's *Lehrstück* version, *Die Mutter*.[29] In both this work and his collaboration with Weill, *Der Jasager*, Brecht created a central character who transforms him/herself through self-knowledge, depicted family relationships and sacrifice that are transcended by the collective cause, and incorporated ritual elements (*Der Jasager* being based on the Noh play *Taniko*). There are obvious parallels here with Bush's opera. Not only is the characterisation of Wat Tyler lacking in psychological depth, but Nancy Bush specifically refers to Tyler's profession as a roof-*tiler*, just as two major peasant characters are simply 'Herdsman' and 'Escaped Serf'; all three are synonymous with their social function.[30] The domestic scene in Act I reveals Tyler's family as a microcosm of society, even in the details of the tax collector's attempted attack on Jennet (sexual exploitation echoing the financial exploitation of the peasantry as a whole). The plot of the opera is ritualised, both in the timelessness of the narrative (especially in the final couplet, 'All that is great in Man still lives/And once again, and once again shall rise!') and, for English audiences, its familiarity.[31] There is no question or suspense surrounding Tyler's martyrdom and the failure of the Revolt (while, at

---

[29] There is a full typescript translation of this version in ABH.
[30] The historical figure's name, too, is said to be a contraction of 'Walter the T[i]ler'.
[31] Libretto, 56.

the same point, the eventual collapse of feudalism is equally apparent); the drama lies in his emergence from the mass of peasants and acceptance of this role. Intriguingly, the mentor/disciple role appears in two relationships in the opera. On the one hand, Tyler is the disciple of John Ball, 'the static, folk-like image of the revolutionary' in *Mother*, who anoints the more active figure of Tyler and leads him to his act of self-sacrifice.[32] On the other hand, Tyler also acts as mentor to Margaret, who in the pivotal love duet of Act I Scene 2 is persuaded to sacrifice her personal feelings of concern for Tyler's safety and embrace the necessity of revolution. Indeed, without Margaret's journey, the element of personal transformation would be virtually lost, given the static nature of Tyler's character.

Wat Tyler then, does show evidence of Soviet aesthetics, but these influences were absorbed over a long period, and from a variety of sources. The libretto and preparatory essays for the music (*English Suite, Piers Plowman's Day*) were written when Bush was still hopeful of the spontaneous emergence of English socialism in solidarity with the new communist nations of the Eastern Bloc, and completing the fusion of national content and the thematic method in his personal style. The evidence of ritual in *Wat Tyler* – both in the narrative structure and the prominent treatment of religion – recalls those characteristic works of that period: *Lidiče* and *The Winter Journey*. Rather than viewing the opera as more or less faithful to the Soviet dictates of 1948, therefore, it is worth resituating it within Bush's immediate post-war project and comparable projects in English culture of the period.

'The Norman Yoke'

Although *Wat Tyler*'s reception has been dominated by concerns over its political content, it was, first and foremost, a historical opera. As has been frequently observed with reference to Britten's *Gloriana*, this genre of post-war English opera was something of a minefield.[33] John Lowerson has argued that *Wat Tyler* was 'the wrong sort of history' because it did not chime with nostalgic post-war portrayals of national heritage.[34] But it is worth looking in more detail at what sort of history Bush did present, however 'wrong'. In the 1930s and 1940s, the Peasants' Revolt was attracting renewed interest as part of a radical new approach to the writing of

---

[32] Clark, *The Soviet Novel*, 67.
[33] See, for example, Wiebe, *Britten's Unquiet Pasts*, 109–50.
[34] Lowerson, 'The Wrong Sort of History'.

history. The CPGB Historians' Group, which contained such figures as Eric Hobsbawm, E.P. Thompson, and Christopher Hill, began meeting in 1946, but it had its origins in earlier events in the life of the British Party. While *The British Road to Socialism* was adopted as CPGB policy only in 1951, the Popular Front period and the events of the war had already given rise to a desire to engage with specifically English concerns. The historians' work encompassed questions relevant to the intellectual life of the Party as a whole, as well as specifically historical matters. As Bill Schwarz has noted, the primary purpose of the Historians' Group was:

> directed much more to the anglicization of the Marxist tradition, demonstrating its compatibility with a native idiom of critical social theory. This radical tradition was conceived as the theoretical framework for a popular political strategy and as a resource for the creation of a politics appropriate to nationally specific conditions. The intention was to reactivate a national-popular consciousness and in this the Group cultivated a profound sense of *Englishness*, which called for a major reassessment of English cultural and political history from the seventeenth century and before.[35]

Thus, the Group sought to construct a radical popular history of England, and indeed one of their foundational texts was A.L. Morton's *A People's History of England*, first published in 1938. In pursuing this project, three preoccupations of the historians identified by Schwarz are relevant here. Firstly, their aims posed the problem of the distinction between 'people' and 'nation'. Rather than the classically Marxist international proletarianism, the Historians' Group were working with the nebulous category of the 'national-popular'. Secondly, the project had implications for the function of the intellectual, which became not only theoretical but also political. As James Klugmann, the much-criticised Party historian said, echoing Dimitrov's 1935 speech to the Seventh Congress of the Comintern:

> We became the inheritors of the Peasants' Revolt, of the left of the English revolution, of the pre-Chartist movement, of the women's suffrage movement from the 1790s to today. It set us in the right framework, *it linked us with the past* and gave us a more correct course for the future.[36]

---

[35] Bill Schwarz, '"The People" in History: The Communist Party Historians' Group, 1946–56' in Richard Johnson, Gregor McLennan, Bill Schwarz, David Sutton (eds.), *Making Histories: Studies in History-writing and Politics* (London: Hutchinson, 1982), 54 (his emphasis).

[36] Cited in Schwarz, '"The People" in History', 56 (his emphasis).

The new history, then, not only created a teleological narrative of English popular history, but also contributed to that narrative, by fostering political consciousness informed by the past. Finally, acting as a caution to the first two problems, the historians desired a historical method that navigated the tensions between historical explanations that explained change in terms of economic or social necessity at the expense of the particular (as a dialectical Marxist model of history may do), and historical explanations that privileged the specific historical event so far as to reject any general theoretical premise.

The 'central text' of the Group that found one virtuosic solution to these problems was Hill's essay 'The Norman Yoke'.[37] Hill's essay explored the notion that England was democratic prior to the Norman Conquest and that the oppressive institutions of the state were imported at this time. Hill traced the theory from the seventeenth century, in the radical groups spawned by the English Revolution, to the present day, while also identifying its origins in the eleventh century. By revealing, according to Blackledge, 'a continuous trajectory of democratic struggle associated with the Norman yoke theory between the seventeenth and the nineteenth centuries', Hill connected previous popular struggles in England with the present, a point reinforced by the observation that the goals of the English Revolution were yet to be completed.[38] Indeed, he drew a direct link between contemporary Marxism and the Norman yoke tradition in the latter's 'recognition of the class basis of politics, its deep sense of the *Englishness* of the common people, of the proud continuity of their lives, institutions and struggles with those of their forefathers, its insistence that a propertied ruling class is from the nature of its position fundamentally alien to the interests of the mass of the people', thus both identifying true Englishness exclusively with the working classes, and subtly presenting Marxism as a home-grown tradition.[39] While Hill did not single out the Peasants' Revolt for particular scrutiny in his essay, its importance to the Historians' Group is unquestionable. Dona Torr – credited by the group with revealing to them the human figures of history as well as its objective basis – identified 1381 as the moment when 'Englishmen became conscious of their common nationhood', and thus the beginning of an unbroken tradition of English radicalism.[40]

---

[37] Christopher Hill, 'The Norman Yoke' in John Saville (ed.), *Democracy and the Labour Movement: Essays in Honour of Dona Torr* (London: Lawrence & Wishart, 1954), 11–67; Paul Blackledge, *Reflections on the Marxist Theory of History* (Manchester: Manchester University Press, 2006), 84.
[38] Blackledge, *Reflections*, 85. [39] Cited in Schwarz, '"The People" in History', 70.
[40] Ibid., 73.

English Radicalism and Historical Time: The Opera

The opera's libretto was completed before the ideas of the Historians' Group reached their full articulation in writings like Hill's 'The Norman Yoke' and Torr's unfinished study of Tom Mann. Nevertheless, the opera may be legitimately compared with them for several reasons. As stated previously, a major source for the libretto was Fagan's *Nine Days That Shook England*. Fagan was linked to the Historians' Group because he was indebted to the work of both Torr and E.A. Kosminsky, with whom Hill had studied in Russia.[41] Moreover, the Historians' work took place within the context of the broader cultural work of the Party. Bush was at the centre of this work through his seat on the NCC and his frequent contributions to Party publications. His views on 'Tasks of Cultural Workers' are strikingly similar to those of the Historians with respect to the political role of popular history, and he wrote much later of his admiration for the Historians' Group at this time:

> Thus we as Marxists believe in making the cultural heritage of mankind available to the people, not as a collection of museum pieces, but as a vivid experience of man's spirit throughout history. But our responsibility does not end there. We also have to set about building the new culture, expressing the fight of progressive mankind *at this stage* of our advance. For Britain this new culture must be in great part British culture. Developed from our British heritage it should have in the main for its content the life of the British people in past periods and today. The history of the British people is extraordinarily rich in heroic and revolutionary events.[42]

Finally, Bush had attempted, and still was attempting, to create comparable English historical narratives within music. 'Towards To-morrow' and the pageant of the Festival of Music for the People were two early attempts (discussed in Chapter 2). In the post-war period, Bush collaborated with A.L. Lloyd on 'The Living English', a pageant of folk songs which evoked an idealised ancient common England. The WMA Singers performed programmes that surveyed the history of English popular music, notably for the Festival of Britain.[43] And Bush had organised the music for the

---

[41] Fagan, *Nine Days That Shook England*, 11–12.

[42] Bush, 'Tasks of Cultural Workers', 52. Bush wrote during the CPGB's crises of 1956 that 'The Historians Group of the Party has been the admiration of all members of the National Cultural Committee for the contribution which they have been making, especially during the past two or three years, where their co-ordinated work has been on a high level. [...] The production of Comrade Thompson's book on "William Morris" is an event of the greatest importance'. Alan Bush to Harry Pollitt, 7 September 1956, ABH.

[43] See V&A Archives EL6/65: Workers' Music Association.

Communist Manifesto Centenary Pageant in 1948. Written by Montagu Slater, the librettist of *Peter Grimes*, this depicted the dialectical progress of history from feudalism through capitalism to the present, interpolated with declamation of sections of the manifesto. Thus, there is ample evidence of Bush's exposure to the historians' ideas and his own efforts to weave Marxism into a specifically English history of music.

The work of the historians illuminates several features of the opera. Much of the language of the libretto draws a contrast between the impact of the ruling classes – the 'Norman Yoke' – and the life of the peasantry. In the Prologue, the Herdsman and Escaped Serf make much of the 'ripe and rotten' and 'mouldering' crops and images of a cruel, hard land, while in Act I Scene 2 Margaret refers to their misfortune 'since the days of Pestilence'.[44] In Act I Scene 3, the turning point from indignation to action, the peasants' initial reference to England's state ('England's furrow groweth wild,/England's fountain is defiled') is succeeded by John Ball's crucial statement:

> Weary the weight of the walls upon me.
> Green fields I longed to look upon.
> Courage fled from me; I was corrupted.[45]

Finally, Wat Tyler's petition to the King for freedom envisages a future for England in which 'Green shall her acres grow again/Under the plough of freeborn men'. Throughout, both the idealised, pre-Norman past and future freedom are associated with the green, natural order of things in England, while Norman rule is associated with man-made stone walls, rottenness, and corruption.

This contrast, which chimes with the 'Norman Yoke' theory, is also reflected in the music. Act II Scene 2 is the only scene exclusively to feature the King and his counsellors. It is framed by the only two distinctly demarcated arias in the opera, the two minstrel songs. In the rest of the opera, the 'historical' musical elements are integrated into Bush's personal musical style. Bush uses parallel fourths and fifths in harmony, avoids the third and leading note at cadences, frequently employs leaps of the fourth and fifth in vocal lines, and with some notable exceptions favours the use of modes rather than major-minor scales, but, as we have seen in previous chapters, these were longstanding features of his style, whether writing chromatic or diatonic music. The use of the 'Cutty Wren' in the Prologue is a notable exception, and yet it is diegetic at that point, and was considered an authentic folk

---

[44] Libretto, 9–10, 24.   [45] Libretto, 32, 36.

Ex. 6.1 Bush, *Wat Tyler*, 'Minstrel song', VS, p. 181.

song of the period. In the minstrel's songs, by contrast, the idiom is ostensibly historical pastiche, which Lew identifies as specifically evoking the medieval French chanson. The harp imitates the lute accompaniment, and the vocal line is highly melismatic, another feature sharply in contrast to the avoidance of melisma in the rest of the opera (Ex. 6.1). The beauty and artifice of the songs is apt for their content: the first song depicts love as the captivity of a wounded animal, while the second song explicitly bespeaks longing for Aquitaine. In response to the first, too, King Richard describes how 'Over the embroidered grass I rode. Silver and white/Were the numberless stars

I ravished'.[46] In both music and text the over-refinement, decadence, corruption, and, above all, *foreignness* of the King is emphasised.

Both the 'Norman Yoke' theory and Torr's timeline of English radicalism evoke a particular conception of historical time. In part, this presents the history of the English people as a dialectical process, drawing on the wider Marxist conception of the historical shift from feudalism to capitalism to (in the imagined national future) socialism. It also evokes an idealised common past and present as both part of, and standing outside, the motion of history and experiences of the working classes. Act II Scene 3 was originally denoted as the Epilogue, a designation Bush was still using in 1952.[47] The Prologue and Epilogue stand outside the concentrated action of the rest of the opera, both in the absence of the protagonist, and in the way they situate the events within a larger historical narrative, the Prologue by showing the growth of unrest, and the Epilogue by pointing to the continuance of hope and struggle after Tyler's death.

Bush's music underscores this narrative. He believed that opera composers since the mid-nineteenth century had aimed at continuous music throughout each act, leading to 'a musical formlessness, which, in a piece of instrumental music, would result in a lack of intelligibility'.[48] While he considered Wagner to have solved the problem, he also believed that by establishing a symphonic orchestral foundation, Wagner reduced the characters on stage to 'declamatory dummies'.[49] Accordingly, 'the persons on stage bear both the dramatic and musical burden', but the Prologue, Act I, Act II, and the Epilogue were also each a coherent musical structure. The Prologue moves from G Dorian to D Mixolydian, Act I from G Mixolydian to D Dorian, Act II from F Mixolydian to E♭ minor, and the Epilogue/Act II Scene 3 from G Aeolian to D major. The tonal centres of G and D also have consistent dramatic associations. The opening of the Prologue is a chorus of lament over the cruelty of serfdom. The opening of Act I similarly depicts the peasantry and townsfolk about to be taxed again, before Wat Tyler's intervention. Finally, the Epilogue opens with the mourning of Margaret and the dispersed rebels following Tyler's death. In each of these instances, G is associated with the depiction of the oppressed peasantry. Bush's choice of mode in each case captures the specific tone

---

[46] Libretto, 40.
[47] In the 1956 published libretto it is designated 'Act II Scene 3', but in the 1952 essay 'Problems of Opera', at which point the opera was complete, Bush was still referring to the scene as the Epilogue. See Bush, 'Problems of Opera', *Music* 1/11 (October 1952), 21.
[48] Ibid., 20. [49] Bush, 'Problems of Opera', 21.

Ex. 6.2 *Wat Tyler*, VS, p. 36.

of the scene: oppression in work; the lighter mood of the marketplace; mourning. By contrast, at the end of the Prologue the Herdsman and peasant chorus have articulated their (covert) plans for rebellion (using the coded language recorded at the time).[50] Act I ends with the decisive marching chorus 'When shall we see the grey goose fly?' as the peasants march to London, and the Epilogue concludes with an expression of hope and determination in the face of defeat. Thus, the tonal centre of D is associated with the radical, fighting and conscious peasantry. In sympathy with Torr's articulation of the Peasant's Revolt as the moment of 'conscious' nationhood, this trajectory is enacted symbolically in the key relations of the opera.

To cement the connections with the English Marxist conception of history, Bush uses the tonal centre of B at significant moments of the work. It is used momentarily in the Prologue when the Herdsman invites the Serf to 'Warm the ague out of your bones'. It is touched upon (as B minor) at the entry of Wat Tyler in Act I Scene 1, a moment which also introduces a significant motif in Tyler's vocal line (Ex. 6.2). The tonal centre is heard again as Tyler urges on the peasants breaking into Maidstone Gaol; as the peasants anoint him as their leader; and at the

[50] Nancy Bush, 'Preface', 2.

Ex. 6.3 *Wat Tyler*, VS, pp. 207–8.

moment of Tyler's petition to Richard. Just as, in the Piano Concerto, Bush used contrasting keys to symbolise the future, utopian state of socialism and the present struggle, here B symbolises the peasants' longed-for freedom, in contrast to the 'fighting' tonal centre of D, particularly in the B major used at the moment of Tyler's appeal to Richard (Ex. 6.3). The reappearance of the motif from Ex. 6.2 at this point has a further significance. It will return again (in D) in the closing bars of the opera (Ex. 6.4), underscoring the fact that the peasants' struggle continues. It is also a motif particularly associated with Tyler himself, given its association with his first appearance (Ex. 6.2). In the opera as a whole, Bush chose three closely related tonal centres – G, B, D – to symbolise the oppression, hope, and rebellion of the peasantry, and their journey through the events of the

Ex. 6.4 *Wat Tyler*, VS, closing bars.

opera from 'unconscious' to 'conscious' nationhood. It is significant that while the centre of B is the tonal midpoint, B major, which appears only at the moment of Tyler's petition, is remote from the determined D Dorian of the fighting chorus 'When shall we see the grey goose fly?'. Like the utopian past and future, B major stands somewhat outside the tonal world of the opera. Nevertheless, in the musical depiction of Tyler and his legacy through a recurrent motif and the symbolic use of keys, a link is forged between a future utopia and the embattled present.

A People's Christ?

A remaining question is the matter of *Wat Tyler*'s modernity, the quality most doubted by English critics of the opera. Certainly, the historical models it engaged with were new in English historiography, and, in the broad sense of the term, it reflects an unquestionably modern conception of time and history. One may think, for example, of Scott Burnham's application to Beethoven's 'heroic' music of the 'spiral time' of German romanticism, 'wherein the path of redemption leads from a prelapsarian golden age to a future golden age – past and future merge mystically'.[51] Indeed, Marx was to inherit this conception of history via Hegel. Yet while Bush's engagement with this model demonstrates the depth of his engagement with Marxist English history as in itself a modern phenomenon, it does not fully answer critiques of the opera. The primary territory on

---

[51] Scott Burnham, *Beethoven Hero* (Princeton: Princeton University Press, 1995), 123.

which the opera's modernity has been questioned is in comparison with the model of modern English opera provided by *Peter Grimes*.

The modernity of Britten's opera may be particularly located in the psychological complexity of Grimes, his anti-heroism, and the ability of the music to capture his alienation from the community. Superficially, these qualities are absent in *Wat Tyler*, but it is fruitful briefly to turn the matter on its head, and consider what the works have in common. There is a direct link between the two works through Slater, who collaborated with Bush on the historical Communist Manifesto Centenary Pageant and who wrote the libretto of *Peter Grimes*. As Humphrey Carpenter has noted, it was in Slater's hands that *Peter Grimes* 'became a story about a community'.[52] It is not simply Grimes' character in itself, but the 'individual against the crowd', as Pears put it, and the parallels between Grimes as 'an introspective, an artist' and Britten's own place in society, that makes the opera compelling.[53] Similarly Wat Tyler is, in some respects, an outsider. Fagan recounts that the covert 'Great Society', which played a crucial role in the uprising, found its best recruits in the independent skilled tradesmen, such as tilers or 'tylers', who wandered from town to town in search of work.[54] Bush's Margaret sings to Tyler: 'Where you go I never may follow./Why will you wander wide in the world?/Why will you leave your hearth for strangers?'[55] When he first appears, Tyler is about to fix a roof, and greets townsfolk following an apparent absence. Tyler's entrance music in the scene, too, is markedly different from the A Dorian chorus that immediately precedes it. Tyler is not synonymous with the crowd, but an individual who allies himself with them.

A further parallel may be drawn between the victimhood of Grimes, hounded to suicide by the community, and Tyler, a willing sacrifice to the cause of revolution. As Lew observes, some reviewers of the first performances of *Peter Grimes* read him as a Christ-like figure, his death as an outsider standing for all those rejected for being different, although Grimes is far more morally ambiguous, and Britten's artistic depiction of innocence more complex, than this would suggest. Brecht and his musical collaborators similarly played on the difference between self-sacrifice in the context of identification with a collective struggle, and the futility of the sacrifice of a single individual, a contrast embodied in the respective figures of the boy in *Der Jasager* and the Young Comrade in *Die Massnahme*. Like Grimes, the boy in *Der Jasager* was (mis)interpreted by some early critics through the lens of Christian teaching, while the Young Comrade was

---

[52] Humphrey Carpenter, *Benjamin Britten: A Biography* (London: Faber, 1992), 181.
[53] Carpenter, *Benjamin Britten*, 203.   [54] Fagan, *Nine Days That Shook England*, 20.
[55] Libretto, 26.

recalled in the figure of the 'Boy' (based on the Polish Jew Herschel Grynszpan, whose assassination of a German diplomat provoked *Kristallnacht*) in *A Child of Our Time*.[56]

These parallels are important, as they connect *Grimes* and *Wat Tyler* to a post-war British tradition of music which invokes ritual and the figure of Christ in order to comment on the possibility of social transformation. While *Grimes* is not overtly ritualistic in the way that *A Ceremony of Carols* is, Christian ritual is depicted as hypocrisy (as it is in *Wat Tyler*) when the Borough folk emerge from Church and form a mob to confront Grimes. The opera is also cyclic in that, in the final scene, the normal life of the Borough resumes with the death of the protagonist rendered insignificant, as it is in *Wozzeck*, with the implications for society left for the audience to infer. In *A Child of Our Time*, Tippett not only played on the possibility of individual sacrifice to achieve collective salvation by depicting the futility of the Boy's act of violence, but invoked ritual through the creation of symbolic characters, the congregational use of the spirituals, and the depiction of a psychological journey towards individual and collective wholeness ('I would know my shadow and my light') as the source of healing for modernity's wounds. Vaughan Williams's *The Pilgrim's Progress*, too, is dramatically ritualistic while rejecting the figure of Christ, with the composer changing the name of Bunyan's protagonist from Christian to Pilgrim to emphasise the universality of the spiritual journey. Yet Pilgrim's allegorical spiritual journey acts, reflecting Vaughan Williams's preferred generic title of morality for the work, as an implicit social directive, with the figure of Bunyan in jail at the end offering his book to the audience. Vaughan Williams also, in his earliest dramatic setting of Bunyan (the 1922 'pastoral episode' *The Shepherds of the Delectable Mountains*), used the hymn tune 'York', associated with the Roundheads. Despite the huge differences between Bush's opera and Vaughan Williams's, in both cases ritual content was combined with material identifying with a tradition of English radicalism.

Bush's allusions to Christian ritual have been noted in relation to *The Winter Journey* and *Lidiče*, and *Wat Tyler* shares with those works the pervasive use of musical archaisms such as parallel fourths, and the use of fire as a metaphor for destruction that can signify rebirth. Fire appears in the Prologue, and the first hint of the 'B' tonal centre occurs as the

---

[56] Stephen Hinton, 'Jasager, Der', *The New Grove Dictionary of Opera. Grove Music Online. Oxford Music Online*. Oxford University Press, accessed 19 August 2016, http://www.oxfordmusiconline.com/subscriber/article/grove/music/O004122.

Herdsman invites the Serf to share the fire. At the end of Act I Scene 2 Tyler sings:

> The forest fire begins to burn.
> Blow, northern wind, blow, blow!
> Drive on the flame that kindles now![57]

In the Epilogue, it is the 'evening glow' that gives the peasants fresh hope that 'the embers of hope still burn'.[58] Bush's perception of the function of ceremonial cultural spectacles like the Communist Manifesto Centenary Pageant is also relevant:

> I am certain that there is no one who either participated in or witnessed the Pageant who will not feel able to fight with redoubled strength and enthusiasm for the victory of Socialism in Britain.[59]

Rather than simply setting a political message, this statement implies that to witness cultural performance is to participate in a ritual, in which one's beliefs are renewed through identification with the events and people depicted. Most significantly, the opera's message of social transformation may be connected, like *The Pilgrim's Progress*, to a landmark work of English religious allegory.

As mentioned previously, some of the music of *Wat Tyler* exists in earlier versions in the symphonic suite *Piers Plowman's Day*, based on Langland's allegorical poem about the mysterious figure of Piers Plowman. As Jill Mann writes, 'Initially he seems to be a simple peasant, a type of honest Christian layman, but as the poem progresses he takes on connotations of the priesthood, of the apostle Peter, of the pope as head of the Church, and of Christ himself'.[60] The poem was certainly familiar to both Alan and Nancy Bush; Nancy used the 'four-footed verse' of the poem as one model for the language of the libretto; she was surely aware of its direct links with the Peasants' Revolt, and of the fact that Piers Plowman was actually cited in letters of John Ball.[61] There are obvious parallels with the characters of Wat Tyler and John Ball in Piers' humble status, his feud with hypocritical clerics (which may be compared with the contrast between Ball's sermon on equality under God and the peasants' condemnation of 'Highborn lord, thieving monk,/Priest and prelate, noble and all!'), and the narrator's vision of Piers Plowman carrying the

---

[57] Libretto, 31. [58] Libretto, 56. [59] Alan Bush to Harry Pollitt, 1 April 1948, ABH.
[60] Jill Mann, 'Allegory and Piers Plowman' in Andrew Cole and Andrew Galloway (eds.), *The Cambridge Companion to Piers Plowman* (Cambridge: Cambridge University Press, 2014), 70.
[61] Helen Barr, 'Major Episodes and Moments in *Piers Plowman* B' in Cole and Galloway, *The Cambridge Companion to Piers Plowman*, 24.

Ex. 6.5 *Wat Tyler*, VS, p. 154.

cross.[62] *Piers Plowman* invites further comparison with the opera because of the poem's mix of references to real and allegorical situations, historical and eschatological time. Alongside the exploration of trenchant issues of Langland's own time, the narrator meets Abraham, witnesses Christ's triumph over Lucifer in Hell, and, ultimately, the coming of the Antichrist and his destruction of the Holy Church, which prompts a renewed search for Piers Plowman. As J.F. Goodridge has stated (also revealing another parallel with *The Pilgrim's Progress*), Langland's pilgrimage:

---

[62] Libretto, 22.

is that of man's individual life and his life in society, as it has to be lived on this middle-earth between the 'Tower of Truth' and the 'Dungeon of Falsehood'. Langland was concerned [...] both with the condition of society and with the history of the human soul struggling to 'cleanse the doors of perception' and come to terms with ultimate truth. [...] this meant translating his visions, at every point, into an art that had an immediate application to practical life.[63]

While the opera's historical vision concerns a utopian socialist future rather than Christian eschatology, Hill commented on both the Norman yoke theory and the myth of the Fall of Man as instances of a 'profound historical truth': that inequality and exploitation have a historical origin, and equality may again return. As Hill points out, these affinities were spelled out in the 1381 peasants' question, subsequently set to music by Bush: 'When Adam delved and Eve span/Who was then the gentleman?' (Ex. 6.5).[64] Moreover, Langland's dual time is strikingly reminiscent of the contrast between the events of 1381 and the motion of history writ large, the individual life and death of Wat Tyler and the ongoing struggle towards the future.

There is a final, most revealing parallel to be made between opera and poem. We have yet to address the place of Act II within the opera (with key relations that fall outside the central G-B-D tonal trajectory of the work) and Alan and Nancy's curious treatment of the King and religious themes. In light of Goodridge's description of a key theme of *Piers Plowman*, it is noteworthy that 'truth' and 'falsehood' also feature prominently in the libretto. In the Prologue, the Herdsman states three revolutionary riddles such as were used during the Revolt:

> John the Miller hath yground small,
> The King's Son of Heaven shall pay for all.
>
> Be ware or you be woe.
> Know your true friend from your foe.
>
> And so bid John Trueman and all his fellows.
> John Trueman doth you to understand
> Falseness and guile have ruled too long.[65]

These opening riddles establish not only that the peasants' struggle is a battle for truth over falseness, but also invoke the figure of Christ as king. Subsequently, an ongoing theme is the peasants' belief that their

---

[63] J.F. Goodridge, 'Introduction' to William Langland, *Piers the Ploughman*, trans. J.F. Goodridge (London: Penguin, 1960), 11.
[64] Hill, 'The Norman Yoke', 12. [65] Libretto, 10–11.

Ex 6.6 *Wat Tyler*, VS, pp. 242–3.

woes are the fault of John of Gaunt and representatives such as Sir Thomas Bampton, and that King Richard II himself will be their deliverer. As Tyler announces in Act I Scene 3: 'Now overleap we lying lords/ And all corrupting counsellors [...] We stand here for our right,/For Richard and the Commons!'[66] The climax of the opera is, however, Richard's meeting with the remnants of the peasants outside Westminster Abbey, the betrayal of his promises to Wat Tyler, and his resolve that serfdom shall continue forever. It is only at this moment that the peasants realise the falseness of the King, and the truth that Wat Tyler (musically entwined with the themes of 'hope' and 'struggle') represents their path to freedom. This last tableau is set to music out of character with the rest of the opera, a sardonic, chromatic, harmonised chant on the 'Te Deum' in F♯ Aeolian, accompanied by twisted fragments of the 'Cutty Wren' in the orchestra (Ex. 6.6).

Lew considers the music here to be a frivolous incursion into a moment of tragedy, which merely 'satirizes the superficiality of royal pomp'.[67] The allusions to *Piers Plowman*, however, present a weightier explanation. Bush selected the following lines from the complete 'Te Deum' text:

Te deum laudamus: te Dominum confitemur.	We praise thee, O God: we acknowledge thee to be the Lord.
Tibi cherubim et seraphim incessabili voce proclamant:	To thee Cherubin, and Seraphin: continually do cry:
Sanctus, Sanctus, Sanctus Dominus, Deus Sabaoth.	Holy, Holy, Holy: Lord God of Sabaoth;
Miserere nostri Domine, miserere nostri.	O Lord, have mercy upon us: have mercy upon us.
In te Domine speravi: non confundar in aeternum.	O Lord, in thee have I trusted: let me never be confounded.[68]

Given the reference to the 'King of Heaven' in the Prologue, and the presence of the 'Cutty Wren' in both scenes, the end of the 'Te Deum' text – 'let me never be confounded' shows the trajectory of the King's falseness in the opera: the peasants' King as Redeemer has been proven false; the 'Te Deum' is undermined because the articulation of faith jars with the reality of the King's actions. In short, Richard in this moment is the equivalent of

---

[66] Libretto, 38. [67] Lew, 'A New and Glorious Age', 531.
[68] Alan Bush, *Wat Tyler: An Opera in Two Acts with a Prologue* [Vocal Score] (London: Novello, 1959), 242–5. Translation from John Henry Blunt (ed.), *The Annotated Book of Common Prayer, Being an Historical, Ritual, and Theological Commentary on the Devotional System of the Church of England* (London: Rivingtons, 1866), 10–13.

Ex 6.7 *Wat Tyler*, VS, pp. 205–6.

Langland's Antichrist: the false saviour who sweeps away the true redeemer, leaving only hope and memory.

There is another dimension to Bush's construction of truth and falsehood in the opera. Although the revelation of falsehood uses the tonal centre of F♯, this is not generally Bush's choice for Richard. His first utterance in Act II Scene 1 uses G♭ Mixolydian, a mode that aptly signifies his remoteness from the peasants (G Mixolydian) as he expresses nostalgia for Aquitaine. The Queen Mother's aria, her news of the rebels and her prescient lament that England 'has, alas, no saviour here', prompts a shift to E♭, the tonal centre later used in the lament over Tyler's body, which in both cases signifies mourning. This is also the tonal centre that heralds the King in Act II Scene 2. In that scene, during the exchange between the King and Tyler, they are sharply distinguished both in tonal centre and vocal line, Tyler's being marked by the 'freedom motif' and Richard's by a motif combining a Phrygian second and rising perfect fifth. When Richard agrees to the rebels' demands, he shifts sharpwards for the first time, but not to Tyler's utopian B major, but G♯ Phrygian, moving to B Phrygian (Ex. 6.7). He also retains his distinctive vocal line in a mechanical utterance, underscored by the bass line that accompanied Bampton's threats to Tyler in Act I Scene 3.[69] Thus, the Phrygian is particularly associated with Richard and his distinctive vocal phrase, not F♯. The F♯ of the final scene's revelation and the 'Te Deum' melody do, however, have a provenance earlier in the opera, in Archbishop Sudbury's advice to the King to pretend to appease the rebels in Act II Scene 1. It is no coincidence that F♯, the key representing false-seeming, is closely related to the utopian B. It is also enharmonically equivalent to the King's initial 'remote' G♭. Just as Tyler is anointed by the true priest, John Ball, the over-refined and distant King is brought to deceit by the hypocritical Sudbury. Thus, the dichotomies of truth/falsehood, strength/weakness, Christ/Antichrist that are embodied in the figures of Tyler and the King underpin the entire opera.

Conclusion

Who, then, is Bush's Wat Tyler: a Soviet 'positive hero', a reinvented Christ, or Piers Plowman? Does he amount to a modern operatic protagonist? Tyler remains, in many respects, the antithesis of the kind of protagonist presented by *Wozzeck* or *Peter Grimes*. Yet he is best understood, not as a fleshed-out individual interacting with society but, like Piers Plowman, as a quasi-allegorical figure alongside others in the opera. Wat

---

[69] Vocal Score, 113–14, 206.

Tyler and the King are not Christ and the Antichrist, or the positive hero and his foil, but they symbolise particular qualities at certain points of the opera. The early reviewers rightly saw in Wat Tyler an undiluted figure of good. However, reading Wat as Piers Plowman, the notional English listener to be impelled towards socialism is not invited to crudely imitate Tyler, but to navigate the attractions of truth and false-seeming, and thus, like Margaret and the Herdsman, to be transformed and to locate his place in history. Again, this remains a model of modern opera remote from *Peter Grimes* in many respects, and potentially repugnant to those who reject Bush's brand of utopianism. Nevertheless, the engagement in the musical and literary language with aspects of mid-century British modernism (in the deliberate archaisms, the images of destruction and rebirth), the ritual structure of the work, its rich tonal symbolism, the radical conception of history and use of time, and the sceptical vision of Christ, all project a concept of English modernity and a self-consciousness about the artist's place within it that bears comparison with Britten's project in *Grimes*. Bush's desire to engage musically with the past in order to construct a model of the future may similarly be associated with broader cultural work in post-war Britain. Unfortunately for Bush, by 1974 the subtleties of his work had undoubtedly been lost in the delays and semi-amateur nature of the British performances, prejudicial beliefs about the conservatism and impersonal nature of communist art, and models of operatic modernity that seemed openly refuted by Bush's opera. Yet if an alternative, socialist, narrative of modernity can be recouped, the allegorical figure of truth who is swept away by deceit presents an intriguing monument to post-war British culture.

7 Bush and East Germany: Opera, Sex, and the Communist Body

> There's nothing wrong with a bit of lovemaking.
> [...]
> Frankly [...] I don't like the idea of dying. I don't! I don't! I just don't!
> Barrie Stavis, *The Man Who Never Died*.[1]

To the litany of *Wat Tyler*'s anti-modernisms discussed in Chapter 6 might have been added its treatment of sex and desire. Opera has, of course, always been a site for cultural exploration of sex and gender through, for example, the use of castrati and trouser roles, the frequent depiction of female sexuality, and the phenomenon of opera fandom.[2] In modernist opera, the portrayal of unhinged or transgressive sexuality is frequently bound up with the use of a modernist musical idiom, as in such canonical examples as *Salome, Erwartung, Lulu, Peter Grimes* and *Death in Venice*. With the exception of the boorish advances of Sir Thomas Bampton towards Jennet Tyler, *Wat Tyler* features no such excessive and destructive manifestations of desire. The only relationship shown is marital; the tension and renewed harmony between Wat and Margaret Tyler is wholly focused on their shared ideals, their ability to put them before the purely personal. Not only sex, but *bodies* are curiously lacking in *Wat Tyler*. The Peasants' Revolt is a subject that could accommodate a visceral dramatic depiction of violence, suffering, and death in such moments as the attempt to punish the Escaped Serf with branding, John Ball's release from prison, and the death of Tyler. Alan and Nancy Bush, however, dwell almost exclusively on the characters' sense of injustice and desire for freedom.

---

[1] Barrie Stavis, *The Man Who Never Died: A Play about Joe Hill* (New York: Haven Press, 1954), 157 and 231.

[2] See, for example, Carolyn Abbate, 'Opera; or, the Envoicing of Women' in Ruth A. Solie (ed.), *Musicology and Difference: Gender and Sexuality in Music Scholarship* (Berkeley and Los Angeles: University of California Press, 1993), 225–58; Corinne E. Blackmer, and Patricia Juliana Smith (eds.), *En Travesti: Women, Gender, Subversion, Opera* (New York: Columbia University Press, 1995); Catherine Clément, *Opera, or the Undoing of Women*, trans. Betsy Wing (Minneapolis: University of Minnesota Press, 1989); Wayne Koestenbaum, *The Queen's Throat: Opera, Homosexuality and the Mystery of Desire* (New York & London: Poseidon Press, 1993).

The absence of sex and the body in *Wat Tyler* chimes with images of communism as joyless, oppressive, and indifferent to personal relationships, as immortalised in Orwell's *Nineteen Eighty-Four*. Yet, curiously, in Bush's final two operas, sex and the body achieved a new prominence. In *The Sugar Reapers or Guyana Johnny*, Bush used the folk music of British Guiana to recreate a dance-based Guianese betrothal ceremony, the Que-Que. Employing sexualised terminology redolent of the early British reception of jazz, Ossia Trilling remarked following the opera's premiere on 'The entire singing and dancing choreographed ensembles, with their samba, rumba and other outlandish dances, both African and Asian in origin, with exemplary abandon, reaching their highpoint in the festive Queque [sic] series during the betrothal ceremony.'[3] *Joe Hill* is another departure. In addition to featuring the eponymous character conducting an affair, the work makes an extraordinary focus on the assault on Joe Hill's body: his being shot, and his confessed fear of the physical process of dying during the protracted depiction of his execution.

It is worth pondering the reasons for this change. The greater prominence of sex and the body in Bush's later operas not only allows enquiry into a stereotype of communist art, but also enables consideration of these works in a complex, shifting social and political reality rather than as manifestations of a static ideology. East Germany, the state most closely associated with the operas, was a society in which ideas about sexual cultures and music were remarkably complex. As Josie McLellan has written, it was common at the time of German reunification for the press to report on events such as the opening of the first sex shop in the East, with the implication that East Germans 'had led lives which were sexually as well as politically repressed'.[4] Yet this stereotype can mask the centrality of sex and gender in East German culture, particularly in relation to those increasing sources of tension between the state and the people: dance music and youth culture. While, as in the case of sex, a traditional assumption has been that the state demonstrated blanket opposition of these phenomena, more recent studies have revealed phases of appeasement or renewed suppression of popular music. Certainly, the ruling communist party, the Sozialistische Einheitspartei Deutschlands (SED), feared the influence of Westernised, commercial dance music upon young people,

---

[3] Ossia Trilling, 'Bush Opera Performed in Leipzig', *Providence Sunday Journal*, 26 March 1967, copy held in ABH.

[4] Josie McLellan, 'Did Communists Have Better Sex? Sex and the Body in German Unification' in David Clarke and Ute Wölfel (eds.), *Remembering the German Democratic Republic: Divided Memory in a United Germany* (Basingstoke: Palgrave Macmillan, 2011), 119.

but they also faced the constant problem, prior to construction of the Berlin Wall, of large numbers leaving for West Germany (*Republikflucht*). The SED was also gripped by the intense desire to demonstrate their superior modernity to the West. Thus, tolerance of popular music, and efforts to appropriate it for socialism, became part of the GDR's ongoing, and ultimately futile, attempts to appease its citizens.[5]

Within this context, it is significant that Bush's last two operas not only show an increased interest in the body, but are also the ones most closely associated with East Germany: they have never been performed in Britain, and they were conceived and composed with East German productions in mind. They are also a departure in their shift away from English national subjects and the rigid socialist realism that had characterised the previous operas. *The Sugar Reapers or Guyana Johnny*, with its extended dance numbers, pervasive use of Guianese folk music, relative lightness of subject, and rhythmic vitality, is reminiscent of the musical, rather than opera. In *Joe Hill*, Bush used spoken dialogue and adopted Joe Hill's own songs with little alteration. Like the American works of Weill, the two operas thus seem to occupy a middle ground between through-composed opera on the one hand and the tradition of the musical absorbing an array of interpolated pre-existing styles and melodies on the other. Bush would have rejected any comparison with Weill and held a resoundingly negative view of commercial popular music. Yet he had always trodden a difficult path as a composer, seeking to create something that was modern and properly socialist, which also tapped into the deepest roots of folk music to create music of real popular resonance. In the 1950s and 1960s, Western commercial popular music was bound up with motions towards sexual liberation and individual expression, and the SED were fighting a losing battle with it. To what extent, then, did Bush give ground, and try to incorporate elements of the latest trends into his operas? Alternatively, do Bush's later operas represent an attempt at an *echt* communist alternative to the new models of sexuality and modernity being presented in popular music?

These questions strike at the heart of Bush's aesthetic project, with its aspirations to populism and modernity. They raise the question not only of how far the requirements of those categories shifted in post-war decades, but how this project really intersected with the cultural agendas of the GDR. The composer's post-war British critics assumed that Bush's success in East Germany was a result of political affinity. But by tracing his

---

[5] On these issues, see Patrick Major, *Behind the Berlin Wall: East Germany and the Frontiers of Power* (Oxford: Oxford University Press, 2010).

articulations of populism and sexual modernity through his operas, a far more complex and contradictory relationship is revealed.

'Unser Freund Alan Bush'

If anything, those who criticised Bush's relationship with the communist regime in East Germany underestimated its extent. It is easy to point to affinities between Bush's stated aesthetic and political positions and those of leading musical organisations in the GDR. Creating culture in the image of their political activity was, from the outset, a priority of the SED, and the Party was able to begin the construction of a German socialist musical culture with the return from exile of Ernst Hermann Meyer in 1948.[6] Meyer was a musician of some calibre, having trained in musicology and composition in Berlin before the Nazis came to power and forced his emigration to Britain as a communist in 1934. As such a capable musician and dedicated supporter of the SED, Meyer quickly secured Party backing to take over planning for music in the GDR and was instrumental in establishing its direction. The founding conference of the *Verband Deutscher Komponisten und Musikwissenschaftler* (Union of German Composers and Musicologists, VDKM) in 1951 was an important milestone. As Toby Thacker has discussed, Meyer's speech on 'Realism, the Vital Question of German music' attacked the avant-garde. Echoing the Soviet call to respect the 'best traditions of Russian and western classical music', Meyer set a mandate to 'encourage realistic music that emphasised musical content over empty form, that cherished the German national musical heritage, and that was in the literal sense *Volksmusik* (music of the people)'.[7]

The parallels between Bush's ideas and those prevalent in East German cultural planning were no coincidence; the composer played an intimate role in the development of East German music. Thacker has observed that friendships between German communist exiles and British musicians between 1933 and 1948 'were important in the evolution of a specifically Marxist theory of music and society later embedded in the musical culture of the GDR'.[8] Bush's papers and MI5 documents reveal the full truth of this

---

[6] Thacker, *Music after Hitler*, 111ff.

[7] Slonimsky, *Music since 1900*, 1360; Elisabeth Janik, *Recomposing German Music: Politics and Musical Tradition in Cold War Berlin* (Leiden & Boston: Brill, 2005), 237.

[8] See Toby Thacker, '"Something Different from the Hampstead Perspective": An outline of selected musical transactions between Britain and the GDR' in Stefan Berger and Norman LaPorte (eds.), *The Other Germany: Perceptions and Influences in British-East German Relations, 1945–1990* (Augsburg: Wißnew-Verlag, 2005), 212.

assertion. In the Security Service's opinion, Meyer was 'a great friend of, and [...] absolutely dominated by, Alan BUSH, without whose authority he will not undertake any duties connected with Communist Party activities'.[9] Given the inflammatory rhetoric they frequently used regarding Bush himself, this judgment must be treated with caution, yet it is true that Bush put activity in Meyer's way – for example helping him to join the LLCU as a conductor – and Meyer considered that he was 'a true and trusted supporter and friend when I was in dire trouble'.[10] More significantly, Meyer appears to have been closely involved in Bush's efforts to theorise the relationship between music and society and to attempt the practical implementation of the findings. Meyer contributed to the Research Panel of the 1938 'Music and Life' Congress, and in wartime he covertly joined the Research Committee of the William Morris Musical Society.[11] As discussed in Chapter 3, the Society was not only, as MI5 believed, a front for political subversion, but also a testing-ground for ideas about how to build socialist musical cultures. It is impossible to know from the surviving documents of the society exactly what Meyer's contribution was, but what is certain is that both were present at these wholesale discussions of how to shape musical culture based on Marxism, as Bush attempted to do in post-war Britain, and as Meyer did in the GDR in 1948.

Moreover, there is plenty of evidence of the importance Meyer and his colleagues attached to Bush's opinion, and his direct influence upon musical émigrés who joined the new socialist German state. Eisler was the most prominent musician in East Germany with whom Bush had an established friendship. The Austrian musicologist Knepler, another wartime émigré in Britain, was invited to move to East Germany in 1949 to establish a Berlin Academy of Music, and he immediately sought Bush's advice.[12] Bush also knew the pianist Eberhard Rebling, who migrated to the GDR from the Netherlands in 1952 and edited the journal *Musik und Gesellschaft* for much of the 1950s. Above all, Meyer remained loyal to Bush and influenced by his thinking. In 1946, while still in England, Meyer wrote a draft memorandum on 'Music in a Future Germany' which had little to say about realism in composition but, like the WMA's *Policy for Music in Postwar Britain*, outlined a comprehensive plan of musical

---

[9] 'Conquest' report, 19 May 1941, TNA/PRO KV 2/3515: Bush, Alan D., Item 26a.
[10] Ernst Hermann Meyer, 'Alan Bush in the Thirties' in Stevenson (ed.), *Time Remembered*, 74–5.
[11] 'Mr Hollis', report, 19 December 1941, TNA/PRO KV 2/3515: Bush, Alan D., Item 20c.
[12] Georg Knepler to Alan and Nancy Bush, 7 August 1949, BL/AB MS Mus. 465: Chronological correspondence May-August 1949.

activity and education.[13] Meyer also wrote a response to the British communist composer Boughton's public endorsement of the Soviet declaration of 1948, condemning his suggestion of returning to nineteenth-century standards of dissonance and urging 'Let us not bar progress and experiment. We must go forward, not back'.[14] As Thacker has asserted, Meyer's dedication to Soviet cultural dictates was always incomplete, and the nuances of his ideas may be traced back to his relationship with Bush.[15]

National and Sexual Identity in the New East Germany

Bush, then, was well situated through personal connections to forge a career in the new German state. Yet this alone does not explain the extent of his success, especially in the field of opera. He also had personal contacts in the Soviet Union and made strenuous efforts to have his operas performed, but only one, *The Sugar Reapers or Guyana Johnny*, ever made it to the USSR, and even then it was a long way from Moscow, with productions in Tartu and Odessa (Fig. 7.1). In 1966, Bush was told by Kaarel Ird, Intendant of the State Theatre in Tartu, that the reason *Wat Tyler* and *Men of Blackmoor* had not been performed in the Soviet Union 'was because there was a generally accepted notion that they were formalistic or had formalistic tendencies'.[16] Although Bush's Russian correspondent, Shneerson, denied that this was the case, one wonders how Ird had gained that impression. His operas faced another hurdle in East Germany in that they occupied an anomalous position with regard to the immediate cultural objectives of the regime. A document written by Max Burghardt, the Intendant of the Leipzig theatres, who would have much to do with Bush's opera career in East Germany, reveals official aims for theatrical repertoire in the city. Burghardt placed the theatres at the service of such goals of the regime as the reunification of Germany, the promotion of world peace, the development of a realistic national culture in opposition to Americanisation, and deepening cultural links with the Soviet Union and 'People's Democracies'.[17] An official review of opera in the GDR made in

---

[13] E.H. Meyer, 'Music in a Future Germany' (Draft Memorandum), 1946, SAAdK Ernst Hermann Meyer Archive, File 386.
[14] Cited in Thacker, *Music after Hitler*, 114–15.   [15] Ibid., 115.
[16] Alan Bush to Grigori Shneerson, 3 January 1966, BL/AB MS Mus. 440: Correspondence with Grigori Shneerson.
[17] Max Burghardt, 'Den Kampf gegen die zersetzenden Einflüsse des imperialistischen Kulturzerfalles und der Kulturbarberei (Amerikanismus)', Stiftung Archiv der Parteien

Opera	Production
Wat Tyler	Leipzig (1953), Rostock (1955), Magdeburg (1959)
Men of Blackmoor	Weimar (1956), Jena (1957), Leipzig (1959), Zwickau (1960)
The Sugar Reapers	Leipzig (1966), Tartu (1969), Odessa (1973)
Joe Hill: The Man Who Never Died	Berlin (1970)

Fig. 7.1 Productions of Bush's operas in the Communist Bloc.

1952 confirmed the need to guarantee a proportion of works from the Soviet Union and the People's Democracies in programmes.[18] What place was there, then, for British opera, however infallibly socialist?

In order to answer this question, we must acknowledge the disparity between the lofty cultural aims expounded by Burghardt and the reality of East Germany's position in the early 1950s. Far from being in a position to restore German unity, East Germany was barely recognised as a nation and almost totally lacking international influence. Prior to 1954, neither East nor West Germany had formally regained sovereignty, and thereafter the Hallstein Doctrine blocked any recognition of the East German state beyond countries of the Communist Bloc. Forging a national identity was not simply a matter of adopting Soviet socialist realism, but an integral part of the struggle with West Germany to prove pre-eminence in economic, cultural, and ideological spheres and to be proven, as Joy Calico has remarked, 'the custodians of true German culture'.[19] Calico emphasises that it was through *Nationaloper* above all that the SED hoped to achieve these goals in the sphere of music. However, they had to navigate a series of problems that made a new national culture all the more difficult to achieve. Firstly, the new state was hampered by a dearth of talent of international stature. The VDKM were only ever able to attract a handful of known communists such as Bush, Serge Nigg, and Nono from the West to its

---

und Massenorganisationen der DDR im Bundesarchiv, Berlin (SAPMO-BArch) NY 4199/69: Nachlass Max Burghardt.

[18] 'Analyse über die Oper in der Deutschen Demokratischen Republik', Bundesarchiv, Berlin (BArch) DR 1/6112: Ministerium für Kultur – Stakuko, HA Darstellende Kunst und Musik, Abteilung Darstellende Kunst; Theaterangelegenheiten (inc. Spielpläne, 1948–53).

[19] Joy Haslam Calico, '"Für eine neue deutsche Nationaloper:" Opera in the Discourses of Unification and Legitimation in the German Democratic Republic' in Celia Applegate and Pamela M. Potter (eds.), *Music and German National Identity* (Chicago and London: University of Chicago Press, 2002), 191.

events.[20] While the new state's great asset was Brecht, the premiere of his *Lucullus* opera was a notorious failure for the East German state, due to the disparity between Brecht's cultural vision and that of the SED.[21] Secondly, there was the matter of how to connect with tradition while rejecting the legacy of fascism and its overt appropriation of the German classics. Thirdly, while the SED had embraced the principle of opposing the 'disintegration of culture' engendered by American influence, this left the problem of how East German culture would embody both modernity and mass appeal. Achieving pre-eminence over West Germany meant, in part, adopting the trappings of 1950s modernity: consumer products and dance music.[22] Consequently, not only did dance music become a hydra that the SED could not defeat, but modern East German national identity was bound up with a form of music strongly associated with the articulation of youth, individuality and counter-culturalism.

Within this labyrinth of cultural and political needs, it is possible to reconsider the premiere and reception of *Wat Tyler* in 1953. It is significant that this performance was arranged to coincide with the Leipzig Fair.[23] As Katherine Pence has observed, the post-war Leipzig Fairs were a significant means by which the GDR sought legitimation, holding a threefold importance in this respect. Firstly, the practice of holding the fair originated in the Middle Ages, so the event offered a valuable link with the historical and cultural traditions of Leipzig. Secondly, it allowed the East to showcase consumer products, economic and industrial growth, and recovery after the war, albeit with mixed success. Finally, the fairs in this period cast Leipzig as 'a "bridge" or a "mediator" between East and West', a miniature international community of nations.[24] The numerous German

---

[20] The minutes of a planning meeting for the founding conference of the VDKM in 1951 shows that only eleven musicians from outside the communist bloc were even invited, including Bush and at least two musicians who subsequently migrated to the GDR. 'Vorbereitendes Büro zur Durchführung der Gründungskonferenz des Verbandes Deutscher Komponisten und Musiktheoretiker vom 2. – 5.4.51 im Kulturbund z.d.E.D: Protokoll der Besprechung vom 31.3.51', SAAdK VKM Archive, File 2745.

[21] See Joy Calico, 'The Trial, the Condemnation, the Cover-up: Behind the Scenes of Brecht/Dessau's *Lucullus* Opera', *Cambridge Opera Journal* 14/3 (2002), 313–42.

[22] Katherine Pence and Paul Betts, 'Introduction' in Katherine Pence and Paul Betts (eds.), *Socialist Modern: East German Everyday Culture and Politics* (Ann Arbor: University of Michigan Press, 2008), 11

[23] The premiere was to have taken place earlier in the year, and was delayed due to the indisposition of the lead singer.

[24] Katherine Pence, '"A World in Miniature": The Leipzig Trade Fairs in the 1950s and East German Consumer Citizenship' in David F. Crew (ed.), *Consuming Germany in the Cold War* (Oxford & New York: Berg, 2003), 22–27.

articles on *Wat Tyler* make myriad connections between these features of the Fair and the opera. As argued in Chapter 6, Bush's opera tapped into efforts to construct a history of specifically English communism, and adumbrated a connection between past (the idealised English commons), present (the initiation of popular revolt in 1381), and future (the advent of English socialism). This feature of the opera was not lost on Rebling. He pointed to the dangers of mere archaism of style in historical opera: if an opera united a historical musical style with an authentic historical depiction it would fail to speak to the people in contemporary life:

> It is [...] essential to portray time and people by means of folk music as well as the music of the ruling classes, and yet to draw on the full range of modern vocal and orchestral techniques, in order to identify the appropriate intonations for the true humanness [*Menschlichkeit*] of the acting characters, and to express the essential content of revolutionary ideas, so that the fighters of today may be won over for progress and feel reaffirmed in their struggle.[25]

Bush, in Rebling's view, not only achieved a 'happy synthesis' of historical and modern elements but, in doing so, constructed a historical narrative that points towards the ongoing revolutionary struggle towards socialism. To underscore that this was not merely good dialectics, but that it was of profound relevance to the young East Germany, Rebling called upon German composers 'to follow the example of Alan Bush' by exploring subjects such as the Peasants' War or the 1848 revolutions in order to create 'progressive, historical-revolutionary opera'.[26] Notably, this mention of the Peasants' War and 1848 predated by a few months the call for composers to use these subjects in seminal articles on the necessary path of *Nationaloper* in leading publications.[27] In a later article following the Leipzig premiere, Rebling specifically described *Wat Tyler* as 'this very significant work for the development of a *Nationaloper*' and 'this outstanding example of the creation of a realistic *Nationaloper*', thus confirming the work's connection to this specifically East German contemporary cultural project.[28]

---

[25] E. R. [Eberhard Rebling], 'Die Oper "Wat Tyler" von Alan Bush: Zur Uraufführung im Berliner Rundfunk', *Musik und Gesellschaft* 2/4 (April 1952), 34.
[26] Ibid., 36.
[27] 'Für eine neue deutsche Nationaloper', *Neues Deutschland* 1 November 1952, 1; 'Für eine neue deutsche Nationaloper', *Musik und Gesellschaft* 2/12 (December 1952), 1.
[28] E.R., 'Die Oper "Wat Tyler" von Alan Bush in Leipzig', *Musik und Gesellschaft* 3/10 (Oct 1953), 16.

Another aspect of Bush's opera that made it so ripe for appropriation to East German cultural goals was the failure of British institutions to mount a production. East German outlets were able to preen themselves over the fact that they had achieved this cultural milestone when Britain could not. *Neues Deutschland* even published an interview with Bush preceding the premiere in which he described the strong economic upswing of the People's Democracies made evident by the Leipzig Fair, and the political significance of the participation of over 100 English industrialists in the event.[29] The *Tägliche Rundschau*, with specific reference to *Wat Tyler*, emphasised that Leipzig possessed not only the most modern factories and machinery, but also the largest and most modern 'theatre-workshop' [*Theaterwerkstatt*] in Germany.[30] Thus the very fact of Leipzig staging an unperformed prize-winning British opera gave the GDR credibility as a promoter of culture and international cooperation.

The premiere of *Wat Tyler* offered one further, and arguably the most important, item of cultural capital to East Germany. Two reviewers, Richard Petzold and Ernst Krause, both mention Bush's support for 'the "other" England, the England of progress and the working classes'.[31] In part, this intriguing phrase separates Bush's work from association with a Western, capitalist nation while affirming its nationalism, yet it is also significant that the phrase occurs in Petzold's account in the midst of a history of English music which traces its development from a rich folk music and medieval tradition, through a decline and focus on foreign imports and market-guided culture under capitalism, through to the re-emergence of a tradition rooted in English choral music and folk song in the late nineteenth century. There is a suggestion that Bush's opera is the product of an undercurrent in English musical culture, one that was diverted by capitalism: the very narrative of English history being constructed by British communist intellectuals at this time.[32] To reinforce the point, Petzold argues that the opera may be 'too modern' for the average opera-goer, because the archaic sources of his style have created an austerity that contrasts sharply with the melodic and colouristic embellishment and 'comfortable sound-world' that Petzold associates with Verdi or

---

[29] Anon., 'Gespräch mit Alan Bush', *Neues Deutschland*, 6 September 1953, 6.
[30] 'Die Leipziger Bühnen in der neuen Spielzeit', *Tägliche Rundschau*, 1 September 1953, 6.
[31] Richard Petzold, 'Musik in England', *Leipziger Theater: Wat Tyler* [1953 production programme]; Ernst Krause, 'Alan Bush und sein "Wat Tyler"', *Aufbau* 11 (1953), 1022.
[32] Prof. Dr. Richard Petzold, 'Einführung', *Alan Bush: Wat Tyler*, Vollständiges Opernbuch (Leipzig: Verlag Philipp Reclam, 1954), 25.

Puccini.³³ The modernity of the opera for Petzold, then, is not just its connection of the distant past with the socialist present, but it is the use of a style which rejects the features of late-bourgeois opera.

An opera whose music and historical narrative circumvented the recent past was of obvious interest to a state attempting to deal with the legacy of fascism. As David Bathrick has written:

> Official antifascism [...] became an important social imaginary for the absolution of guilt [...] for many living in the GDR. [...] As a story of genesis, the SED history of the period 1933 to 1949 was structured to associate the heritage, if not the very existence, of the GDR with a (vastly mythologized) working-class resistance to fascism. For those not in the resistance [...] there was also a saving grace. Given that fascism was the highest state of capitalism, and given that the elimination of capitalist property relations [...] in the Soviet Zone had supposedly removed the material and hence the political grounds for fascism, the building of socialism in the GDR came to represent de facto a form of overcoming the past.³⁴

If fascism were the highest realisation of capitalism, and the founders of the GDR had eradicated fascism both politically and socio-economically, *Wat Tyler* had the potential to strike the keynote of the early years of the new state. The SED's mythology – that its working-class citizens were the heirs of an anti-capitalist popular struggle dating back to the Middle Ages – was constructed, metaphorically, in *Wat Tyler*. The fact that Bush was known to have worked with the leading musicians of the GDR in exile from Nazism cemented the relevance of the opera to the new, anti-fascist state.

Finally, one of the strengths of the opera, mentioned by a number of reviewers, was that it deepened sympathy with the individual protagonists while representing the people. The socialist state, on the Soviet model, demanded the synonymous growth towards socialism of the individual and the state as a whole. As McLellan points out, the early post-war years were inauspicious for personal relationships, as the SED expected citizens 'to defer individual pleasures and devote themselves to the massive task of building the "better Germany"'.³⁵ Yet this goal, in itself, demanded not so much the rejection of family and sexual relations as the cultivation of proper socialist ones. Again, the legacy of fascism presented difficulties in

---

³³ Ibid., 26.
³⁴ David Bathrick, *The Powers of Speech: The Politics of Culture in the GDR* (Lincoln & London: University of Nebraska Press, 1995), 12–13.
³⁵ Josie McLellan, *Love in the Time of Communism: Intimacy and Sexuality in the GDR* (Cambridge: Cambridge University Press, 2011), 5.

this regard. Germany's catastrophic defeat 'caused a deep crisis in conceptions of masculinity', and required a 'remasculinisation' of both new Germanies.[36] Yet Nazi, not to mention Prussian, culture had contrasted an overtly militaristic model of German masculinity with a domesticated model of femininity. Meyer was concerned that this needed to be part of the discussion of East German musical culture:

> Already long before Hitler there have existed in the musical life of Germany, tendencies to cultivate music in connection with chauvinist and militarist politics. For many decades military marches and the so-called 'patriotic' songs have been of an importance as in no other country. The songs have often been of a musical character which suited their aggressive and imperialist or arrogant and brutalising texts.[37]

Wat Tyler, on the contrary, was a strong, active, proletarian character who would find many parallels in the masculine heroes of the early GDR, such as Ernst Thälmann, the former stoker-turned-communist leader executed by the Nazis in 1944, and Adolf Hennecke, an East German miner and Stakhanovite figure made famous by his extraordinary capacity for increased production.[38] Some of the language used about Thälmann – 'The flame that surrounds us, that glows in our hearts, that fills our spirits, will accompany us like a guiding light on the battlefields of our lives' – is strongly reminiscent of the imagery that suffuses *Wat Tyler*.[39] Margaret Tyler, too, represents a transformed image of femininity, because Wat and Margaret's personal desires are subsumed by their mutual commitment to revolution.

It is of course a bitter irony that by the time of *Wat Tyler*'s premiere, stories of heroes of production stood in sharp contrast to the rising quotas and falling wages that contributed to the June 1953 riots, and that such heroes in part valorised individual effort in opposition to worker solidarity. While this highlights the cynicism of the regime, it does not alter the value *Wat Tyler* had for the construction of a German socialist culture. The fact that the opera was succeeded by historical operas based on heroes of the German Peasants' war – Paul Kurzbach's *Thomas Münzer* (performed June 1955) and Jean Kurt Forest's *Der arme Konrad* (performed October 1959) – and the wealth of new opportunities offered to Bush confirm the evidence already given.

---

[36] Mark Fenemore, *Sex, Thugs and Rock 'n' Roll: Teenage Rebels in Cold-War East Germany* (New York & Oxford: Berghahn Books, 2007), 44–5.
[37] Meyer, 'Music in a Future Germany'.
[38] Fenemore, *Sex, Thugs and Rock 'n' Roll*, 46–8.   [39] Ibid., 38–9.

Violence and Masculinity

Given the extraordinary suitability of *Wat Tyler* for East Germany's cultural goals, it must be asked why his operas were not even more successful. *Wat Tyler* and *Men of Blackmoor* each achieved a number of productions; why were none of them in Berlin, even after *Wat Tyler* was broadcast by Berlin Radio in 1952? In the case of *Blackmoor*, this is doubly curious given that Burghardt, the Leipzig Intendant who staged *Wat Tyler*, moved to the Deutsche Staatsoper in 1954, and that many aspects of Bush's second opera were ideally suited to the new state. The subject was a miner's strike in nineteenth-century Northumberland, and, like *Wat Tyler*, it combined folk music with Bush's own idiom.[40] The subject of mining was an especially happy one for the opera's prospects. Fenemore has pointed out that, in addition to Hennecke's celebrity, the East German mining towns in the early years of the GDR enjoyed a reputation as a lawless frontier akin to the Wild West; miners presented an exciting and masculinist image of postwar reconstruction that could also act as a socialist alternative to some of the glamorous mass cultural products of the West.[41]

In fact, Bush's opera *was* auditioned at the Staatsoper in November 1954, an event attended by Burghardt, Krause and others. At this point in GDR history, music-making was monitored not by Meyer's VDKM but by the Staatliche Kommission für Kunstangelegenheiten der DDR (State Commission for Artistic Affairs, *Stakuko*), an organisation run by SED functionaries and succeeded, in 1954, by a Ministry for Culture (MfK) whose Music Department followed the same policies with virtually the same staff.[42] As Thacker has revealed, the nature of *Stakuko*'s repressive control of musical life is often misunderstood, consisting of 'a strange mixture of hectoring and whingeing', rather than outright bans, and also limited in its work by a small number of staff with a vast remit.[43] Nevertheless, their respective assessments of *Wat Tyler* and *Blackmoor* are revealing. Regarding the former, the report made some technical criticisms, yet on the strength of the Berlin Radio broadcast the head of the Music Department of *Stakuko*, Rudolf Hartig, asked for the recording and score to be made available to interested Intendants of opera

---

[40] For a detailed discussion of this dimension of the opera, see John Lowerson with Joanna Bullivant, 'Trouble down t'pit: Marxist Politics, Industrial Stereotypes and Northern Sources in Alan Bush's Opera, *Men of Blackmoor* (1954)' in Rachel Cowgill, Dave Russell and Derek Scott (eds.), *Music and the Idea of the North* (forthcoming).
[41] Fenemore, *Sex, Thugs and Rock 'n' Roll*, 4. [42] Thacker, *Music after Hitler*, 157ff.
[43] Ibid, 159.

houses.⁴⁴ By contrast, the report on *Blackmoor* by the new leader of the Music Department, Hans-Georg Uszkoreit, criticised the fact that, in the opera, 'the resolution of the conflict did not lead to a peaceful and optimistic conclusion'.⁴⁵ While Uszkoreit acknowledged the difficulties presented by a piano arrangement, he nevertheless complained of the dissonances (*dissonierende Härten*) it produced. He concluded that the opera was not suitable for performance at the Staatsoper, but might find a place in another theatre of the GDR.

Uszkoreit's account is curious in several respects. If the ending of the opera was insufficiently peaceful and optimistic, why was this a problem at the Staatsoper but not elsewhere in the GDR? Why, too, did he employ the awkward term '*dissonierende Härten*', a phrase that redundantly jumbles together two terms for dissonance? Uszkoreit was a functionary rather than a professional musician, but it also seems an excessive response to an inappropriate arrangement, and not one that should sink the entire opera. In a previous instance of a problematic new opera – Brecht/Dessau's *Lucullus* – Calico has argued that the music was criticised to disguise official embarrassment over the real problem of the text, one that could not be admitted due to Brecht's international status.⁴⁶ When we look more closely at Bush's libretto, it is clear that it too could have been unacceptable. Firstly, the heroic image of the miner in the GDR was of the excessively productive comrade serving the state. Bush's miners, on the other hand, are on strike for the entire duration of the work. Secondly, the libretto shows a level of violence on the part of the heroes not seen in *Wat Tyler*, and there is evidence that it was altered to reduce this after the Berlin audition. In the original, never published version, the hero Daniel sabotages the pit machinery, endangering the lives of the strikebreaking leadminers still in the mine, who never re-emerge. In the altered, final version, the overseer Fletcher's warning over the damaged shaft that 'there'll be death in it' is answered by Daniel:

> No death for them! They'll see the light of day,
> And live to crawl the way they came,
> Like rats that run to lair!

---

⁴⁴ Rudolf Hartig, 'Über die Oper "Wat Tyler" von Alan Bush', 27 March 1952, BArch DR 1/190: Ministerium für Kultur, Hauptabteilung Musik: Komponisten und Musikwissenschaftler, 1952–1957; Rudolf Hartig to Prof. Rudolf [sic] Pischner, 27 March 1952, BArch DR 1/190.
⁴⁵ Hans-Georg Uszkoreit, 'Vermerk!', 15 November 1954, BArch DR 1/190.
⁴⁶ Calico, 'The Trial, the Condemnation', 340–1.

> Nor hope, for all your bribes and threats,
> They'll work the pit again.[47]

Nancy Bush also added a hopeful refrain near the beginning and end of the opera that reinforced the sense that the miners' struggle was looking to a future revolution.

Given the context of the audition, only a year after the June 1953 uprising and its brutal suppression, it seems highly likely that an opera that deals intensively with a single strike (in contrast to the historical vista of *Wat Tyler*), and which encouraged identification with workers engaging in violent strikes, could not be stomached as a prospect for the main Berlin opera house. Despite the superficial affinities with *Wat Tyler*'s perfect articulation of GDR aspirations, *Blackmoor* presented a different, unpalatable, face of popular revolt. With the extraction of much of the violence and a reassuring nod to dialectical history, the opera could be taken up elsewhere in the GDR (including Hennecke's hometown of Zwickau), yet, unsurprisingly, it generated the sort of criticisms of mildness that had dogged *Wat Tyler* when it eventually reached England in two amateur productions.[48] Clearly, the different fates of *Wat Tyler* and *Blackmoor* demonstrate both the inflexibility of new models of socialist masculinity in the GDR and the subtleties that could secure approval or rejection for even the most auspicious of socialist artworks.

Communism and Youth Culture

The differing treatment of Bush's early operas reveals another crucial facet of the East German regime. While its repressive nature remains clear, the SED was also locked into a process of give-and-take between its own ideals and the shifting tastes and ideologies of the populace, especially in the face of the Party's powerlessness over key aspects of life in the GDR. *Wat Tyler* married well with official notions of music both populist (in its use of folk tunes and subject matter) and modern (in its articulation of socialist historical progress). Yet especially among a younger generation growing up in the 1950s and 1960s, what was modern and popular in music was understood very differently. Due to the proximity to West Germany, the SED could not control the ability of young East Germans to listen to Western radio or, before the construction of the Wall in 1961, to travel

---

[47] Several copies of the original libretto in typescript with sheets of 'additions', dated 1955, are in ABA.
[48] See, for example, Desmond Shawe-Taylor, 'More Mild than Bitter', *Sunday Times*, 4 December 1960.

to clubs in West Berlin. Worse for the SED, the music being embraced by young people was largely commercial and American: dance music, jazz, beat, and rock 'n' roll. It was not merely that such music did not match the SED's vision of a German socialist musical culture which celebrated labour in the cause of building the new nation from the ashes of Nazism. It was also bound up with a raft of more alarming social manifestations of post-war modernity: participation in a global youth culture outside state control, the desire for commercial goods ('Coca-colonisation'), sexual liberation (in particular, female sexuality), and above all, the possibility for young people of 'withdrawing from official incorporation strategies by submerging themselves into their own separate worlds of hobbies, youth-specific interests and subcultures'.[49]

Mounting appropriate official responses was trickier than may at first appear. The SED could, and did, make alarmist denunciations of dance music, often emphasising its non-realism and decadence, sometimes with racist and sexist overtones. One report, for example, labelled girls who danced to jazz as 'Veronikas', using the derogatory name given to women consorting with (implicitly, black) American GIs in the immediate post-war period.[50] Yet such attacks came at a cost. Racist descriptions of dance music conflicted with East Germany's goal of enlightened internationalism, its support for decolonisation, and its frequent efforts to establish diplomatic relations with newly independent countries in Africa and Asia.[51] A repressive attitude to the sexual liberation of young people sat at odds with the impulses in East Germany towards increased rights for women and relaxation of attitudes towards premarital sex.[52] Finally, the East German government, through *Stakuko*, had proved totally incapable of doing anything to stop the pervasive enjoyment of dance music and the performance of similar music throughout the GDR. Not only was attempting to do so (through measures such as enforcing fines, issuing permits and guidelines) a bureaucratic nightmare, but demands for a realist culture amid the harsh realities of daily life in East Germany offered nothing to compare with the seductive escapism and glamour of dance music.[53] Escapism was a matter for concern, not only because of the concomitant lack of focus on the realities of building socialism, but because of the real

---

[49] Fenemore, *Sex, Thugs and Rock 'n' Roll*, 12.   [50] Ibid., 22.

[51] See William Glenn Gray, *Germany's Cold War: The Global Campaign to Isolate East Germany, 1949–1969* (Chapel Hill and London: The University of North Carolina Press, 2003).

[52] Dagmar Herzog, 'East Germany's Sexual Evolution' in Pence and Betts (eds.), *Socialist Modern*, 73.

[53] Thacker, *Music after Hitler*, 198–9.

threat of flight. As Fenemore points out, in 1955, a Politbüro meeting expressed alarm at the levels of *Republikflucht* among young people.[54] Consequently, the SED's attitude to dance music and other forms throughout the 1950s and 1960s consisted of waves of liberalisation and repression.

It should be stressed that anxiety over sexual liberation and popular music was by no means confined to East Germany. West Germany, equally, went through moral quandaries over the correct response to youth culture. The notorious British association between communism and homosexuality discussed in Chapter 3 notwithstanding, the CPGB contained a good deal of 'native revolutionary priggishness' that was bolstered by Soviet emphasis on family values after the Second World War.[55] Bush's own attitudes were complex. Early publications of the WMA included articles on jazz, and the organisation continued to support one branch of popular music in the spirit of the 1960s in the form of the folk revival.[56] Bush was also keenly interested in socialism and youth, attending a string of the postwar World Youth Festivals held in locations throughout the Communist Bloc.[57] However, he endorsed the broad rhetoric of anti-Americanism that characterised the 'Battle of Ideas' in terms redolent with fears of unbridled sexuality:

> Comic strips, American Digests, novels, films, are marketed under the favourable conditions in the world of capitalist competition which subservient governments provide for them. Cultural coca-colonisation is a real factor in our every-day lives. As is well known U.S.A. comic strips, films, novels and plays have reached appalling depths of degradation, sadism, neurosis, sensationalism, and scarcely veiled pornography.[58]

While he was slow to link such ideas to any specific brand of popular music, the era of Beatlemania provoked a more extreme response:

> People [in Prague] have a rather different idea of how an audience ought to behave. They will not stand for teenagers breaking up the chairs and generally making themselves destructive of socialist property. You may think this is rather a stuffy notion, though I hope you won't. I will not go further into this rather awkward subject, apart from mentioning that in the more raucous dives over here where pop-groups perform, it is quite a routine for the chairs to be washed the next morning, in order to remove the traces of urine that the teenage girls have left behind them in their extasy (I have spelt that word

---

[54] Fenemore, *Sex, Thugs and Rock 'n' Roll*, 103.
[55] Kevin Morgan, Gidon Cohen and Andrew Flinn, *Communists in British Society, 1920-1991* (London, Sydney & Chicago: Rivers Oram Press, 2007), 127.
[56] See BL/AB MS Mus. 657: Correspondence with the WMA, 1960-1969.
[57] See N. Bush, *Alan Bush*, 52-8.   [58] Bush, 'Tasks of Cultural Workers', 54.

wrong). I don't say this is the fault of the groups, but I do say that these results are not such as people in the socialist countries want to encourage.[59]

Again such reactions were not purely socialist: an almost identical description of young female fandom as bestial (with loss of bladder control) and excessively sexual (ecstasy) appeared in a police report on a beat concert in West Berlin in 1965, and the urban myth that such behaviour took place at Beatles' gigs persists even now.[60]

Notable in Bush's assertion is his confidence that such a phenomenon was entirely confined to capitalist countries, certainly not a confidence shared by the SED. Yet there is reason to suppose that Bush shared their anxiety about the path of popular culture. Firstly, the very extremity of his reaction bespeaks uncertainty, and the context for his anecdote is a correspondence with a Young Communist, with the undoubted intention of influencing youthful opinion. Secondly, the popularity of music that Bush implicitly associated with 'Coca-colonisation' threatened the national dimension of his work and that of the WMA. A statement by the latter in 1961 lamented the fact that 'with the enormous growth of commercialised music through various mass media, many young people are more conversant with American people's songs than their own'.[61] By the mid-1960s, Bush's personal involvement with working-class groups, and the WMA's activities, had declined significantly in comparison with the 1940s highpoint. In 1975 Bush lamented the decline of working-class musical culture since 1951. Even where the WMA and its offshoot, Topic Records, were successful in capturing the contemporary mood, as with the publication of *Songs for the Sixties* by Peggy Seeger and Ewan MacColl, those singers were hardly central figures in the WMA.[62] They refused Bush's invitation to perform at a benefit to raise money to stage *Wat Tyler* in the 1970s, citing their musical differences with Bush.[63] At the heart of all these uncertainties and complaints lay a deep anxiety about the lack of success of some of

---

[59] Alan Bush to Peter Carter [Chairman of the Young Communist League], 22 October 1966, BL/AB MS Mus. 665: Correspondence with the Communist Party of Great Britain.

[60] Fenemore, *Sex, Thugs and Rock 'n' Roll*, 170. See also http://www.huffingtonpost.com/2014/08/05/beatles-things-you-didnt-know_n_5648410.html.

[61] 'Revised draft of letter to T.U.C. General Secretary (George Woodcock)', 18 April 1961, BL/AB MS Mus. 657.

[62] Peggy Seeger and Ewan MacColl (eds.), *Songs for the Sixties* (London: Workers' Music Association, 1961).

[63] Alan Bush to Peggy Seeger and Ewan MacColl, 3 November 1973, BL/AB MS Mus. 629: Correspondence concerning proposed performances of *Wat Tyler* at Sadler's Wells, 1950–73.

Bush's most cherished principles of socialist musical culture. His theory of music, developed through the 1930s and 1940s, was predicated on the need for politically informed organisation of musical culture, and on Bush's belief in the inherent connection of his musical materials and compositional method with the workers it was supposed to inspire. Despite the WMA's insistence on the role they needed to play in guiding the folk revival in the 1960s, they had little influence over their artists. For Bush himself, an added frustration must have been the lack of professional productions of his operas and consequently the loss of a role in British musical life such as he envisaged in the 1940s. Both British and East German communists, then, were horrified by the course of popular culture in the 1950s and 1960s, yet acutely conscious of its power in reaching new generations.

A Socialist Alternative?

It is within this context of revulsion at the direction of popular culture and desire for real popular appeal that Bush's third opera, *The Sugar Reapers or Guyana Johnny*, should be considered. In contrast to the first two operas, it is set in the remote South American colony of British Guiana,[64] and it was inspired by the real-life struggle for independence from Britain that was still being waged when the opera was written. Bush even travelled to the colony in 1959 in order to research the music for the work and gain a firsthand impression of the independence movement.[65]

---

[64] I will use the adjective 'Guyanese' throughout to refer to both British Guiana and independent Guyana.

[65] Bush's experiences attempting to conduct his research are a Cold War story in themselves. Thanks to their surveillance of the CPGB's headquarters, MI5 were aware of Bush's plans well in advance and were convinced that his intentions in travelling to British Guiana were political and subversive. When Bush first attempted to travel in 1957, they successfully lobbied the Governors of Trinidad and British Guiana to bar Bush from entering. After being forced to turn back, Bush garnered much support and publicity, even having a question asked in Parliament. The Labour MP Konni Zilliacus asked John Profumo, then Secretary of State for the Colonies, why Bush had been refused entry 'in order to record folk songs of the territory', and commented that the whole affair had 'an awful smell of something'. Profumo, while brushing off the challenge, made the revealing comment that 'Mr. Bush was deemed to be an undesirable visitor in both territories under the respective Immigration Ordinance'. The ban was rescinded and he was able to travel, albeit still the subject of covert surveillance, in 1959. While there is no full published account of the complete story, an overview is given in N. Bush, *Alan Bush*, 79–81. Bush's own handwritten accounts are in ABH. For documents relating to MI5, see TNA/PRO KV 2/3519: Bush, Alan D. For the Hansard record of the parliamentary discussion, see http://hansard.millbanksystems.com/commons/1957/jun/27/mr-alan-bush-entry-permit.

British Guiana, Britain's only South American colony, had originally been a sugar-producing colony using the labour of slaves brought over from Africa. Following the abolition of slavery, the colony gained a population of indentured servants from regions of Eastern India. These two ethnic groups made up the majority of the population in the 1950s, with Indo-Guyanese largely concentrated in villages as sugar workers, and Afro-Guyanese tending to form the majority of the urban population. In 1953, Cheddi Jagan, a sophisticated and well-travelled Indo-Guyanese married to an American, and Forbes Burnham, an Afro-Guyanese leader, won a landslide election result for the left-wing and pro-independence People's Progressive Party (PPP), causing Britain to dispatch a warship to the colony to assert British rule. In the years that followed, anxieties over Jagan's political sympathies, imperialist British scepticism regarding the possibility of Guyanese self-determination, and American fears of a 'second Cuba' produced a degree of interference and exploitation of ethnic tensions that eventually deposed Jagan and installed Forbes Burnham as virtual dictator until the 1990s.[66]

Bush made considerable efforts to recreate the distinctive features of British Guiana in his opera. The setting is a village populated by Indo-Guyanese and Afro-Guyanese sugar workers living side by side. The main character, Johnny, is Afro-Guyanese and a leader of the Popular Party (based on the PPP) in his village, while his brother Joseph eschews responsibility and aims to make his own fortune quickly. Sumintra is Indo-Guyanese and in love with Johnny, but she is being pursued by the overseer, Ganesh Maraj, who is also backed by her father, Panasar. Johnny and Sumintra's betrothal is celebrated on the night in which the Popular Party win a landslide victory in the first free elections in British Guiana. Five months later, the British government has imposed emergency rule and dispatched a warship to the colony (a development based on real events). Political meetings are now illegal; Joseph is caught stealing and betrays his brother, confirming his attendance at a meeting, to avoid prison. Johnny and Sumintra's wedding is interrupted as Johnny is arrested and taken to prison. At the end of the opera, Sumintra forgives Joseph and leads the village in patience and defiance awaiting Johnny's release.

In many respects, the work actively cultivates the features of post-war popular music that made it so alluring in East Germany. In contrast to the

---

[66] See Stephen G. Rabe, *U.S. Intervention in British Guiana: A Cold War Story* (Chapel Hill: University of North Carolina Press, 2005).

dour realism of the first two operas, *The Sugar Reapers or Guyana Johnny* is suffused with exoticism, presenting a cast of African and Indian characters, a setting in a rural sugar-growing community in a distant South American land, and a score influenced by the folk music of Guyana.[67] The opening scene, featuring Ella, an Afro-Guyanese, and several other girls, is representative. The setting for the scene of gathering water and singing of work and rest while observing nature is typically exoticist, while the style of chorus with an ornamented solo line over the top would be familiar to Bush from, say, the spiritual. Ironically, the ostinato figure of the accompaniment and parallel fourths in the chorus lend an exoticism to the music using the same techniques that produced archaism in *Wat Tyler*.[68] The Indian wedding scene in Act II is a similarly evocative appropriation of Indian music; at the beginning of the scene, for example, we hear a repetitive rhythmic line on the bongo drums and a heavily ornamented melody on the oboe in the style of the Indian *shahnai* (later heard on the flute);[69] subsequently a chorus of Indian young men enter in procession, singing what Bush identifies in his sketches as the Gujarati song 'Vagya Changhadia Avi Jan' over a drone-like pedal (Ex 7.1). In addition to such set-pieces, the Afro-Guyanese and Indian-Guyanese are consistently characterised with the 'intonations' of their respective musical cultures, in the case of the former frequently using pentatonicism and, in the latter, through Bush selecting specific Indian scales and *rāgas* for the main Indian-Guyanese characters. Bound up with its exoticism, a further feature of the opera that mimicked something of post-war popular culture was its light-heartedness (at least in comparison to Bush's English operas), its unprecedented dance content and physicality. The overture to the opera incorporates ostinato rhythms, shifting time-signatures, and even saxophones in an effort to capture the spirit of South American dance. The Que-Que, an Afro-Guyanese betrothal celebration, consists of an extended sequence of dances based on melodies adopted from Guyanese folk music, and is an element more characteristic of the musical than modern opera. The wedding scene even favourably presents something of the dancing female body, with the Tartu production, featuring costumed Indian dancers.[70]

---

[67] The notable precedent is Delius's opera *Koanga* (1895–7).
[68] *The Sugar Reapers* or *Guyana Johnny*, Opera in Two Acts (Six Scenes) by Alan Bush, libretto by Nancy Bush, vocal score [VS], 1ff.
[69] Bush actually marks it as such, VS, 222.
[70] A range of photographs of this production may be viewed at http://www.alanbushtrust.org.uk/gallery/gallery.asp?room=Gallery.

Despite these efforts on Bush's part, what might be considered concessions to the spirit of post-war popular music were consistently at loggerheads with both socialist realist aesthetics and his own discomfort with the nature of post-war popular culture. Exoticism sat uncomfortably within socialist realism, inviting criticism for escapism, eroticism, and primitivism (arguably, the very factors that made it attractive). Consequently, both Bush and East German reviewers were constantly at pains to assert the work's authenticity, both as a depiction of the

Ex. 7.1 Bush, *Sugar Reapers*, wedding scene, VS 228–9.

Ex. 7.1 (cont.)

Guyanese struggle and in terms of the musical material used. The *Leipziger Volkszeitung* reviewer defended the work against the strawman of all three dangers of exoticism. He compares it favourably with Krenek's *Jonny spielt auf* (in which 'It is difficult to feel that [Krenek] showed any desire for the liberation of the oppressed Negroes'); remarks that Bush's use of Guyanese folk music 'gives his music essential impulses, in no sense purely exotic tone-colour'; and observes that he writes 'simple but in no respect primitive melody'.[71] Revealing another dimension of East German approbation, Dietrich Wolf wrote in the official programme for the Leipzig premiere that 'Guyana represents the whole colonial-ruled portion of humanity, with which Bush has declared himself in solidarity'.[72] Not only did this statement situate the opera's depiction of Guyana within a Marxist narrative in which imperialism is an extension of capitalism and thus opposed by communism, but it also implied East Germany's role as patron and comrade of nations seeking independence – the very role that was so elusive in reality. In East German discourse, then, the exotic elements of the opera could be distanced from jazz (as in *Jonny spielt auf*) and comfortably situated within anti-capitalist ideology and East German foreign policy.

For Bush's part, the exotic appeal of the opera was justified by the authenticity of music and subject matter:

> we Marxists warn against exoticism, and rightly so, if it is a matter of the exotic for its own sake. In *Guayana Johnny* [the German title of the opera], however, there really is a political struggle, which specifically takes place in a country where, for us Europeans, even the everyday seems appealing owing to its peculiarity'.[73]

Yet Bush's choices in selecting Guyanese music during his visit reveal the limitations of his enthusiasm for exoticism. Bush was initially frustrated in his search for Guyanese music, and in at least one instance discovered communities singing American songs heard on the radio.[74] In his search for what was distinctively Guyanese, he was, in the end, partly indebted to Vesta Lowe, a Guyanese collector of folk song who had published a collection of Afro-Guyanese songs.[75] It is notable that Bush's evocation of modern Guyana did not permit the inclusion of music that reflected the impact of modernity or commercialism. His musical characterisation of his main Indian characters is also telling. Ex. 7.2 shows some of the scales and *rāgas* used respectively in the solo music of Sumintra, Panasar, and Ganesh Maraj (Ex. 7.2). All of Sumintra's scales have a Western modal equivalent (Dorian, Phrygian, and Mixolydian), such as Bush used

---

[71] Werner Wolf, '"Guayana Johnny". Erfolgreiche Uraufführung von Alan Bushs Oper', *Leipziger Volkszeitung*, 14 December 1966.

[72] Dietrich Wolf, 'Nicht vom Schreibtisch aus', *Guayana Johnny: Oper von Alan Bush* [programme for the 1966 Leipzig Production], n.p.

[73] Alan Bush to Karl Kayser, 10 May 1965, BL/AB MS Mus. 633: Correspondence concerning the 1966 production of *The Sugar Reapers*.

[74] Interview with Dr Rachel O'Higgins, 1 July 2010.

[75] ABA contains a picture of Bush with Vesta Lowe, and a copy of her published collection of folk songs *Guiana Sings* (Delaware, Ohio: Cooperative Recreation Service, 1959).

Ex. 7.2a *Sugar Reapers*, Sumintra's scale and *raga*. Reprinted by permission.

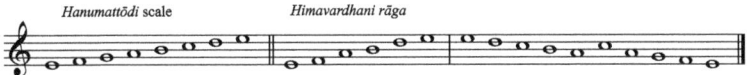

Ex. 7.2b *Sugar Reapers*, Panasar's scale and *raga*.

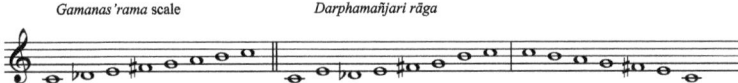

Ex. 7.2c *Sugar Reapers*, Ganesh Maraj's scale and *raga*.

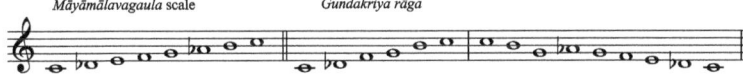

freely in his earlier operas. His depiction of her may be seen in contrast with Johnny's pentatonic melodic lines in Act I Scene 2 (Ex. 7.3). The villain Ganesh Maraj, in contrast, consistently uses a *rāga* derived from the *Māyāmālavagaula* scale characterised by alternating semitones and augmented seconds, which invests his vocal line with a distinctive, exotic sound throughout. In the case of Panasar, the more morally ambivalent character, one of his *rāgas* corresponds to the Lydian mode, and we hear him using this in Act I Scene 1 when he laments his under-employment. Yet when he orders Sumintra to marry Ganesh Maraj later in the same scene, believing that this will secure his own future, the melodic collection he uses is much closer to the *Gamanas'rama* scale, which contains, like the Lydian, the interval of the augmented fourth. Looking at the *rāga* Bush associated with this scale for Panasar, however, there is no direct leap of an augmented fourth in either ascending or descending forms, so according to Bush's understanding of *rāga* theory, as a strict pattern ascending and descending, this interval should not be used. Yet as he argues with Sumintra, the augmented fourth forms a dissonant accompaniment figure, and also characterises his agitated vocal line (Ex. 7.4). Thus, Guyanese music could be rendered akin to Bush's existing national idiom and, where it is most strikingly different and exotic, could reinforce the musical identification of characters most identified with imperialism and oppression. The exotic is, then, once again tainted with suspicion.

Ex 7.3 *Sugar Reapers*, Act I Scene 2, VS 78–9.

Ex. 7.4 *Sugar Reapers*, Act I Scene 1, VS, 42.

A similar ambiguity surrounds the depiction of women in the opera, in the context of post-war culture. On the one hand, as previously stated, the staged opera depicted Indo- and Afro-Guyanese women dancing to exotic music, seemingly overcoming some of the racial and sexual fears that guided East German attitudes to female sexuality and popular music. On the other hand, the figure of Sumintra is not only characterised musically using those Indian scales closest to Western modes, but she is also a model of socialist femininity as depicted in the earlier operas: virginal, committed to marriage, and able to put communal political needs ahead of personal desires. This depiction of femininity strikes at the heart of the opera's ambivalence towards post-war youth cultures, and it also reveals why such efforts were ultimately doomed to failure. The exoticism, escapism, and commercialism of post-war popular music, whether American or British, imported or homegrown, was not simply attractive as a refreshing alternative to the hardships of life under socialism. Rather, popular music offered a space where an individual sense of self (*Eigensinn*) beyond the control of the state could be formed and reinforced by sexual and social behaviour (seeking pleasure, withdrawing from state-directed activities) and consumption (such as possession of records).[76] In drawing elements of the bodily or the exotic into state-sanctioned opera, Bush and the approving East German authorities articulated anxieties about the young people embracing the forms of modernity offered by popular musics. Yet that combination of popular virtues and the same overarching narrative of collective progress and action was a circle that could not be squared.

Communist Lateness

While *Wat Tyler* created, for East Germany at least, an operatic space in which socialist models of modernity and national culture could dwell together, *The Sugar Reapers or Guyana Johnny* marks the point at which these two forces were tugging apart. An individualist, consumerist model of modernity could no longer be joined to a collectivist narrative of national progress. And it is curious to reflect that this was not merely the case in East Germany. Wiebe has written of Britten's *War Requiem* that it stands as his 'most ambitious attempt to integrate art and national culture, and to connect the individual voice with a notion of cultural citizenship'.[77] Yet the *War Requiem*, as has been frequently observed, also marked the end of this period of Britten's artistic life and the composition of a series of late works of what Mitchell denoted 'parable-art', in which national elements were still present – in *Curlew River*, for example, but stripped down to their essentials and mingled with Far Eastern influences, invoking rituals remote in both time and space (whether it be mediaeval England or Japan), and thus rendered both strange and intimate.

In an insightful essay, Edward Said has explored the concept of late style in the crowning work of this period in Britten's artistic life: *Death in Venice*. For Said, there is a notion that age can produce 'a new spirit of reconciliation and serenity often expressed in terms of a miraculous transfiguration of common reality' in an artist's late works.[78] What fascinates Said is, on the contrary, artistic lateness as unprecedented difficulty and contradiction, manifest in works which 'tear apart the career and the artist's craft and reopen the questions of meaning, success, and progress that the artist's late period is supposed to move

---

[76] Fenemore, *Sex, Thugs and Rock 'n' Roll*, 12.
[77] Wiebe, *Britten's Unquiet Pasts*, 224–5.
[78] Edward W. Said, *On Late Style: Music and Literature against the Grain* (London: Bloomsbury, 2006), 6.

beyond'.⁷⁹ Two elements of Said's identification of lateness in *Death in Venice* will prove pertinent here. Firstly, he observes that Britten's subject of the aging artist, fear of the loss of creative power, and his intense desire for the beautiful youth Tadzio invites biographical parallels. Yet the finished opera also represents Britten's artistic triumph over the physical degeneration and unreturned passion to which Aschenbach succumbs. Thus the distance between aesthetic object and artist is as important as their commonalities. Secondly, Said argues that Venice, the repository of cultural memory and symbol of both inspiration and decay, acts allegorically as both a point of artistic return and as the site of a struggle between the Apollonian and the Dionysian, played out in a musical language drawing on Britten's own musical past as well as his later non-European sources. For Said, the essence of the work's lateness is the distance between Aschenbach, representing the subjective impulse, and Tadzio, symbolic of the 'fractured landscape' with which the subjective engages. Quoting Adorno, Said concludes that Britten 'does not bring about their harmonious synthesis. As the power of dissociation, he tears them apart in time, in order, perhaps, to preserve them for the eternal. In the history of art late works are the catastrophes'.⁸⁰

While in many respects Bush's final opera, *Joe Hill*, is a world away from *Death in Venice*, I will argue that it repays consideration as a late work, the crowning effort of a new phase in Bush's artistic trajectory. *Joe Hill* is the only opera on which he worked with a librettist other than his wife. Barrie Stavis's *The Man Who Never Died: A Play about Joe Hill* was completed in the early 1950s; thus, like Thomas Mann's *Death in Venice*, it is by no means a late work.⁸¹ The subject was the Swedish-American trade unionist and songwriter Joe Hill, who was tried and executed in controversial circumstances in 1915. Hill's last words were said to be 'Don't mourn for me – organize!' and with these he became a martyr and legend of the organised labour movement. The idea that Hill lived on because of his legacy became an important theme, crystallised in Alfred Hayes' 1925 poem 'I dreamed I saw Joe Hill last night', set to music by Earl Robinson in 1936.⁸² The opera depicts Joe's union activities in Utah and his success as musician and political organiser; his affair with a married woman; the

---

⁷⁹ Ibid., 7.   ⁸⁰ Ibid., 160.

⁸¹ Stavis, born in 1906, was in his late forties at the time. The play received its world premiere in 1955 at Hamline College, St Paul, Minnesota, and another run in New York, 1957–8.

⁸² For a detailed account, see Barrie Stavis's preface to the revised edition of the play: Barrie Stavis, *The Man Who Never Died*, revised edition (Cranbury: Barnes, 1972), 13–32.

accusation of murder that led to his arrest; and finally his trial, execution, and legacy. Stavis's play had generated interest in East Germany as the basis for an opera as early as 1957 and Bush, then engaged on *The Sugar Reapers or Guyana Johnny*, initially advised Stavis about developing such an opera with a range of other possible composers.[83] When in 1965, Bush received independently the offer of a commission from the Berlin Staatsoper, he invited Stavis to work with him, and the adaptation of the play as opera libretto began.

When considering *Joe Hill* as a late work, it is important to note that, as Donald Mitchell remarked of *Death in Venice*, things could have been otherwise.[84] The opera is not a *last* work. At many stages both Bush and Stavis considered collaborating elsewhere. There was also at one point a plan that Nancy Bush would adapt the play, but Stavis took over when it became clear that she intended to shape it into a standard operatic format of acts and scenes, rather than preserving the montage-like juxtaposition of brief scenes of the original.[85] Nevertheless, what emerged was a considerable aesthetic departure from Bush's earlier through-composed operas: a work combining spoken, semi-sung, and fully developed operatic scenes; a much-reduced role for the chorus; far more nuanced psychological insight into the lead character; and a succession of rapidly shifting and fragmentary scenes.

The opera features several of the qualities of lateness that may be found in *Death in Venice*. The subject is recapitulatory and autobiographical. Where Peter Grimes and Wat Tyler were implicitly artists, as discussed in Chapter 6, Joe Hill, like Aschenbach, is *actually* an artist. Joe Hill, too, is an artist in the way that Bush was at the time of his earliest musical-political endeavours in the 1930s: a songwriter and agitator, working directly with political groups. Conceivably, Bush might have embraced the first model of lateness embodied by Said, the 'miraculous transfiguration of common reality', by creating a valedictory portrait of the roots of his artistic life via an implicit comparison with the immortalised trade unionist composer. I suggest, on the contrary, that *Joe Hill* is a work that indeed reopens 'the questions of meaning, success, and progress that the artist's late

---

[83] Stavis approached Paul Dessau and, at Bush's suggestion, Claudio Santoro. See BL/AB MS Mus. 441: Correspondence with Barrie Stavis and BL MS Mus. 1699: Correspondence between Barrie Stavis and Ossia Trilling.

[84] Donald Mitchell, 'An Introduction in the Shape of a Memoir' in Donald Mitchell (ed.), *Benjamin Britten: Death in Venice* (Cambridge: Cambridge University Press, 1987), 21.

[85] Barrie Stavis to Reinhard Mieke, 16 February 1961, BL MS Mus. 1699.

period is supposed to move beyond'. The opera betrays an obsession with the process of Hill's immortalisation, particularly the role his songs played in the labour movement. In Act I Scene 3, Ed Rowan, one of Joe's union friends, refers to his 'wonderful song' 'Casey Jones' in the midst of a strike meeting, after which Joe is able to call for unity in action (Ex. 7.5).[86] In Act I Scene 2, Moody, the local copper magnate, and Tom Sharpe, a member of the union who is betraying Joe, hear the song 'Pie in the Sky', set to a familiar hymn tune, and comment on Joe's compositional process and influence upon the workers: 'He puts songs to ev'rything. Whatever people know' (Ex. 7.6).[87] In Act I Scene 6 Ed tells Joe: 'We need you and your songs'.[88] Thus, the opera is suffused with precise references to the process by which Joe's songs inspire action and solidarity. It is striking that these form part of an opera composed not only when Bush's vision of national-cultural renewal and consensus was increasingly anachronistic, but as he justified his belief in the ability of music to foster national and popular cohesion using an ever more elaborate theoretical apparatus. In a 1969 paper, he drew on Ernest Ansermet's theories of perception and Deryck Cooke's *The Language of Music* in support of his argument for the universality of tonality and its ability to articulate and communicate emotion.[89] In one sense, then, the opera is a revisitation, an anxious reassertion of Bush's beliefs about musical language. This also brings the opera in line with Bush's other major late works: the *24 Preludes* and Symphony No. 4, op. 98 (the 'Lascaux', 1983), inspired by the cave paintings discovered in southern France, which meditates on the origins of human artistic expression.

The lateness and questioning nature of the opera is also revealed in the transfiguration of Joe Hill, and the autobiographical parallels that this both invites and refutes. Like Wat Tyler, Joe Hill is a popular Christ, with a mythology that long predates Stavis's play surrounding his sacrifice for the sake of the movement and 'resurrection' in the form of his legacy

---

[86] *Joe Hill: The Man Who Never Died*, Opera in Two Acts by Alan Bush, libretto by Barrie Stavis, full score (FS), vol. I, 82i–82l. The full score is unpublished, but deposited in the British Library as BL/AB MS. Mus. 392-3. There is also a manuscript vocal score, in unknown hand, with German translation only and with many differences from the full score, extant in ABH. These examples have been prepared with reference to both sources, but references will be made to the manuscript, given hereafter as FS, with a volume number referring to MS Mus. 392 (vol. I) and 393 (vol. II).

[87] FS, vol. I, 76-8.   [88] FS, vol. I, 353.

[89] The most complete exposition of these ideas is Bush's 1969 paper 'National Character an Essential Ingredient in Musical Art Today'. It is published in Bush, *In my Eighth Decade*, 67–80.

Ex. 7.5 Bush, *Joe Hill*, Act I Scene 3, 'Casey Jones'.

Ex. 7.6 *Joe Hill*, Act I Scene 2.

and songs.[90] Comparisons with Christ are manifold in the opera. In the original play, the unionist Ben Winton casts Christ as progenitor of the union movement:

> Remember another organizer? His name was Jesus Christ. He was a carpenter. He was an organizer. And He went among the poor and the lowly and the downtrodden. And He said, 'Rise up against your oppressors'. And He said, 'Drive the money changers from the temple'. And that's why they nailed Jesus Christ to the bleeding cross. And I'm not blaspheming when I say, 'Jesus Christ is you. Joe Hill is you'.[91]

In the play this speech follows Ed's speech accusing the authorities of framing Hill because he sings for 'the poor and the downtrodden', but in the opera (Act II Scene 3) the two speeches are juxtaposed, reinforcing the image of Joe Hill as 'organizer' Christ (Ex. 7.7).[92] In a further departure from the play, in the opera the simultaneous speeches are taking place at two separate meetings in the union hall, which coalesce as the chorus of workers become conscious of their identity with Joe Hill/Christ. In addition, Joe's doubt-ridden night vigil before his execution (Act II Scene 6) mirrors Christ's soliloquy in the Garden of Gethsemane (Ex. 7.8).[93] Ed's response to his anxieties about dying, cited at the head of this chapter, is rich in Christian allusion:

> Don't mortify yourself. The fall from grace is not a fall from grace. It's what you've done all your life that gives you grace, not what you do in the last moments of your agony.[94]

Finally, Joe Hill is eulogised in the Epilogue with a chorus 'Blessed is work', alluding to the Biblical Beatitudes.[95]

Although the final chorus makes it clear that Joe Hill's legend is intact, the sense of human tragedy threatens to overwhelm the final,

---

[90] For a comparison of Joe Hill and Steinbeck's Jim Casy, for example, and discussion of the Christology of both figures, see Stephen Bullivant, '"That's him. That shiny bastard:" Jim Casy and Christology', *Steinbeck Studies* 16/1–2 (2005), 15–31.
[91] Stavis, *The Man Who Never Died*, 195.   [92] FS, vol. II, 562–3.   [93] FS, vol. II, 847–51.
[94] Stavis, *The Man Who Never Died*, 232.
[95] These aspects of the opera suggest another operatic parallel: between Joe Hill and Britten's Billy Budd. Melville's narrative is explicitly Christological, and Billy's cry before his execution – 'Starry Vere, God bless you!' – is beatific. However, Billy's innocence, refusal to sanction mutiny, and acceptance of his fate stands in sharp contrast to Hill's worldliness and realism. See also Mervyn Cooke, 'Hermann Melville's *Billy Budd*' in Mervyn Cooke and Philip Reed, *Benjamin Britten: Billy Budd*, Cambridge Opera Handbooks (Cambridge: Cambridge University Press, 1993), 22–4.

Ex. 7.7 *Joe Hill*, Act II Scene 3.

muted assertion of his immortality. Bush's Wat Tyler was, like the exemplary positive hero of socialist realism, sanguine about the possibility of death and unflinching in putting revolution before personal priorities. Joe Hill, on the contrary, is flawed. Like Aschenbach, he experiences illicit passion, in his case through an affair with a married woman, and this passion is his downfall. The affair results in both the incriminating gunshot wound and the lack of an alibi that allow Joe to be executed for murder. Moreover, Joe muses extensively over the physical process of dying and the personal loss it represents: he mourns for Martha (the married woman he loves) and fears that in his last moments 'I'll be turned into a fighting, screaming animal': 'ev'ryone will know the reasons why I died [...] But how do you balance that off against the fact that you're so alone when you die'.[96] Indeed, Bush's colleague Bernard Stevens, upon hearing a 1979 BBC broadcast of the opera, complained to Bush about this very aspect of the work in relation to communist theatrical precedents: 'Joe Hill's aria before his execution was very beautiful and moving but really religious in character. Brecht would have made him a much more wily and cunning figure'.[97] This comment is all the more revealing because many aspects of the opera draw on the Brecht-Eisler model of didactic music theatre that meant so much to Bush in the 1930s. The musical and political unification of the chorus in Act II Scene 3 is Brechtian. In contrast to the grand operatic forces of the previous operas, the large orchestra in *Joe Hill* is frequently used, in Eislerian style, as a chamber ensemble with a wide expressive palette to provide a gestic commentary on the action, as in Act I Scene 4 when Joe is shot and Martha Weber abducted to a sparse orchestral accompaniment of flutter-tonguing woodwind, muted trumpets and pizzicato strings.[98] The critic Trilling, a friend of Stavis, remarked that the chorus 'We shall not be moved' was sung first 'with vigorous realism' outside the place of execution, and second over loudspeakers just before the rifle shots as Joe Hill is killed, in an example of a Brechtian technique of distancing.[99] Yet Joe Hill's transfiguration as a popular Christ, and the powerful sense of the physical destruction of the human being, are the exact opposite of the elision

---

[96] FS, vol. II, 855–64.
[97] Bernard Stevens to Alan Bush, 1 August 1979, BL/AB MS Mus. 444: Correspondence with Bernard Stevens.
[98] FS, vol. I, 273–6.   [99] Ossia Trilling, 'Joe Hill', *The Guardian*, 6 October 1970.

Ex. 7.8 *Joe Hill*, Act II Scene 6, Joe's soliloquy.

Ex. 7.8 (cont.)

of the individual, the inversion of Christ's sacrifice, that was adumbrated by Brecht and Eisler in *Die Massnahme*.

The opera thus engages with Bush's aesthetic past in complex ways. We may recall Said's observation that Britten's opera stands as an aesthetic triumph in contrast to Aschenbach's terminal decline. Similarly, reinforced by the opera's Christology, Joe Hill achieves immortality, and his songs achieve the miraculous unifying and energising political effect on the workers that always lay at the heart of Bush's aesthetic project. Yet by resisting musical identification with Joe Hill by maintaining a distance between Hill's songs and his own music, and by confounding the Brechtian parallels the opera establishes, and, finally, by surviving beyond that peculiar point of musical-political possibilities in the 1930s and 1940s, Bush casts an anxious, self-reflective glance back over his aesthetic project, in a profound instance of artistic lateness.

Conclusion

Joe Hill presents Bush's final word on a theme running throughout his work and reputation: self-sacrifice. In the course of his career, Bush was accused of sacrificing his artistic self to the detriment of his music, or, contrariwise, in left-wing assessments, praised for practising self-improvement for collective gain. Like Britten, he has been written into his works, and was invested in that process himself. Just as Aschenbach or Grimes draw comparison with Britten's artistic sensitivity and difference within a hostile society, Tyler and Joe Hill embody Bush's capacity for personal sacrifice in the service of a chosen people. In both cases, too, the limits of such comparisons are significant. Britten's artistic championing of the individual always existed in tension with his astonishingly successful career and enormous contribution to modern British culture, and these contradictory impulses interacted in ways that were not easy to predict. The implicit social critique of *Peter Grimes* secured Britten's future as an opera composer, while *Gloriana*, a commission bound up with the project of announcing a new era of modern British history, failed to match the dominant vision of the 'New Elizabethans'.[100] For Bush's part, the *idea* of submitting himself to the collective goal of building socialism – and thus identifying with Wat Tyler or Joe Hill – was undoubtedly powerful. Yet that idea was played out in Bush's music in ways that were historically and geographically situated. The high point of his career, like Britten's, was bound up with the construction of a national musical culture in which all could participate. His political music, his modernist critiques of the concert hall, and his lobbying for state planning in the 1930s built towards this; *The Winter Journey*, the *English Suite*, and *Wat Tyler* represented the most complete engagement with this idea; in the climate of the 1960s, in which unified national cultures could not hold in either England or East Germany, it collapsed. The mass, working-class audience for whom Bush's activities held appeal contracted rapidly from this point. Nor did Bush exert a powerful influence on younger generations of radical composers seeking a rapprochement between progressive music and politics in the 1960s: while he admired the ideas of Cornelius Cardew, affinities between their musical styles and intellectual dialogue between the two were negligible.[101]

The collapse of Bush's vision of national culture should not be taken as further evidence of the aesthetic and ideological failures of communism. Bush's concept of artistic selfhood and social responsibility, his investment in national culture, his complex relationship

---

[100] See Wiebe, *Britten's Unquiet Pasts*, 109ff.
[101] For details of their interactions, see Tilbury, *Cornelius Cardew* and Alan Bush to Boris Kotliarov, 11 February 1975, BL/AB MS Mus. 435, Correspondence with Boris Kotliarov.

with English historical, religious, and musical traditions: all of these mark him as profoundly modern and intimately linked with the most important issues in British culture in the mid-twentieth century. The fact that the works that resulted from this rapprochement, bound up with Bush's radical politics, were frequently unacceptable in Britain should not detract from their importance. Both the works themselves, with their unavoidable political content, and the composer's justified demands for a public space for his music, prompted prolonged reflection in many quarters over the proper purpose and meaning of music. Bush's music was often rejected by individuals and organisations as contrary to their aesthetic and political values – the BBC reports, for example, are littered with discussions of musical autonomy and the ideological content of the works. Yet as a provocative individual, Bush also helped to define those values. By variously evaluating, rejecting, or embracing Bush's works and ideas, individuals and organisations in Britain gained a clearer sense of what their aesthetic position was, whether that meant tolerating the Piano Concerto in the interests of freedom of expression, or embarrassment over the fact that an opera by a communist was a prizewinner for the Festival of Britain.

All of this should not only modify our impressions of Bush, but prompt reflection on the role of communists in British cultural life, and indeed more widely in twentieth-century Western society. Bush has been viewed, accurately, as among the most inflexibly Stalinist of leading Party members. Despite this rigidity, and his unapologetic loyalty to the Soviet regime, his realisation of these ideas in his music was subjective, personal, rooted in his previous practices, conditioned by practical circumstances and the realities of British life, and distinct from the work of fellow musicians – from Eisler and Weill to Nono and Cardew – who shared similar ideas. Bush should not be absorbed into modern British culture unproblematically. He saw his music as a radical alternative to the main thrust of that culture, and remains, politically and aesthetically, a figure on the margins. However, the fact of his contribution to national culture, and his navigation of a complex subjectivity – personal, national, socialist – should highlight the dangers of viewing a communist musician as extraneous to British culture. On the contrary, in all their contradictions, Bush's works show us precisely what British music is.

Appendix 1 Developments in CPGB policy, 1939–41

Date	Event
23 August 1939	Signing of Non-Aggression Pact between Soviet Russia and Nazi Germany (Molotov-Ribbentrop Pact); welcomed by CPGB newspaper the *Daily Worker*.
3 September 1939	Outbreak of war; CPGB Central Committee calls for support of 'all necessary measures to secure the victory of democracy over fascism'.
25 September 1939	CPGB learn of Comintern description of the war as 'imperialist'.
4 October 1939	CPGB Central Committee announces new anti-war position.
January 1941	People's Convention
22 June 1941	German invasion of the Soviet Union; immediate call for 'a people's war against fascism and a people's peace'.[2]
4 July 1941	CPGB supports the Churchill government.
17 September 1941	Alan Bush called up and enters the Royal Army Medical Corps.

Appendix 2 Bush, Selected Works, 1939–47

	Year(s) composed	Forces	Commission/first performance
Orchestral/Band			
Symphony in C, op. 21	1939–40		First performance: Promenade concert, 24 July 1942.
Russian Glory for Military Band – Military March on Soviet Songs, op. 20	1942		BBC commission.
Overture Festal Day, op. 23	1942		BBC commission as part of a series of programmes celebrating the 70th birthday of Ralph Vaughan Williams, broadcast 12 October 1942.
Fantasia on Soviet Themes for Military Band, op. 24	1942		BBC commission, performed at Promenade concert, 27 July 1945 in arrangement for orchestra.
Overture: Resolution, op. 25	c. 1943		BBC broadcast, Home Service, BBC Symphony Orchestra/Clarence Raybould (cond.), 1 February 1944.
Homage to William Sterndale Bennett, op. 27	1945–6	For string orchestra	London String Orchestra, Wigmore Hall, London, two broadcasts in 1945, London String Orchestra/ Alan Bush (cond.).
English Suite, op. 28	1945–6	For string orchestra	London String Orchestra, Wigmore Hall, London, 9 February 1946, excerpts broadcast by BBC in 1946.

(cont.)

	Year(s) composed	Forces	Commission/first performance
Chamber			
Meditation on a German Song of 1848, op. 22	1941	For violin and piano	London Contemporary Music Centre, 15 May 1944, Alan Bush and Max Rostal.
Esquisse: Le Quatorze Juillet	1943	Piano solo	
Lyric Interlude, op. 26	1944	For violin and piano	Concert of Bush's own works, Queen Mary Hall, London, 6 January 1945, Alan Bush and Max Rostal. Several BBC broadcasts in 1946.
Three Concert Studies for Piano, Violin and Cello, op. 31	1947		
Workers' songs			
'Against the People's Enemies' (text: Randall Swingler)	1939		Martin Lawrence (baritone), Workers' Music Association, 15 December 1939.
'Unite and Be Free' (text: Alan Bush)	1941		
'The Great Red Army' (text: Randall Swingler)	1942		BBC broadcast: 30/31 August 1942, 'London Labour Choir' [WMA Singers]/Alan Bush (cond.), *Britain Sings*, Overseas – North American Transmission.
'Britain's Part' (text: Alan Bush)	1942		WMA Singers, 24 October 1942.
'Toulon' (text: Nancy Bush)	1942		Commissioned by the Birmingham Anglo-Soviet Unity Group, first performed: WMA concert, Birmingham, 26 May 1943.
'Song of the Commons of England' (text: Maurice Carpenter)	1944		Concert of Bush's own works, Queen Mary Hall, London, WMA Singers, 6 January 1945.

(cont.)

	Year(s) composed	Forces	Commission/first performance
Other choral			
Freedom on the March	1943	For solo, mixed chorus and symphony orchestra	Combined choirs and London Philharmonic Orchestra, cond. Alan Bush (British-Soviet Unity Demonstration), Royal Albert Hall, 27 June 1943.
The Winter Journey (text: Randall Swingler)	1946	Cantata for Soprano and Baritone Soli, SATB, string quintet and harp.	Commission; Alnwick Choral Society, Alnwick Parish Church, Northumberland, 14 December 1946, simultaneously broadcast on the BBC Third Programme.
Lidiče (text: Nancy Bush)	1947	Unaccompanied SATB	WMA Singers, Lidiče, August 1947.
Pageant			
The Living English (arrangement of folk songs), songs selected by A.L. Lloyd.	1946		London Co-operative Society, performed 26 October 1946 as part of the Folk Song and Dance Festival.

Appendix 3 *Wat Tyler*, Characters and Synopsis

Characters

Wat Tyler	*Baritone*
John Ball	*Bass*
Herdsman	*Bass*
Escaped Serf	*Tenor*
Elderly Peasant	*Tenor*
King Richard II	*Tenor*
Sir Thomas Bampton	*Bass-Baritone*
Archbishop Sudbury	*Bass*
Walworth, Lord Mayor of London	*Bass-Baritone*
Earl of Salisbury	*Baritone*
Minstrel	*Tenor*
Herald	*Tenor*
Retainer	*Tenor*
Clerk	*Tenor*
Margaret, wife of Wat Tyler	*Lyric Dramatic Soprano*
Jennet, daughter of Wat Tyler	*Soprano*
Fishwife	*Mezzo-Soprano*
Queen Mother	*Mezzo-Soprano*

Peasants, Townsfolk, Nobles

Prologue

The edge of a forest in Kent, end of May, 1381

A serf returning from work attempts to escape. A Herdsman tries to dissuade him, suggesting that 'great things are stirring' in Kent. Peasants enter for a secret meeting of the 'Great Society', singing a traditional song, the 'Cutty Wren'.

Act I

Scene 1: Maidstone Market Place, early June, 1381

Townspeople and peasants have been summoned to Maidstone to be listed for the Poll Tax. One of them, Wat Tyler, has their support when he declares that they must refuse to pay a second time. The crowd resists Sir Thomas Bampton, the royal commissioner. He is chased from the stage when the peasants are roused following brutal treatment of the now recaptured serf.

Scene 2: A room in Tyler's Cottage near Maidstone, the same evening

Tyler returns home to give the news to his wife and daughter. Bampton and his Clerk knock on the door and ask for shelter. Bampton becomes drunk and insults Jennet, Tyler's daughter, whereupon Tyler strikes him to the ground. Bampton threatens Tyler before leaving, and Tyler goes out to rouse the men of Kent.

Scene 3: Maidstone Market Place, a week later, early morning

The Peasant Army march into the square, acclaim Tyler as their leader and declare they will seek their freedom from the King alone. They set free John Ball, a priest famous for his sermons against serfdom, by storming Maidstone Prison. He preaches to them, and leads the Army to London with Tyler.

Act II

Scene 1: A Room in the Tower of London, a few days later

The young Richard II sits listening to a minstrel with members of his Council in attendance. The Queen Mother enters distraught, having been turned back from her pilgrimage to Canterbury by peasants on the march. She upbraids the King and nobles for inaction. After discussion by Walworth, Lord Mayor of London and the Earl of Salisbury, Archbishop Sudbury suggests a meeting between the king and the rebels, at which Richard will agree to the peasants' demands.

Scene 2: An open field at Smithfield, three days later

The King and nobles await the people's petition. Tyler and the Herdsman enter alone. Tyler addresses the King, his request for freedom from serfdom is granted and charters promising this are carried to the waiting crowd. As Tyler turns to go, he is insulted by Bampton. He draws his dagger impatiently and is instantly surrounded by the nobles. Walworth stabs him and he falls. The King declares himself the leader of the people and goes out to them. John Ball and a few peasants, hastening on to the deserted stage, sing a dirge over Wat Tyler as he lies dead.

Scene 3: Outside Westminster Abbey, the end of June

A deputation of peasants awaits the King. The charters have not been honoured, and, unable to believe that Richard has deceived them, they wish to appeal to him in person. As they wait, Margaret, Tyler's wife, mourns her lost love. The King and nobles enter for a thanksgiving service. The King pauses to read the charter, tears it in pieces, and declares that serfdom shall continue forever. A Te Deum sounds from the Abbey. The doors close behind the triumphal royal procession. The peasants are at first desolated; then turning away from the Abbey and heartened by the Herdsman, they break into a chorus of hope for future freedom.

Select Bibliography

Archives, newspapers, and music periodicals consulted are listed here, alongside major printed sources consulted. Detailed references to items in archives and individual pieces of journalism, such as concert reviews, may be found in the notes.

Archives Consulted

Alan Bush Archive, Histon, Cambridge
Arts Council of Great Britain Archives, V & A Archive of Art and Design, London
BBC Written Archive Centre, Caversham
British Library, Alan Bush Collection
Bundesarchiv, Berlin
Archives of the Communist Party of Great Britain [www.communistpartyarchive.org.uk]
The National Archives: Public Record Office, Kew
Stiftung Archiv der Akademie der Künste, Berlin
University of Essex, Frederick Warner Collection

Newspaper Sources

Aufbau
Daily Express
Daily Herald
Daily Telegraph
Daily Worker
Left Review
Leipziger Volkszeitung
The Listener
Modern Quarterly
Monthly Musical Record
Music and Life
Musical Opinion
Musical Times
Musik und Gesellschaft
Neues Deutschland
New Statesman
Our Time

Select Bibliography

Radio Times
The Spectator
Sunday Times
Tägliche Rundschau
The Times

Published Sources

Aaronovitch, David, *Party Animals: My Family and Other Communists* (London: Jonathan Cape, 2016).

Abbate, Carolyn, 'Opera; or, the Envoicing of Women' in Ruth A. Solie (ed.), *Musicology and Difference: Gender and Sexuality in Music Scholarship* (Berkeley and Los Angeles: University of California Press, 1993), 225–58.

Abraham, Gerald, *This Modern Stuff: A Fairly "Plaine and Easie" Introduction to Contemporary Music* (London: D. Archer, 1933).

Adlington, Robert, *Louis Andriessen: De Staat* (Aldershot: Ashgate, 2004).

(ed.), *Red Strains: Music and Communism Outside the Communist Bloc*, Proceedings of the British Academy (Oxford: Oxford University Press, 2013).

Albright, Daniel (ed.), *Modernism and Music: An Anthology of Sources* (Chicago and London: University of Chicago Press, 2004).

Anderson, Benedict, *Imagined Communities: Reflections on the Origin and Spread of Nationalism*, rev. ed. (London and New York: Verso, 2006).

Andrew, Christopher, *The Defence of the Realm: The Authorized History of MI5* (London: Allen Lane, 2009).

Antokoletz, Eliot, *A History of Twentieth-Century Music in a Theoretic-Analytical Context* (New York: Routledge, 2013).

Banfield, Stephen (ed.), *The Twentieth Century*, The Blackwell History of Music in Britain, vol. xi (Oxford: Blackwell, 1995).

Barr, Helen, 'Major Episodes and Moments in *Piers Plowman* B' in Andrew Cole and Andrew Galloway (eds.), *The Cambridge Companion to Piers Plowman* (Cambridge: Cambridge University Press, 2014), 15–32.

Bathrick, David, *The Powers of Speech: The Politics of Culture in the GDR* (Lincoln and London: University of Nebraska Press, 1995).

Bell, Nicolas, 'The Function of Music in the Socialist Pageant in Inter-War Britain', unpublished paper delivered at the Institute of Historical Research, London, 18 October 2004.

Betz, Albrecht, *Hanns Eisler: Political Musician*, trans. Bill Hopkins (Cambridge: Cambridge University Press, 1982).

Blackledge, Paul, *Reflections on the Marxist Theory of History* (Manchester: Manchester University Press, 2006).

Blackmer, Corinne E., and Patricia Juliana Smith (eds.), *En Travesti: Women, Gender, Subversion, Opera* (New York: Columbia University Press, 1995).

Bowers, Timothy, Sleeve Notes to *Alan Bush: Chamber Music*, The London Piano Quartet (Epoch CDLX 7130, 2003).

Brecht, Bertolt, and Hanns Eisler, 'Note to the Audience' in John Willett and Ralph Mannheim (eds.), *Bertolt Brecht Collected Plays* vol. 3 pt. 2 (London: Methuen, 1997), 232–3.

Brett, Philip, *Music and Sexuality in Britten: Selected Essays*, ed. George E. Haggerty (Berkeley and Los Angeles: University of California Press, 2006).

Briggs, Asa, *The History of Broadcasting in the United Kingdom, Vol. 3: The War on Words* (London: Oxford University Press, 1970).

Bullivant, Joanna, 'Modernism, Politics and Individuality in 1930s Britain: The Case of Alan Bush', *Music & Letters* 90/3 (August 2009), 432–52.

Bullivant, Stephen, '"That's him. That shiny bastard:" Jim Casy and Christology', *Steinbeck Studies* 16/1–2 (2005), 15–31.

Burnham, Scott, *Beethoven Hero* (Princeton: Princeton University Press, 1995).

Bush, Alan, 'Arbeiterbewegung und moderne Musiker' [1935] in 1re *Olympiade Ouvrière Européenne: de musique et de chant. 8-10 Juin 1935, Strasbourg* [festival programme], 19–27, ABH.

'Chopin', *Poetry and the People* 20 (1940), 19–20.

'The Crisis of Modern Music', Keynote 1/4 (Summer 1946), 4–7.

'Eisler Demonstration', *Left Review* 1/8 (May 1935), 330–2.

In My Eighth Decade and Other Essays (London: Kahn & Averill, 1980).

'Marxism and Music', typewritten MS, undat. [1942], 7–8, ABH.

'Music' in C. Day-Lewis (ed.), *The Mind in Chains: Socialism and the Cultural Revolution* (London: Frederick Muller, 1937), 123–43.

'Music and the Working-Class Struggle', *Left Review* 2/2 (November 1935), 646–51.

Music in the Soviet Union (London: Workers' Music Association, 1944).

'A Musical Journey through the Balkans', *Changing Epoch* 1 (1947), 11–22, copy in ABH.

'A Musician in Eastern Europe' (undat.) [*c.* 1947], ABH.

'My Studies and Friendship with John Ireland' [article written for a John Ireland Centenary Programme broadcast by the BBC in October 1979], ABH.

'The National Government and Hitler' [1939], unpublished typescript article, ABH.

'Notes on the Problems of Workers' Music', typewritten MS for study classes delivered under the National Council of Labour Colleges, February–March 1936, ABH.

'Obituary: Franz Reizenstein, 1911–68', *The Royal Academy of Music Magazine* 196 (Midsummer 1969), 24–5.

'Our Music', *Red Notes* [official organ of the LLCU] 4 (January 1937), Copy held in Sir Frederick Warner Collection, Albert Sloman Library, University of Essex, Colchester, National Cataloguing Unit for the Archives of Contemporary Scientists no. 144/1/06, A.80.

'The Outlook for the British Composer', *The Author, Playwright and Composer* LII/1 (Spring 1941), 63–5.

'Planning a Workers' Festival', typewritten MS, undat. [*c.* 1936], ABH.

'Problems of Opera', Music 1/11 (October 1952), 19–21.

'Problems of Soviet Musical Theory', *Modern Quarterly* 5/1 (1949–50), 38–47.

'A Remarkable Document', *Anglo-Soviet Journal* 10/3 (Autumn 1949), 19–20.

'Soviet Music', *Anglo-Soviet Journal* 10/1 (Spring 1949), 32–4.

Strict Counterpoint in the Palestrina Style: A Practical Textbook (London: Joseph Williams, 1948).

'The Structure and Expression of Modern Music' [1948], ABH, [photocopy of original typescript article held by National Library of Scotland, Ronald Stevenson Musicological Correspondence, Inventory Acc. 11567].

'Tasks of Cultural Workers', *Communist Review* (February 1951), 49–55.

'Understanding Modern Music', handwritten MS, undat. [1930s], ABH.

'"Wat Tyler" and the Purpose of Opera', *Opera* 25/6 (June 1974), 488–91.

'What Is Modern Music?', *Proceedings of the Musical Association* 63rd Session (1936–7), 21–37.

Bush, Alan, and Nancy Bush, *Alan Bush: Wat Tyler*, with an Introduction by Richard Petzoldt, Vollständiges Opernbuch (Leipzig: Verlag Philipp Reclam, 1954).

Bush, Alan, and Randall Swingler (eds.) with members of the Workers' Music Association and the Left Book Club Musicians' Group, *The Left Song Book* (London: Victor Gollancz, 1938).

Bush, Nancy, *Alan Bush: Music, Politics and Life* (London: Thames Publishing, 2000).

Calder, Angus, *The Myth of the Blitz* (London: Jonathan Cape, 1991).

Calico, Joy Haslam, '"Für eine neue deutsche Nationaloper:" Opera in the Discourses of Unification and Legitimation in the German Democratic Republic' in Celia Applegate and Pamela M. Potter (eds.), *Music and German National Identity* (Chicago and London: University of Chicago Press, 2002), 190–204.

'The Trial, the Condemnation, the Cover-up: Behind the Scenes of Brecht/Dessau's *Lucullus* Opera', *Cambridge Opera Journal* 14/3 (2002), 313–42.

Callaghan, John, and Ben Harker (eds.), *British Communism: A Documentary History* (Manchester: Manchester University Press, 2011).

Carpenter, Humphrey, *Benjamin Britten: A Biography* (London: Faber, 1992).

Chowrimootoo, Christopher, 'Bourgeois Opera: Death in Venice and the Aesthetics of Sublimation', *Cambridge Opera Journal* 22/2 (2011), 177–218.

'The Timely Traditions of Albert Herring', *Opera Quarterly* 27/4 (2011), 379–419.

Clark, Edward (ed.), *Tribute to Alan Bush on His Fiftieth Birthday* (London: Workers' Music Association, 1950).

Clark, Katerina, *The Soviet Novel: History as Ritual* (Chicago: University of Chicago Press, 1981).

Clément, Catherine, *Opera, or the Undoing of Women*, trans. Betsy Wing (Minneapolis: University of Minnesota Press, 1989).
Cobbe, Hugo (ed.), *Letters of Ralph Vaughan Williams, 1895–1958* (Oxford and New York: Oxford University Press, 2008).
Cooke, Mervyn, and Philip Reed, *Benjamin Britten: Billy Budd*, Cambridge Opera Handbooks (Cambridge: Cambridge University Press, 1993).
Croft, Andy, *Comrade Heart: A Life of Randall Swingler* (Manchester and New York: Manchester University Press, 2003).
  (ed.), *A Weapon in the Struggle: The Cultural History of the Communist Party in Britain* (London: Pluto, 1998).
Deery, Philip, and Neil Redfern, 'No Lasting Peace? Labor, Communism and the Cominform: Australia and Great Britain, 1945–50', *Labour History* 88 (May 2005), 63–86.
Dennis, David B., *Beethoven in German Politics, 1870–1989* (New Haven and London: Yale University Press, 1996).
Dent, Edward J., *TERPANDER or Music and the Future* (London and New York: K. Paul, Trench, Trubner; Dutton, 1926); repr. as *The Future of Music* (Oxford: Pergamon Press, 1965).
Desbruslais, Simon, The Identity, Application and Legacy of Paul Hindemith's Theory of Music, DPhil thesis, University of Oxford (2013).
Doctor, Jennifer, *The BBC and Ultra-Modern Music, 1922–1936: Shaping a Nation's Tastes* (Cambridge: Cambridge University Press, 1999).
  'The Parataxis of "British Musical Modernism"', *Musical Quarterly* 91/1–2 (Spring/Summer 2008), 89–115.
Doctor, Jennifer and David Wright (eds.), *The Proms: A New History* (London: Thames & Hudson, 2007).
Douzinas, Costas, and Slavoj Žižek (eds.), *The Idea of Communism* (London and New York: Verso, 2010).
Edmunds, Neil, *The Soviet Proletarian Music Movement* (Oxford: Peter Lang, 2000).
  'William Glock and the British Broadcasting Corporation's Music Policy, 1959–73', *Contemporary British History* 20/2 (June 2006), 233–61.
Eisler, Hanns, 'Some Tips for Rehearsal of "The Decision"' in John Willett and Ralph Mannheim (eds.), *Bertolt Brecht Collected Plays* vol. 3 pt. 2 (London: Methuen, 1997), 233–4.
Eisler, Hanns, and Ernst Bloch, 'Avantgarde-Kunst und Volksfront' [1937] in Günter Mayer (ed.), *Hanns Eisler: Musik und Politik. Schriften 1924–1948* (2nd edn, Leipzig: Deutscher Verlag für Musik, 1985), 397–405.
  'Die Kunst zu Erben' [1938] in Günter Mayer (ed.), *Hanns Eisler: Musik und Politik* (2nd edn, Leipzig: Deutscher Verlag für Musik, 1985), 406–14.
Esty, Jed, *A Shrinking Island: Modernism and National Culture in England* (Princeton and Oxford: Princeton University Press, 2004).
Fagan, Hyman, *Nine Days That Shook England: An Account of the English People's Uprising in 1381* (London: Victor Gollancz, 1938).

Fenemore, Mark, *Sex, Thugs and Rock 'n' Roll: Teenage Rebels in Cold-War East Germany* (New York and Oxford: Berghahn Books, 2007).

Freedman, Jean R., *Whistling in the Dark: Memory and Culture in Wartime London* (Lexington: University Press of Kentucky, 1999).

Fischer, Ernst, *The Necessity of Art: A Marxist Approach*, trans. Anna Bostock (London, 1963).

Fitzpatrick, Sheila, *Everyday Stalinism: Ordinary Life in Extraordinary Times: Soviet Russia in the 1930s* (New York and Oxford: Oxford University Press, 1999).

Foreman, Lewis (ed.), *From Parry to Britten: British Music in Letters 1900–1945* (London: Batsford, 1987).

Fox, Christopher, 'After the Fludde: Ambitious Music for All-Comers' in Peter Wiegold and Ghislaine Kenyon (eds.), *Beyond Britten: The Composer and the Community* (Woodbridge: Boydell Press, 2015), 26–44.

Frogley, Alain, 'H.G. Wells and Vaughan Williams's *A London Symphony*: Politics and Culture in Fin-de-Siècle England' in Chris Banks, Arthur Searle, and Malcolm Turner (eds.), *Sundry Sorts of Music Books: Essays on the British Library Collections Presented to O.W. Neighbour on his 70th Birthday* (London: British Library, 1993), 299–308.

Frolova-Walker, Marina, '"National in Form, Socialist in Content": Musical Nation-Building in the Soviet Republics', *Journal of the American Musicological Society* 51/2 (1998), 331–71.

  'Stalin and the Art of Boredom', *Twentieth-Century Music* I/1 (March 2004), 101–24.

  Stalin's Music Prize: Soviet Culture and Politics (New Haven and London: Yale University Press, 2016).

Gardner, James, 'The Battle of Ideas and the Importance of Theory', *Communist Policy to Meet the Crisis*, Report of the 21st National Congress of the Communist Party, November 1949, Marxists Internet Archive, accessed 5 February 2014, www.marxists.org/history/international/comintern/sections/britain/congresses/21/05.htm.

Garratt, James, *Music, Culture and Social Reform in the Age of Wagner* (Cambridge: Cambridge University Press, 2010).

Gillies, Malcolm, *Bartók in Britain: A Guided Tour* (Oxford: Clarendon Press, 1989).

Gloag, Kenneth, *Tippett: A Child of Our Time* (Cambridge: Cambridge University Press, 1999).

Grabs, Manfred (ed.), *Hanns Eisler: A Rebel in Music. Selected Writings of Hanns Eisler* (1978; repr. London: Kahn & Averill, 1999).

Gray, Cecil, *Predicaments, or Music and the Future: An Essay in Constructive Criticism* (London: Oxford University Press; Humphrey Milford, 1936).

Gray, William Glenn, *Germany's Cold War: The Global Campaign to Isolate East Germany, 1949–1969* (Chapel Hill and London: The University of North Carolina Press, 2003).

Grimley, Daniel M., 'Landscape and Distance: Vaughan Williams, Modernism and the Symphonic Pastoral' in Matthew Riley (ed.), *British Music and Modernism, 1895-1960* (Aldershot: Ashgate, 2010), 147-74.

Guttsman, W.L., *Workers' Culture in Weimar Germany. Between Tradition and Commitment* (New York, Oxford and Munich: Berg, 1990).

Hall, Duncan, *'A Pleasant Change from Politics': Music and the British Labour Movement between the Wars* (Cheltenham: New Clarion, 2001).

Hardy, Lisa, *The British Piano Sonata, 1870-1945* (Woodbridge: Boydell, 2001).

Harper-Scott, J.P.E., *Edward Elgar: Modernist* (Cambridge: Cambridge University Press, 2006).

The Quilting Points of Musical Modernism: Revolution, Reaction, and William Walton (Cambridge: Cambridge University Press, 2012).

Hellbeck, Jochen, *Revolution on My Mind: Writing a Diary under Stalin* (London and Cambridge, MA: Harvard University Press, 2006).

Hill, Christopher, 'The Norman Yoke' in John Saville (ed.), *Democracy and the Labour Movement: Essays in Honour of Dona Torr* (London: Lawrence & Wishart, 1954), 11-67.

Hindemith, Paul, *The Craft of Musical Composition*, Book I: Theoretical Part, trans. Arthur Mendel (New York: Associated Music Publishers, 1941).

Hinton, Stephen, "Jasager, Der." *The New Grove Dictionary of Opera. Grove Music Online. Oxford Music Online.* Oxford University Press, accessed 19 August, 2016, www.oxfordmusiconline.com/subscriber/article/grove/music/O004122.

Hutchings, Arthur, 'Music in Britain: 1918-1960' in Martin Cooper (ed.), *The Modern Age, 1890-1960*, The New Oxford History of Music in Britain, vol. X (London: Oxford University Press, 1974), 503-68.

Hyde, Douglas, *I Believed: The Autobiography of a Former British Communist* (London: Heinemann, 1950).

Hynes, Samuel, *The Auden Generation: Literature and Politics in England in the 1930s* (London: Bodley Head, 1976).

Janik, Elizabeth, *Recomposing German Music: Politics and Musical Tradition in Cold War Berlin* (Leiden and Boston: Brill, 2005).

Jenks, John, *British Propaganda and News Media in the Cold War* (Edinburgh: Edinburgh University Press, 2006).

Judt, Tony, *Postwar: A History of Europe since 1945* (London: Pimlico, 2007; Penguin, 2005).

Kemp, Ian, *Tippett: The Composer and His Music* (Oxford and New York: Oxford University Press, 1987).

King, Francis, and George Matthews (eds.), *About Turn: The British Communist Party and the Second World War. The Verbatim Record of the Central Committee Meetings of 25 September and 2-3 October 1939* (London: Lawrence and Wishart, 1990).

Koestenbaum, Wayne, *The Queen's Throat: Opera, Homosexuality and the Mystery of Desire* (New York and London: Poseidon Press, 1993).

Langland, William, *Piers the Ploughman*, translated into modern English and with an introduction by J.F. Goodridge (London: Penguin, 1960).

LeMahieu, D.L., *A Culture for Democracy: Mass Communication and the Cultivated Mind in Britain between the Wars* (Oxford: Clarendon Press, 1988).

Lesure, F., *Le Sacre du Printemps: Dossier de Presse* (Geneva: Minkoff, 1990).

Lew, Nathaniel, 'A New and Glorious Age: Constructions of National Opera in Britain, 1945–1951', PhD thesis, University of California, Berkeley (2001).

Lowe, Vesta, *Guiana Sings* (Delaware, Ohio: Cooperative Recreation Service, 1959).

Lloyd, A.L., 'Prehistoric Music', *Vox Pop* 2/5 (May 1945), 7–8.

Lowerson, John, 'The Wrong Sort of History? The Problems and Productions of Alan Bush's *Wat Tyler*', paper delivered at the Institute of Historical Research, London, 11 May 2009.

Lowerson, John, with Joanna Bullivant, 'Trouble down t'pit: Marxist Politics, Industrial Stereotypes and Northern Sources in Alan Bush's Opera, *Men of Blackmoor* (1954)' in Rachel Cowgill, Dave Russell and Derek Scott (eds.), *Music and the Idea of the North* (Routledge, forthcoming).

Mann, Jill, 'Allegory and Piers Plowman' in Andrew Cole and Andrew Galloway (eds.), *The Cambridge Companion to Piers Plowman* (Cambridge: Cambridge University Press, 2014), 65–84.

Mason, Colin, 'Alan Bush in High Middle Age', *The Listener*, 26 May 1960, 954.

Major, Patrick, *Behind the Berlin Wall: East Germany and the Frontiers of Power* (Oxford: Oxford University Press, 2010).

Maw, David, '"Phantasy mania:" Quest for a National Style' in Emma Hornby and David Maw (eds.), *Essays on the History of English Music in Honour of John Caudwell: Sources, Style, Performance, Historiography* (Woodbridge: Boydell, 2010), 97–121.

Mayer, Günter, (ed.), *Hanns Eisler: Musik und Politik. Schriften 1924–1948* (2nd edn, Leipzig: Deutscher Verlag für Musik, 1985).

  'Leben und Kunst unter dem Primat der Politik: Über zwei Konflikttypen bei Hanns Eisler' in Harry Goldschmidt, Georg Knepler, Konrad Niemann (eds.), *Komponisten, auf Werk und Leben befragt: ein Kolloquium* (Leipzig: Deutscher Verlag für Musik, 1985), 286–302.

  Sleeve Notes to *Hanns Eisler: Historic Recordings*, Boris Blacher, cond., Gesang Studioorchester (Berlin Classics BER 92302, 1996).

McCabe, John, *Alan Rawsthorne: Portrait of a Composer* (Oxford: Oxford University Press, 1999).

McIlroy, John, and Alan Campbell, 'Histories of the British Communist Party: a User's Guide', *Labour History Review* 68/1 (April 2003), 33–59.

McLellan, Josie, 'Did Communists Have Better Sex? Sex and the Body in German Unification' in David Clarke and Ute Wölfel (eds.), *Remembering the German Democratic Republic: Divided Memory in a United Germany* (Basingstoke: Palgrave Macmillan, 2011), 119–30.

  Love in the Time of Communism: Intimacy and Sexuality in the GDR (Cambridge: Cambridge University Press, 2011).

Mellor, Leo, *Reading the Ruins: Modernism, Bombsites and British Culture* (Cambridge: Cambridge University Press, 2011).

Mitchell, Donald, 'An Introduction in the Shape of a Memoir' in Donald Mitchell (ed.), *Benjamin Britten: Death in Venice* (Cambridge: Cambridge University Press, 1987), 1–25.

Mitchell, Donald, and Philip Reed (eds.), *Letters from a Life: The Selected Letters and Diaries of Benjamin Britten 1913–1976*, vol. I (London: Faber, 1991).

Moi, Toril, 'From Femininity to Finitude: Freud, Lacan, and Feminism, Again,' *Signs: Journal of Women in Culture and Society* 29/3 (Spring 2004), 841–78.

Morgan, Kevin, *Against Fascism and War: Ruptures and Continuities in British Communist politics, 1935–41* (Manchester and New York: Manchester University Press, 1989).

Harry Pollitt (Manchester: Manchester University Press, 1993).

Morgan, Kevin, Gidon Cohen, and Andrew Flinn, *Communists in British Society, 1920–1991* (London, Sydney and Chicago: Rivers Oram Press, 2007).

Morris, R.O., *Contrapuntal Technique in the Sixteenth Century* (London: Oxford University Press, 1922).

Newsinger, John, 'Review: Recent Controversies in the History of British Communism', *Journal of Contemporary History* 41/3 (July 2006), 557–72.

Nielinger-Vakil, Carola, *Luigi Nono: A Composer in Context* (Cambridge: Cambridge University Press, 2015).

O'Higgins, Rachel (ed.), *The Correspondence of Alan Bush and John Ireland, 1927–1961* (Aldershot: Ashgate, 2006).

Ottaway, Hugh, and Alain Frogley, 'Vaughan Williams, Ralph', *Grove Music Online. Oxford Music Online.* Oxford University Press, accessed 27 May 2014, www.oxfordmusiconline.com/subscriber/article/grove/music/42507.

Payne, Anthony, 'Alan Bush', *Musical Times*, 105/1454 (April 1964), 263–5.

Pence, Katherine, '"A World in Miniature": The Leipzig Trade Fairs in the 1950s and East German Consumer Citizenship' in David F. Crew (ed.), *Consuming Germany in the Cold War* (Oxford and New York: Berg, 2003), 21–50.

Pence, Katherine, and Paul Betts (eds.), *Socialist Modern: East German Everyday Culture and Politics* (Ann Arbor: University of Michigan Press, 2008).

Péteri, György (ed.), *Nylon Curtain: Transnational and Trans-Systemic Tendencies in the Cultural Life of State-Socialist Russia and East-Central Europe* (Trondheim, Norway: Program on East European Cultures and Societies, 2006).

Pirie, Peter J., *The English Musical Renaissance* (London: Gollancz, 1979).

Plant, Andrew M., *The Life and Music of Philip Christian Darnton* (PhD diss., University of Birmingham, 2002).

Pollitt, Harry, *How to Win the Peace* (London: Communist Party of Great Britain, 1944).

Pople, Anthony, 'Vaughan Williams, Tallis and the Phantasy Principle' in Alain Frogley (ed.), *Vaughan Williams Studies* (Cambridge: Cambridge University Press, 1996), 47–80.

Rabe, Stephen G., *U.S. Intervention in British Guiana: A Cold War Story* (Chapel Hill: University of North Carolina Press, 2005).

Rapson, Jessica, 'Mobilising Lidice: Cosmopolitan Memory between Theory and Practice', *Culture, Theory and Critique* 53/2 (2012), 129–45.

Riley, Matthew (ed.), *British Music and Modernism, 1895–1960* (Aldershot: Ashgate, 2010).

Robinson, Suzanne, 'From Agitprop to Parable: A Prolegomenon to *A Child of Our Time*' in Suzanne Robinson (ed.), *Michael Tippett: Music and Literature* (Aldershot: Ashgate, 2002), 78–121.

Roscow, Gregory (ed.), *Bliss on Music: Selected Writings of Arthur Bliss 1920–1975* (Oxford: Oxford University Press, 1991).

Roseberry, Eric, 'Britten's Piano Concerto: The Original Version', *Tempo* 172 (March 1990), 10–18.

 'The Concertos and Early Orchestral Scores: Aspects of Style and Aesthetic' in Mervyn Cooke (ed.), *The Cambridge Companion to Benjamin Britten* (Cambridge: Cambridge University Press, 1999), 233–44.

Rumph, Stephen C., *Beethoven after Napoleon: Political Romanticism in the Late Works* (Berkeley and London: University of California Press, 2004).

Rupprecht, Philip, *British Musical Modernism: The Manchester Group and Their Contemporaries* (Cambridge: Cambridge University Press, 2015).

Russell, Dave, *Popular Music in England, 1840–1914, A Social History*, 2nd edn (Manchester and New York: Manchester University Press, 1997).

Sachs, Curt, *The Rise of Music in the Ancient World* (originally published 1943; London: J.M. Dent & Sons, 1944).

Said, Edward, *On Late Style: Music and Literature against the Grain* (London: Bloomsbury, 2006).

Samuel, Raphael, *The Lost World of British Communism* (London and New York: Verso, 2006).

Sayle, Alexei, *Stalin Ate My Homework* (London: Sceptre, 2010).

Schaarwächter, Jürgen, *Two Centuries of British Symphonism: From the Beginnings to 1945: A Preliminary Survey* (Hildesheim: Georg Olms Verlag, 2015).

Schafer, R. Murray, *British Composers in Interview* (London: Faber & Faber, 1963).

Schmelz, Peter J. (ed.) Special Cold War Issue of the *Journal of Musicology* 26/1 (Winter 2009).

Schoenberg, Arnold, *Theory of Harmony*, trans. Roy E. Carter (Berkeley: University of California Press, 1978).

Schwarz, Bill, '"The People" in History: The Communist Party Historians' Group, 1946–56' in Richard Johnson, Gregor McLennan, Bill Schwarz, David Sutton (eds.), *Making Histories: Studies in History-Writing and Politics* (London: Hutchinson, 1982), 44–95.

Schwarz, Boris, *Music and Musical Life in Soviet Russia, 1917–1970* (London: Barry & Jenkins, 1972).

Seeger, Peggy, and Ewan MacColl (eds.), *Songs for the Sixties* (London: Workers' Music Association, 1961).

Shreffler, Anne, 'Berlin Walls: Dahlhaus, Knepler, and Ideologies of Music History', *The Journal of Musicology* 20/4 (Autumn 2003), 498–525.

Sinfield, Alan, 'Private Lives/Public Theater: Noel Coward and the Politics of Homosexual Representation', *Representations* 36 (Autumn 1991), 43–63.

Slonimsky, Nicolas, *Music since 1900* (London: Cassell, 1972).

Stavis, Barrie, *The Man Who Never Died: A Play about Joe Hill* (New York: Haven Press, 1954).

Steele, Brent J., *Alternative Accountabilities in Global Politics: The Scars of Violence* (London and New York: Routledge, 2013).

Stehlík, Eduard, *Lidice: The Story of a Czech Village*, trans. Peter Kurfürst (Praha: For the Lidice memorial by Jitka Kejřová, 2004).

Stewart, Stanley, 'Was Wittgenstein a Closet Literary Critic?', *New Literary History*, 34/1 (2003), 43–57.

Stevenson, Ronald, 'Alan Bush: Committed Composer', *Music Review* 25/4 (November 1964), 323–42.

—— (ed.), *Time Remembered. Alan Bush: An 80th Birthday Symposium* (Kidderminster: Bravura Publications, 1981).

Stone, Dan (ed.), 'Editor's Introduction: Postwar Europe as History' in *The Oxford Handbook of Postwar European History* (Oxford: Oxford University Press, 2012), 1–36.

Stonor Saunders, Frances, *Who Paid the Piper? The CIA and the Cultural Cold War*, 2nd edn (London: Granta, 2000).

Taylor, Charles, *Sources of the Self: The Making of Modern Identity* (Cambridge: Cambridge University Press, 1989).

Thacker, Toby, *Music after Hitler, 1945–1955* (Aldershot: Ashgate, 2007).

—— '"Something Different from the Hampstead Perspective": An Outline of Selected Musical Transactions between Britain and the GDR' in Stefan Berger and Norman LaPorte (eds.), *The Other Germany: Perceptions and Influences in British-East German Relations, 1945–1990* (Augsburg: Wißnew-Verlag, 2005), 211–24.

Thomson, George, *Marxism and Poetry* (London: Lawrence & Wishart, 1945).

Thorpe, Andrew, *The British Communist Party and Moscow, 1920–43* (Manchester: Manchester University Press, 2000).

—— 'Communist Party History: A Reply to Campbell and McIlroy', *Labour History Review*, 69/3 (December 2004), 363–5.

Tilbury, John, *Cornelius Cardew (1936–1981): A Life Unfinished* (Matching Tye, Essex: Copula, 2008).

Tomoff, Kiril, *Creative Union: The Professional Organization of Soviet Composers, 1939–1953* (Ithaca, NY: Cornell University Press, 2006).

Tovey, Donald, *Essays in Musical Analysis*, ii: Symphonies (II), Variations and Orchestral Polyphony (London: Oxford University Press, Humphrey Milford, 1935).

Van Gyseghem, André, 'British Theatre in the Thirties: An Autobiographical Record' in Jon Clark, Margot Heinemann, David Margolies, and Carole Snee (eds.), *Culture and Crisis in Britain in the Thirties* (London: Lawrence and Wishart, 1979), 209–18.

Walls, David, 'Billy Bragg's Revival of Aging Anthems: Radical Nostalgia or Activist Inspiration?', paper presented to the Working Class Studies Association conference, St. Paul, Minnesota, Friday, 15 June 2007, accessed 4 May 2011, www.sonoma.edu/users/w/wallsd/smm-aging-anthems.shtml.

Waters, Chris, *British Socialists and the Politics of Popular Culture, 1884–1914* (Manchester: Manchester University Press, 1990).

'Disorders of the Mind, Disorders of the Body Social: Peter Wildeblood and the Making of the Modern Homosexual' in Becky Conekin, Frank Mort, and Chris Waters (eds.), *Moments of Modernity: Reconstructing Britain, 1945–64* (London and New York: Rivers Oram, 1999), 134–51.

Waters, Julie Anne, '"Against the Stream": Intersections of Music and Politics in the Conception, Composition and Reception of Alan Bush's First Three Symphonies', PhD thesis, Monash University (2012).

Watson, Ian, 'Alan Bush and Left Music in the Thirties: An Introduction and an Interview', *Gulliver* 4 (1978), 80–90.

Song and Democratic Culture in Britain: An Approach to Popular Culture in Social Movements (London: Croom Helm, 1983).

Werth, Alexander, *Musical Uproar in Moscow* (London: Turnstile Press, 1949).

Wiebe, Heather, *Britten's Unquiet Pasts: Sound and Memory in Postwar Reconstruction* (Cambridge: Cambridge University Press, 2012).

Willett, John (ed. and trans.), *Brecht on Theatre: The Development of an Aesthetic* (London: Methuen, 1964).

'*Die Massnahme*. The Vanishing *Lehrstück*' in David Blake (ed.), *Hanns Eisler: A Miscellany* (Luxembourg: Harwood Academic, 1995), 79–90.

Wittgenstein, Ludwig, *Culture and Value: A Selection from the Posthumous Remains*, ed. Georg Henrik von Wright and Heikki Nyman, trans. Peter Winch (Oxford: Blackwell, 1998).

Workers' Music Association, *A Policy for Music in Post War Britain* (London: Workers' Music Association, 1945).

Young, Percy M., *A History of British Music* (London: Benn, 1967).

Index

Abraham, Gerald, 20
Adorno, Theodor W., 3, 7–8, 14
Allinson, Francesca, 66–7
Anderson, Benedict, 67, 142
Andriessen, Louis, 8
Ansermet, Ernest, 235
Antokoletz, Elliot, 168
Arts Council of Great Britain, 2, 109, 149, 177–8, 181–2
Attlee, Clement, 109

Bach, Johann Sebastian, 50, 52, 104, 123
Bantock, Granville, 86
Barr, Margaret, 88
Bartók, Bela, 5, 30, 34, 47, 104, 112
    Second Violin Sonata, 35
Bax, Arnold, 86
BBC (British Broadcasting Corporation), 2, 5, 10, 13, 19, 35, 45, 46–7, 97, 102, 111–14, 118, 130, 138, 163, 177–8, 182, 240, 244, 246–8
Beatles, The, 222
Beethoven, Ludwig van, 23, 36, 46, 51–6, 57, 59, 89, 90, 92–4, 159, 194
    Choral Fantasia, 46
    Fidelio, 92–3
    Missa Solemnis, 52, 159
    Ninth Symphony, 53, 54–6
Benjamin, Arthur
    A Tale of Two Cities, 181
Berg, Alban, 18, 19, 25, 26, 68, 112, 140, 155, 156, 212
    Lulu, 11, 205
    Lyric Suite, 113
    Wozzeck, 25, 38, 179, 196, 203
Betz, Albrecht, 50, 68, 79
Blake, William, 52, 69
Bliss, Arthur, 21–4
    Clarinet Quintet (1932), 21
Bloch, Ernest, 104
Blume, Friedrich, 1
Boden, F.C., 34

Boughton, Rutland, 34, 38, 66, 69, 104, 210
    'Song of Liberty', 66
Boult, Adrian, 46
Boyce, William, 136
Brecht, Bertolt, 1, 17, 34, 36, 37, 43, 47, 49, 59, 76–9, 184, 195, 212, 218, 240, 242
    Der Jasager, 184, 195
    Die Massnahme, 34, 36, 50–1, 52, 69, 76, 79, 195, 242
    Die Mutter, 37, 184
Brett, Philip, 8, 18–19
Bridge, Frank, 6
British Council, 112
British Guiana, 206–7, 223, 224, 228
Britten, Benjamin, 1–4, 6, 8, 15, 18–19, 46, 57, 85, 94, 109, 116, 118, 120, 123, 126, 140, 147, 163, 178, 180, 185, 195, 204, 232–4, 238, 242, 260, 261
    A Ceremony of Carols, 118, 121, 123, 126, 196
    Ballad of Heroes, 46, 85, 121
    Curlew River, 232
    Death in Venice, 6, 205, 232–4
    Gloriana, 180, 185, 243
    Noye's Fludde, 94
    Our Hunting Fathers, 18, 46
    Our Hunting Fathers (1936), 18
    Peter Grimes, 19, 88, 178–80, 189, 195, 203, 204–5, 234, 243
    Piano Concerto, op. 13, 46
    Russian Funeral, 46
    War Requiem, 116, 119, 120, 121, 232
Bülow, Hans von
    'Bundeslied', 68, 87
Bunyan, John, 196
Burghardt, Max, 210, 217
Burnham, Forbes, 194, 224
Bush, Alan
    24 Preludes, 175, 235
    'Against the People's Enemies', 106, 247
    and communist selfhood, 143, 151–4

and Festival of Britain opera commissioning
  scheme, 2, 177, 181–2, 244
and folk music, 2, 31, 67, 88–9, 92, 111–13,
  146–7, 148–9, 155, 160, 162, 168, 179, 185,
  196, 206–7, 213–14, 217, 219, 221, 223,
  225, 227, 228, 248
BBC ban, 2, 16, 46, 96–7, 102
Britain's Part, 110, 117, 247
Byron Symphony, 46
Communist Manifesto Centenary Pageant,
  189, 197
Concert Piece, 17, 28, 29, 33, 41, 43,
  56, 157
'Cutty Wren', 92, 147, 164, 170, 172–3, 183,
  189, 201, 249
Dialectic, 4, 17–18, 30, 32, 40, 45, 47, 49, 63,
  141, 156–7, 161, 164, 166, 169, 172, 174
English Suite, 161–76
Fantasia on Soviet Themes, 112, 116, 136,
  246
Freedom on the March, 248
Homage to William Sterndale Bennett, 246
'In Nomine', 164, 168, 172
Joe Hill, 177, 205–7, 232–42
'Labour's Song of Challenge', 81
Lascaux Symphony, 235
Lidiče, 116, 129, 130–4, 135–6, 140, 183, 185,
  196, 248
Lyric Interlude, 116–17, 132, 137, 247
'Machine Ballet', 89
'Make Your Meaning Clear', 62, 70, 74, 75,
  83
Meditation on a German Song of 1848, 247
Men of Blackmoor, 141, 177–8, 210, 217
Nottingham *Symphony*, 2, 140–1, 146
Overture Festal Day, 246
Overture Resolution, 136
Pageant of Labour, 64, 85
Peace and Prosperity, 58
Phantasy for Violin and Piano, 166
Piano Concerto, 2, 40, 45–60, 64, 82, 94, 110,
  152, 159, 193, 244
Piano Sonata in B minor, 27
Piers Plowman's Day, 138, 183, 185, 197
Quartet for Piano and Strings, 27–8, 30
'Question and Answer', 62, 81
Relinquishment, 17, 30, 40, 47
Russian Glory, 112, 246
service in the armed forces, 100–1
'Song of the Commons of England', 247

'Song of the Hunger Marchers', 62, 74, 77
'Song to Freedom', 62
Songs of the Doomed, 26, 34
Strict Counterpoint in the Palestrina Style, 1,
  162
String Quartet in A minor, 27–8, 31
Sugar Reapers, 177, 206–7, 210, 223, 225,
  228–30, 231–2, 234
Symphonic Impression, 32
Symphony in C, 2, 113–15
'The Great Red Army', 110, 112, 247
'The Living English', 188
thematic method, 154–61
Three Concert Studies for Piano, Violin and
  Cello, 247
Three Contrapuntal Studies, 40, 79–80, 146
'To the Men of England', 70, 71, 72–3, 75
'Toulon', 247
'Towards To-morrow' (pageant), 64, 85,
  87–9, 92, 188
'Truth on the March', 104
'Unite and Be Free', 106–7, 247
Violin Concerto, 152
Wat Tyler, 2, 16, 46, 92, 164, 177–83, 185,
  189–90, 191–8, 200, 201–2, 205–6, 210,
  212, 213–19, 222, 225, 232, 234, 235, 249
Winter Journey, 116, 118–29, 130–1, 132–3,
  136, 183, 185, 196, 243, 248
workers' music, 16, 18, 39, 49, 62–6, 68–9,
  72, 75–7, 79, 81–4, 90, 93–4, 100, 110, 112,
  117, 129, 130, 146, 149, 160, 170, 188, 222,
  247
Bush, Nancy, 1, 34, 47, 116, 130–3, 136, 177,
  180–4, 192, 197–9, 205, 209, 219, 225, 234,
  247–8
  Lidiče (text), 130–6
Busoni, Ferrucio, 46–7
  Piano Concerto, 46

Calico, Joy, 211–12, 218
Calum Macdonald. *See* Macdonald, Malcolm
Calvocoressi, M.D., 33, 40
Capell, Richard, 19, 21–3
Cardew, Cornelius, 8, 94, 243
  The Great Learning, 94
Caudwell, Christopher, 158–60, 166
CEMA (Committee for Encouragement of
  Music and the Arts), 101, 109, 149
Chamberlain, Neville, 98, 100, 105
Chełmno, 129

Chopin, Frederic, 51
Chowrimootoo, Christopher, 6
Churchill, Winston, 96–7, 99, 108, 245
CIA (Central Intelligence Agency), 139
Clark, Edward, 18, 35, 47, 63, 85, 88, 104, 183, 185
Clark, Katerina, 183–4
Clifford, Hubert, 112
Cobbett, W.W., 166
Comintern (Communist International), 74, 97, 99, 108, 115, 186, 245
concert-demonstration, 69, 78
Congress for Cultural Freedom, 139
Cooke, Deryck
  The Language of Music, 235
Cooper, Martin, 140–2, 146, 176, 179
CPGB (Communist Party of Great Britain), 1, 9, 13, 15, 17, 35, 64, 96–100, 102, 103, 106, 107–9, 115, 142–4, 151, 158, 160, 186, 188, 221, 223, 245
  'Battle of Ideas', 144, 221
  cultural policy, 105–8
  Historians' Group, 186–8
  Music Group, 144
  NCC (National Cultural Committee), 96, 144, 151, 188
Croft, Andy, 9, 58, 87, 94, 119

Daily Worker, 24, 106, 245
Darnton, Christian, 85
DASB (*Deutsche Arbeiter-Sängerbund*), 62, 67–8
Davies, Peter Maxwell, 164
  First Fantasia on an In Nomine of John Taverner, 164
  Seven in Nomine, 164
Dent, Professor Edward J., 24, 104
Dessau, Paul, 212, 218, 234
Dessoir, Max, 1
Dimitrov, Georgi, 74, 99, 186
Doctor, Jenny, 5
dodecaphony. *See* twelve-note method
Drew, David, 177–9
Dunayevsky, Isaak, 112
  Song of the Motherland, 112

Earle, Ben, 7
East Germany, xvii, 2–3, 13–16, 151, 177–8, 205–6, 207–21, 223–4, 226, 228, 231–2, 234, 243, 253, 262
Edmunds, Neil, 6, 35, 45, 48, 84

Eichmann, Adolf, 129
Eisler, Hanns, 1, 17, 24, 34, 36–7, 45, 47, 49–51, 52, 55, 59–60, 63, 68–79, 81–2, 85, 87, 90, 93, 145, 184, 209, 240, 242, 244, 254, 259
  'Ballad of To-day', 69
  Cantata of Exile, 85
  Die Massnahme, 34, 36–51, 52, 68–9, 76, 79, 195, 242
  Die Mutter, 37, 184
  'Einheitsfrontlied', 69, 87
  'In Praise of Dialectics' from *Die Mutter*, 37
  'In Praise of Learning', 69
  News from Vienna, 1938, 85
  Prison House Cantata, 85
  'Report on the Death of a Comrade', 69
  'Solidaritätslied', 70, 75
  'The Party's in Danger', 69
Elgar, Edward, 2–3, 5, 7, 15, 20, 66, 136
  King Olaf, 66
Eliot, T.S., 5–6, 120–1
  The Waste Land, 120
Ellenberg, David, 181, 183
English Civil War, 92
English Peasants' Revolt, 92, 147, 164, 170, 180, 184–7, 197, 205
ENSA (Entertainments National Service Association), 101, 149
Esperanto, 20, 22
Esty, Jed, 6
Evans, Peter, 18

Fagan, Hyman, 181, 188, 195
  Nine Days That Shook England, 181, 188
fascism, 15, 19, 22, 42, 57, 59, 76, 90–4, 97–9, 108–9, 112–13, 119, 129–31, 136, 137, 140, 151, 212, 215, 245
Fenemore, Mark, 215–17, 220–2, 232
Festival of Music for the People, 23, 35, 64, 73, 77–8, 81–5, 89, 90–4, 181–2, 188
Fletcher, Stuart, 25, 83–4
Forest, Jean Kurt
  Der arme Konrad, 216
formalism, 139–40, 153
Forster, E.M., 6
Frankel, Benjamin, 103, 109, 144
Freedman, Jean R., 110, 119
Frogley, Alain, 5
Froissart, Jean, 181
Frolova-Walker, Marina, 8–9, 148
Futurism, 88

Index

Gagarin, Yuri, 183
Gallacher, William, 108–9
GDR (German Democratic Republic). *See* East Germany
Gebrauchsmusik, 6–7, 80, 146
German invasion of the Soviet Union, 97, 99, 108, 110, 115, 245
Goldschmidt, Berthold
  Beatrice Cenci, 182
Gorky, Maxim
  Mother, 184–5, 249
Gow, Dorothy, 6
Gray, Cecil, 22–3, 220
Greene, Graham, 120, 124
Griffiths, Paul, 178
Grimley, Daniel M., 5
Guyana. *See* British Guiana
Gyseghem, André van, 87–8

Hallstein Doctrine, 211
Handel, G.F., 94
  Belshazzar, 64, 91–3
Harper-Scott, J.P.E., 3, 5, 7, 10–12
Hartig, Rudolf, 217–18
Hellbeck, Jochen, 14, 151–2, 159, 175
Hendry, James Findlay, 25–6, 38
Hennecke, Adolf, 216–17, 219
Hepokoski, James, 5
Hey, Robin, 24, 66
Heydrich, Reinhard, 129
Hildebrandt, Egbert, 34
Hill, Christopher, 186–7
Himsworth, Norman, 100
Hindemith, Paul, 5, 6, 19, 22–3, 140, 145, 156, 158, 159, 160, 161, 162, 174
  Craft of Musical Composition, 159, 162
  Ludus Tonalis, 176
Hitler, Adolf, 25, 42, 98–9, 105, 108, 113, 129–30, 139, 178, 208, 210, 216–17, 220
Hobsbawm, Eric, 186
Holst, Gustav, 7, 157
Hughes, Spike, 24

imperialism, 7, 87, 91, 99, 112, 114, 228, 229
'Internationale' (political song), 62, 69, 86–7, 111
Internationale der Arbeitersänger (International of Worker-Singers), 68
Ird, Kaarel, 210

Ireland, John, 1, 17, 27, 42, 47, 113, 116, 136–8, 147, 152, 163
  These Things Shall Be, 138
ISCM (International Society for Contemporary Music), 19–20, 23, 35

Jagan, Cheddi, 224
jazz, 12, 22, 75, 84, 111, 206, 220–1, 228
Jennings, Humphrey, 129
Judt, Tony, 108, 119, 131

Kemp, Ian, 17
Khachaturian, Aram, 139
  Poem about Stalin, 112, 138
Khrennikov, Tikhon, 140, 145
Klugmann, James, 186
Knepler, Georg, 8, 17, 37, 209
Kosminsky, E.A., 188
Krenek, Ernst, 140
  Jonny spielt auf, 227, 228
Kurzbach, Paul
  Thomas Münzer, 216

Lacan, Jacques, 12
Langland, William, 183, 199
  Piers Plowman, 197–203
lateness, 232, 234, 235, 242
Left Song Book, 64, 69, 75, 82–3, 87–8
Leigh, Walter, 6–7
Leipzig Fair, 212, 214
Lew, Nathaniel, 4, 177, 179, 182, 190, 195, 201
Lidiče (Czech village), 129–36, 138
LLCU (London Labour Choral Union), 2, 34, 63–72, 75–7, 89, 91, 106, 209, 254
Lloyd, A.L.
  'The Living English', 188
'Lord Balbus', 66–7, 68
London Labour Speaking Chorus, 79
London String Orchestra, 112, 163–6, 246
Lowe, Vesta, 228
'Lowlands, my Lowlands', 169–70
Lowerson, John, 47, 182, 185, 217
Lukács, Georg, 37
Lutyens, Elisabeth, 6, 18, 85, 104

Macdonald, Malcolm, 4
Maconchy, Elizabeth, 85
Mason, Colin, 4
McLellan, Josie, 206, 215

Index

McNaught, William, 20–1
Mellers, Wilfrid, 18, 62, 63, 163
Mellor, Leo, 119–20, 132, 260
Men of Blackmoor, 177, 179, 217–19
Messiaen, Olivier, 140
Meyer, Ernst Hermann, 17, 63, 208–10, 216–17
MI5 (British Intelligence Organisation), 13, 96, 98, 100–2, 105, 115, 138, 208–9, 223
Mitchell, Donald, 18, 232, 234
Moi, Toril, 12
Morgan, Kevin, 99, 129, 221
Morris, R.O., 162
Morris, William, 69, 107, 188
Morton, A.L.
  A People's History of England, 186
Mozart, Wolfgang Amadeus, 147
Mundy, John, 66
Muradeli, Vano, 139
  The Great Friendship, 139
Murrill, Herbert, 156
Mussorgsky, Modest, 147

Nash, Paul, 5
Nazism, 36, 90, 105, 113, 129–30, 149, 215, 220
Nazi-Soviet pact, 97, 245
Nigg, Serge, 211
Nono, Luigi, 8, 33, 211, 244

O'Higgins, Rachel, 13, 42, 47, 113, 116, 136, 228
Operation Barbarossa. *See* German invasion of the Soviet Union
Orga, Ates, 47
Orwell, George
  Nineteen Eighty-Four, 206
Owen, Wilfred, 121
  'Futility', 120
  'The Seed', 121

Payne, Anthony, 4
'The Peat-Bog Soldiers', 93
People's Convention, 2, 96, 99, 102–6, 108, 245
Petzold, Richard, 214–15
Pirie, Peter J., 4
Pollitt, Harry, 97, 99, 106, 109, 129, 188, 197
Popular Front, 87, 99, 106, 186
Prague Congress (1948), 143–5, 150, 155, 159
  Declaration, 145
Pro Musica (journal), 79–80
Prokofiev, Sergei, 139

Proms (Promenade concerts), 5, 113
Purcell, Henry, 104, 136, 165, 166

Que-Que, 206, 225

RAM (Royal Academy of Music), 1
  RAM New Music Society, 34
RAMC (Royal Army Medical Corps), 100–1, 245
Rankl, Karl
  Deirdre of the Sorrows, 182
Rawsthorne, Alan, 6, 46, 85, 104, 130
  A Rose for Lidiče, 130
  Piano Concerto No. 1, 46
Rebling, Eberhard, 209, 213
Redgrave, Michael, 104
Robinson, Suzanne, 17
Rostal, Max, 116
Rupprecht, Philip, 3, 6–7, 18, 116, 164
Russell, Dave, 65, 217

Sabaneev, Leonid, 21–2
Said, Edward, 232, 234, 242
Schafer, R. Murray, 36, 139–41, 152
Scherchen, Hermann, 34
Schmelz, Peter J., 8–9
Schnabel, Artur, 1
Schoenberg, Arnold, 6–7, 18–19, 21–4, 26, 30, 35–8, 45, 49, 60, 85, 90, 141, 145, 155–7, 160, 174
  Erwartung, 38, 205
  Klavierstück, op. 33a, 35, 156
  Peace on Earth, 85
  Pierrot Lunaire, 45
  Theory of Harmony, 160
Schwarz, Bill, 140, 186–7
SCR (Society for Cultural Relations with the USSR), 143
Searle, Humphrey, 7
SED (Sozialistische Einheitspartei Deutschlands), 206–8, 211–12, 215, 217, 219–22
Sharp, Cecil, 168
Shneerson, Grigori, 111, 143, 181, 210
Short, Ben, 24
Shostakovich, Dmitri, 8, 24–6, 38, 139, 143
  'Leningrad' Symphony, 115
  24 Preludes and Fugues, 176
  Lady Macbeth of the Mtsensk District, 24–6, 38

Index

Shreffler, Anne C., 8
Sibelius, Jean, 5–6, 22
Siegmeister, Elie
  Music and Society, 149
Slater, Montagu, 88, 189, 195
  Communist Manifesto Centenary Pageant, 189, 197
socialist realism, 8, 25, 36, 60, 146, 148, 154, 179, 182–4, 207–8, 211, 226, 240
Solovyov-Sedoi, Vasily, 112
Soviet Resolution, 1948, 143–6, 150, 152–3
Soviet Union, 2, 10, 13, 26, 35, 62, 82, 89, 93, 96–9, 102, 105, 108, 110, 115, 137, 140, 143, 145, 151, 153, 175, 210, 245
Stakhanov, Alexey, 183
Stakuko (Staatliche Kommission für Kunstangelegenheiten der DDR), 211, 217, 220
Stalin, Joseph, 8–9, 14, 99, 138, 139, 148, 151, 183
Stavis, Barrie, 177, 205, 233–5, 238, 240
Steele, Brent J., 131
Stevens, Bernard, 10, 63, 114, 145, 240
  Symphony of Liberation, 114, 119
Stevenson, Ronald, 4, 26, 33, 46–7, 63, 158, 181, 209
Stone, Dan, 108
Stonor Saunders, Frances, 139, 142
Strauss, Richard
  Salome, 205
Stravinsky, Igor, 6, 12, 19, 22–3, 34, 140, 155, 162
  Les Noces, 35
  Oedipus Rex, 34
  Ragtime, 23
Stross, Barnett, 130
Swingler, Randall, 58, 64, 69, 82–4, 87, 91, 104, 106, 110, 118, 130, 247, 248
  'Against the People's Enemies', 106
  Peace and Prosperity, 58
  'The Great Red Army', 110
  'Truth on the March', 104
  Winter Journey, 118–29

Taruskin, Richard, 7
Taverner, John, 164
  Gloria tibi Trinitas, 164

Thacker, Toby, 139, 178, 208, 210, 217, 220
Thälmann, Ernst, 216
theosophy, 1
Thompson, E.P., 186, 188
Thorpe, Andrew, 97, 108
Tippett, Michael, 1, 2, 4, 10, 17–18, 46, 52, 61, 63, 121, 127, 147, 162
  A Child of Our Time, 17, 19, 121, 126, 181, 196
Topic Records, 64, 222
Torr, Dona, 187–8, 191, 192
Trilling, Ossia, 206, 234, 240
twelve-note method, 6, 15, 18, 20–1, 23, 35, 39, 40, 85, 153, 155, 160

Uchytilová, Marie, 131
Uszkoreit, Hans-Georg, 218

Vaughan Williams, Ralph, 2–3, 5, 7, 15, 25, 32, 62, 85, 96–7, 155, 156–7, 162, 163, 168, 169, 170, 196, 246
  A Pastoral Symphony, 5
  Fantasia on a Theme of Thomas Tallis, 168
  Fourth Symphony, 25
  'London' Symphony, 5
  Pilgrim's Progress, 196–7
  The Shepherds of the Delectable Mountains, 196
VDKM (Union of German Composers and Musicologists), 208, 211, 212, 217
VOKS (the All-Union Society for Cultural Ties Abroad), 111, 143

Walton, William, 3, 11, 12, 86
Warlock, Peter
  Capriol Suite, 104
Waters, Chris, 65
Waters, Julie, 4, 144–7
Watson, Ian, 63–4
Weill, Kurt, 11, 207, 244
  Der Jasager, 184, 195
Weimar Republic, 1, 6, 17, 90
Wells, H.G., 5
Wiebe, Heather, 6, 109, 116, 120, 123, 126, 178, 185, 232, 243
William Morris Musical Society, 100, 107, 115, 209
Wittgenstein, Ludwig, 20, 262

WMA (Workers' Music Association), 2, 63, 77, 84, 100, 109, 130, 150, 154, 170, 177, 209, 221–3, 247
  1937 Composers' Group, 84, 86
  WMA Singers, 77, 112, 130, 136, 188, 247–8
Woolf, Virginia, 5–6

Young Workers' Ballet, 79
Young, Percy, 4, 18

Zacharov, Vladimir, 112
Zhdanov, Andrey, 2, 139–40, 144
Zhdanovshchina, 139–40

For EU product safety concerns, contact us at Calle de José Abascal, 56–1°,
28003 Madrid, Spain or eugpsr@cambridge.org.

www.ingramcontent.com/pod-product-compliance
Ingram Content Group UK Ltd.
Pitfield, Milton Keynes, MK11 3LW, UK
UKHW050711260326
469255UK00031B/447